The Beautiful Mysterious

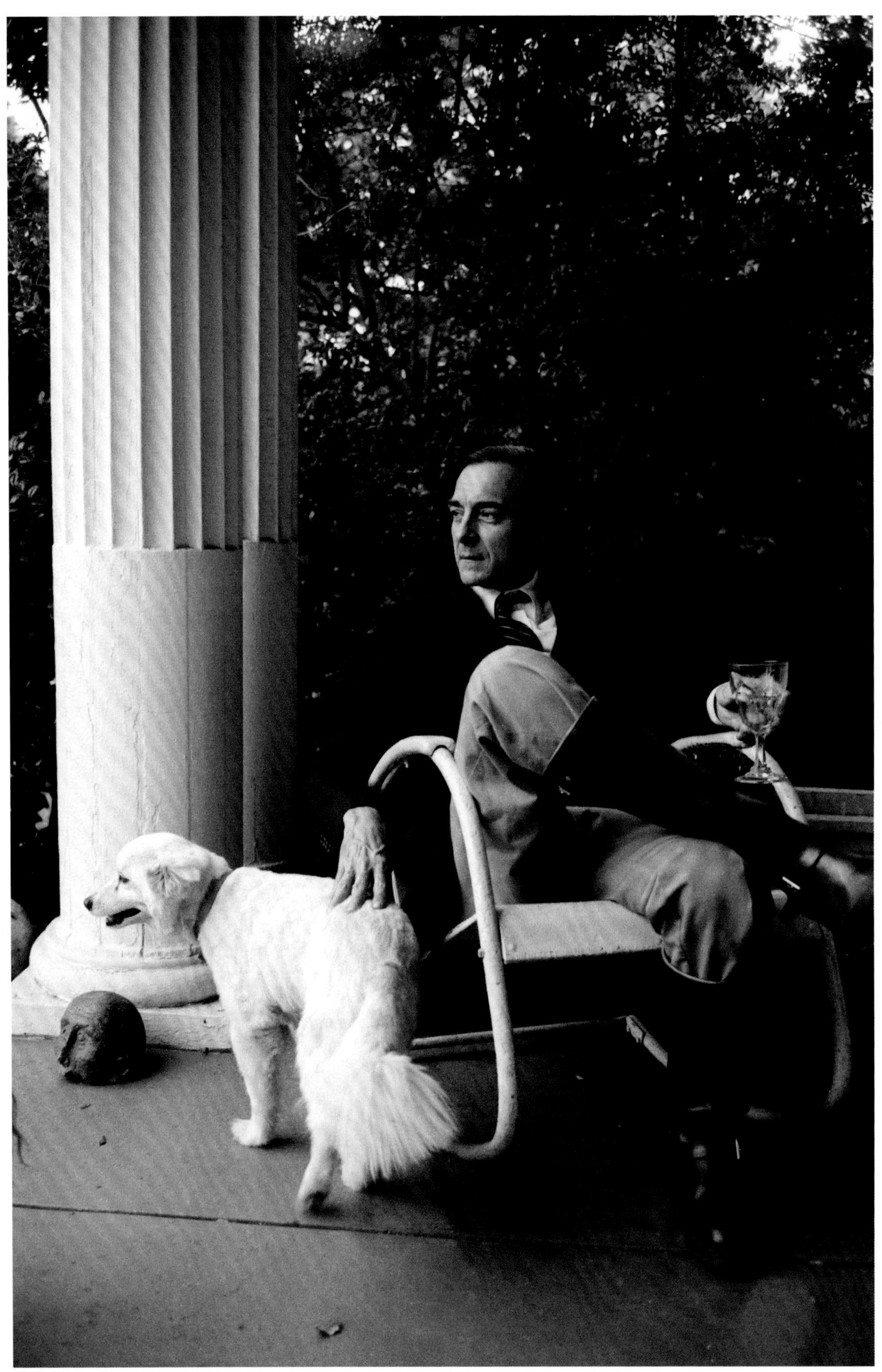

Everett McCourt. *William Eggleston, Memphis*, 1989.

The Beautiful Mysterious

THE EXTRAORDINARY GAZE OF WILLIAM EGGLESTON

ROBERT SAARNIO, Director

MARTI A. FUNKE, Collections Manager

ANN J. ABADIE, Editor

University of Mississippi Museum and Historic Houses Series / Volume 1

University Press of Mississippi, Jackson
in association with the University of Mississippi Museum and Historic Houses

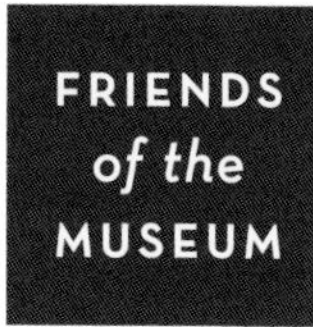

Publication of this book was made possible by funds from Friends of the Museum.

The University Press of Mississippi is the scholarly publishing agency of the Mississippi Institutions of Higher Learning: Alcorn State University, Delta State University, Jackson State University, Mississippi State University, Mississippi University for Women, Mississippi Valley State University, University of Mississippi, and University of Southern Mississippi.

www.upress.state.ms.us
The University Press of Mississippi is a member of the Association of University Presses.

Designed by John Langston
Manufactured in China
First printing 2019
∞

Library of Congress Cataloging-in-Publication Data
Names: Saarnio, Robert, author of introduction. | Funke, Marti A., contributor. | Abadie, Ann J., editor.
Title: The beautiful mysterious : the extraordinary gaze of William Eggleston / Robert Saarnio; Marti A. Funke and Ann J. Abadie.
Description: Jackson : University Press of Mississippi, [2019] | Series: University of Mississippi Museum and Historic Houses Series ; volume 1 | Includes bibliographical references and index. |
Identifiers: LCCN 2018042649 (print) | LCCN 2018044906 (ebook) | ISBN 9781496822413 (epub single) | ISBN 9781496822420 (epub institutional) | ISBN 9781496822437 (pdf single) | ISBN 9781496822444 (pdf institutional) ISBN 9781496822345 (hardcover : alk. paper)
Subjects: LCSH: Eggleston, William, 1939– | Photographers—United States—20th century. | LCGFT: Illustrated works. | Informational works.
Classification: LCC TR654 (ebook) | LCC TR654 .B417 2019 (print) | DDC 770.92—dc23
LC record available at https://lccn.loc.gov/2018042649
British Library Cataloging-in-Publication Data available

Contents

Director's Introduction and Acknowledgments

ROBERT SAARNIO

The University of Mississippi Museum is exceptionally pleased to share in these pages one of its most significant collection holdings, the fifty-five prints by photographer William Eggleston that were given to us by William Ferris, Joel R. Williamson Eminent Professor of History at the University of North Carolina at Chapel Hill and founding director of the Center for the Study of Southern Culture at the University of Mississippi. This publication establishes a transformative moment in the Museum's history, as it not only celebrates this extraordinary photographic print collection but also constitutes the first in what will be a series of publications highlighting the diverse collections of artworks and artifacts held by the Museum.

Museum staff and I were highly privileged to have worked closely with William Ferris in recent years as we developed the exhibition shown in our galleries September 13, 2016–February 18, 2017: *The Beautiful Mysterious: The Extraordinary Gaze of William Eggleston*. Since my appointment as Museum director in 2012, Professor Ferris has extended to me a profound degree of warm-spirited collegiality that has significantly advanced my capacity to lead this academic museum, and I want to take this opportunity to thank him for such great depth of kindness and thoughtfulness. His generosity and his vision in behalf of the Museum over four decades have had impacts of extraordinary meaning to the communities we serve, both academic and public, that will be felt for generations to come.

In conjunction with the exhibition, the Museum hosted a symposium in October 2016 with a morning panel that included William Ferris, novelist and guest curator Megan Abbott, and photographer Maude Schuyler Clay, moderated by author Lisa Howorth. An afternoon panel featured Emily Ballew Neff, executive director of the Memphis Brooks Museum; Richard McCabe, curator of photography at the Ogden Museum of Southern Art; and University of Mississippi art historian Kris Belden-Adams, with William Ferris as moderator. Two programs in February 2017 featured Anne Wilkes Tucker, curator of photography emerita, Museum of Fine Arts, Houston, and New York–based filmmaker Michael Almereyda. Tucker presented a lecture considering the Southernness of Eggleston and his body of work. Almereyda screened his documentary film *William Eggleston in the Real World* and participated in a Q&A moderated by photographer and art professor Brooke White. Our successful exhibition, symposium, and public programs encouraged us to publish this catalog of our Eggleston photographs.

We are highly indebted to several organizations and individuals who have both inspired and supported these initiatives, beginning with William Ferris himself as donor and guiding participant along the way. *The Beautiful Mysterious* exhibition was entirely underwritten through the generous sponsorship of Friends of the Museum. Dorothy Howorth, former president of the Friends' Board, took an early and inspirational lead in advocating for the exhibition and the catalog; without her tireless dedication and fundraising acumen, these outcomes would have been on a much longer pathway to realization. We are deeply indebted to Ms. Howorth and the entire Friends of the Museum Board. We also extend sincere thanks for support from the University of Mississippi Lecture Series and to the planning committee for the symposium, the guest lecture, and the film screening and discussion: Dorothy Howorth, Carlyle Wolfe, Lynn Wilkins, Brooke White, Rebecca Phillips, Marti Funke, and Ann Abadie. The publication of this volume has benefited greatly from the guiding efforts and support initiatives of the Friends' publication committee: John Hardy, Dorothy Howorth, Mary Thompson, Lynn Wilkins, Carlyle Wolfe, and Ann Abadie.

We also must thank the Friends of the Museum for their collective support of this book project. The board stepped forward to allocate support from the proceeds of their highly successful annual fundraising event Harvest Supper, recognizing the significance of the Eggleston catalog. These sponsors have made the book you hold in your hands entirely possible by providing the essential resources to make this project happen.

This publication is very significantly the result of the contributions of its editor and project manager, Ann Abadie, associate director emerita of the University's Center for the Study of Southern Culture. On a voluntary basis she has overseen this project, managed its production calendar, and edited every text element and all images with a sharp and highly experienced eye. She has been guide, mentor, and advisor at every stage of the production. This beautiful tribute to the Museum's Eggleston Collection would not have been possible without Ann's professionalism and many years of publishing experience. We are all exceptionally grateful to her.

Within the University, the Museum exists in an ecosystem of support that makes everything we do possible. The board of trustees of the Institutions of Higher Learning of the State of Mississippi has supported this museum since the 1974 transfer of the City of Oxford's Mary Buie Museum to University stewardship. Chancellor Jeffrey S. Vitter has been a devotedly steadfast friend of the Museum, as has Noel E. Wilkin, provost and executive vice chancellor for academic affairs. The Museum is indebted to Chancellor Vitter and Provost Wilkin for their belief in the enriching power of the arts and culture on our campus. They stand at the forefront of a University leadership team that not only understands the meaning of a teaching museum to its academic community but also enables and encourages us daily to extend our service beyond campus boundaries to the families and communities of Oxford, the state of Mississippi, and our Southeast region.

To our publishing partner, the University Press of Mississippi, we extend heartfelt thanks. Director Craig Gill and designer John Langston were essential partners from the origin of this project, and the coherence and beauty of the outcome are very significantly a result of their talents and the University Press's many years of national leadership in academic publishing.

This project would not have been possible without the considerable assistance of the William Eggleston Artistic Trust and its director, Winston Eggleston. Throughout the process he has made himself readily available, and the guidance of the Trust that he represents has been invaluable, given its role as the steward of the legacy of the artist himself, William Eggleston. Additional assistance came from the David Zwirner Gallery of New York City and its staff members Julia Joern and Ashley Tickle, to whom we are also indebted and extend our sincere gratitude.

Last, but far from least, is the talented and extraordinarily dedicated professional staff of this Museum. This is a team that is notable for its vision, its collective body of wide-ranging skills, and its individual areas of expertise. Specific thanks must be extended to former Collections Manager and Exhibitions Coordinator Marti Funke, whose professionalism and tireless energy stand at the heart of all she does. The special activities that curator of education Emily McCauley developed for participants of all ages in conjunction with the Eggleston exhibition provided inspiration for museum programming that reached hundreds of participants of all ages both on- and off-site from September 2016 to February 2017. The Museum's preparator Taylor Kite assisted in the hanging and installation of *The Beautiful Mysterious* exhibition, an initial project for this highly skilled colleague in his first week of joining our team in 2016. Taken as a whole, this is a staff that not only sustains me; they inspire me.

I close by celebrating our members and supporters and the University and general public communities to whose enrichment we dedicate all that we do. The Museum exists for you, and we thrive in direct proportion to your participation and your involvement in securing our future. This museum is committed to serving widely diverse audiences, and we work daily to earn their appreciation for our efforts to inspire community engagement with the art and cultural treasures that we hold in public trust.

Please enjoy this exceptional publication, *The Beautiful Mysterious: The Extraordinary Gaze of William Eggleston*, produced in the Museum's eightieth year of existence. It is a source of compelling pride to celebrate this signature collection and this brilliant American artistic genius, with a beautiful catalog that launches a series of publications that will bring the University's collections to wider audiences.

Note on the Collection

MARTI A. FUNKE

William Ferris met William Eggleston in 1975 while spending the summer making films in Memphis at the Center for Southern Folklore. The two Bills became close friends, visiting in Memphis and in Oxford beginning in 1979 after Ferris became director of the Center for the Study of Southern Culture at the University of Mississippi, where Eggleston was enrolled as a student from 1958 through 1960.

Early on, Ferris began to purchase Eggleston photographs and later contributed fifty-five to the University of Mississippi Museum. The Museum exhibited thirty-six of these photographs in *The Beautiful Mysterious: The Extraordinary Gaze of William Eggleston* for four months, from September 13, 2016, to February 18, 2017, along with sponsoring a symposium, a guest lecture, a film, and a variety of educational activities for all ages. The exhibition traveled to the Mennello Museum in Orlando, Florida, as the first stop on a national tour. The University Museum had sponsored two previous exhibitions from the Ferris Collection, one in 1991 and the other in 2004.[1]

At the symposium for *The Beautiful Mysterious* exhibition held in October 2016 and transcribed in this volume, Bill Ferris gave a detailed account of his friendship with Eggleston and talked about purchasing the photographs he eventually gave to the University Museum. Briefly, he said that these "are images that I saw on Bill's piano, admired, and picked up. . . . They were whatever he had shot and printed when we visited. I selected only a few out of probably 1,000 or more that I looked at during my visits with Bill."

The Eggleston photographs Ferris donated to the University Museum are important for many reasons. The images were selected by a longtime friend and an important figure in Southern Studies during visits at Eggleston's home from the personal collections of photographs he made and developed or had printed. Bill Ferris looked through the photographs and made these selections. Thus, this is a collection selected and curated by the artist's close friend. A collection doesn't really get more extraordinary than that.

In addition, the images have Eggleston's handwritten notes on them about location, people, dates, and/or projects. Many have notes written directly to Bill Ferris regarding their time together at that location or Ferris's interest in the photograph. Seven of the photographs in the collection are early black and whites, five that have never been exhibited or published.[2] The *Moose Lodge* dye transfer depicting a building near Greenwood, Mississippi, in 1972 is one of the very first color dye transfers Eggleston attempted. Eggleston's cousin and protégée Maude Schuyler Clay says this one was made in Chicago, and she remembers its being the first or, at the least, one of the first. Thus, the University Museum's collection has rare Eggleston photographs, including little- or never-shown black and whites and one of the first dye transfers the Father of Color Photography produced.

Designing the exhibition of *The Beautiful Mysterious: The Extraordinary Gaze of William Eggleston* was a tremendous responsibility. The collection includes marvelous photographs by one of the greatest photographers in the world. Eggleston's work has been the subject of more than one hundred solo exhibitions at prominent institutions worldwide, is held in major international museum collections, and is published in more than seventy portfolios, monographs, and exhibition catalogs. Each photograph selected by William Ferris and curated by author Megan Abbott needed to be highlighted. The walls were painted aubergine with ample space between the photographs to light each one individually and to accentuate the white border Eggleston preserved on each photograph. Instead of large mats around the photographs, the frames precisely match their dimensions. The viewer sees the unequal borders, the dye bleeds, notes to William Ferris, and notes about a print itself.

Significantly, Ferris collected photographs that Eggleston made between 1961 and 1989. During that time Eggleston worked in black and white, began experimenting with color, made dye-transfer prints, exhibited seventy-five color photographs at the Museum of Modern Art, took part in the famed *Election Eve* series, joined eight other photographers to photograph on the set of John Huston's film *Annie*, developed his *Louisiana Project* during the World's Fair in New Orleans, and made iconic photographs of Memphis and landscapes in and around the Mississippi Delta. Eggleston's ties to famed musicians are represented in the patio scene of rock musician Sid Selvidge's grandmother's home. Also included is a photograph of Eggleston's longtime friend and fellow photographer William Christenberry made in Waterford, Mississippi, on a day when the two of them and Bill Ferris were riding around together photographing the area. Many of the photographs Ferris collected feature north Mississippi and Eggleston's native areas, the subjects many regard as his most iconic.

There are Eggleston photographs in many collections all over the United States and in Europe, but this collection offers an intimate selection of Eggleston photographs, curated by an incredible writer, and given by a gracious collector. This collection highlights Eggleston's development from his first days of taking photographs into his famed career and showcases his personal relationships with his family, friends, and place.

Notes

1. *William Eggleston: Artist's Choice* displayed twenty photographs from October 29 to December 15, 1991. Eggleston was present at the opening reception on Friday, November 8, accompanied by his son Winston and friends from Memphis. Dashingly dressed in a dark suit and colorful tie, the photographer declined to speak during an interview session prior to the opening but graciously greeted friends and played selections from his favorite composers on the grand piano overlooking the gallery where his photographs were displayed. The 2004 exhibition included seventeen Eggleston photographs shown in 1991 plus two by William Christenberry and one by Eggleston's cousin and protégée Maude Schuyler Clay.

2. The University Museum's 1962 black-and-white photograph of a young man with an ice cream cone was published for the first time on page 41 of Steidl's 2010 book *Before Color*. The University Museum's 1965 black-and-white photograph of a service station on Union Avenue was shown for the first time in the 2014 exhibition *William Eggleston: From Black and White to Color* sponsored by Fondation Henri Cartier-Bresson and the Musée de l'Elysée in Paris. The photograph is published on page 155 of the exhibition catalog.

The Beautiful Mysterious: The Extraordinary Gaze of William Eggleston

The University of Mississippi Museum, Oxford, Mississippi
September 13, 2016–February 18, 2017

Megan Abbott, Exhibition Curator

Maude Schuyler Clay, Consulting Advisor

Sponsored by the University of Mississippi Museum and Friends of the Museum

"The most beautiful thing we can experience," Albert Einstein once said, "is the mysterious." Nowhere does this feel more true than in the photographs of the legendary William Eggleston. While his subjects—a parking lot, a jukebox, a sunbaked road sign—may seem, on the surface, mundane, the photos themselves exert a powerful, enigmatic force.

"When you see a picture he's taken," artist Edward Ruscha noted, "you're stepping into some kind of jagged world that seems like Eggleston World." But Eggleston World, it turns out, is also ours. Why else would we be so affected? So troubled, so moved? A blue parking lot fills us with romantic loneliness. A worn towel on a clothesline, a hole in its center staring at us, ghostlike, inspires a sense of nameless peril. The young man with a double ice cream cone, lost in thought, summons an exquisite melancholy.

"Things don't matter," Eggleston has said. "I don't take pictures of things." Instead, his photographs feel like moments captured from a much larger narrative—one that remains just beyond our reach. It is not surprising that so many writers and filmmakers—from David Lynch to Donna Tartt—point to Eggleston's influence. They sense a story at work. But it's a story that derives from, and remains in, the unconscious. He drops us in at the middle, or near a shuddering climax, or in the chilly moments after.

Standing before these photos, we are never mere observers. We experience them. We feel them. We close our eyes and still see them. We're forever seeing them. Look at an Eggleston photograph once and you are forever altered. Suddenly, you are in it. It is in you.

—Megan Abbott

Photographs are from the collection William Ferris donated to the University of Mississippi Museum and are reproduced courtesy of the William Eggleston Artistic Trust/David Zwirner.

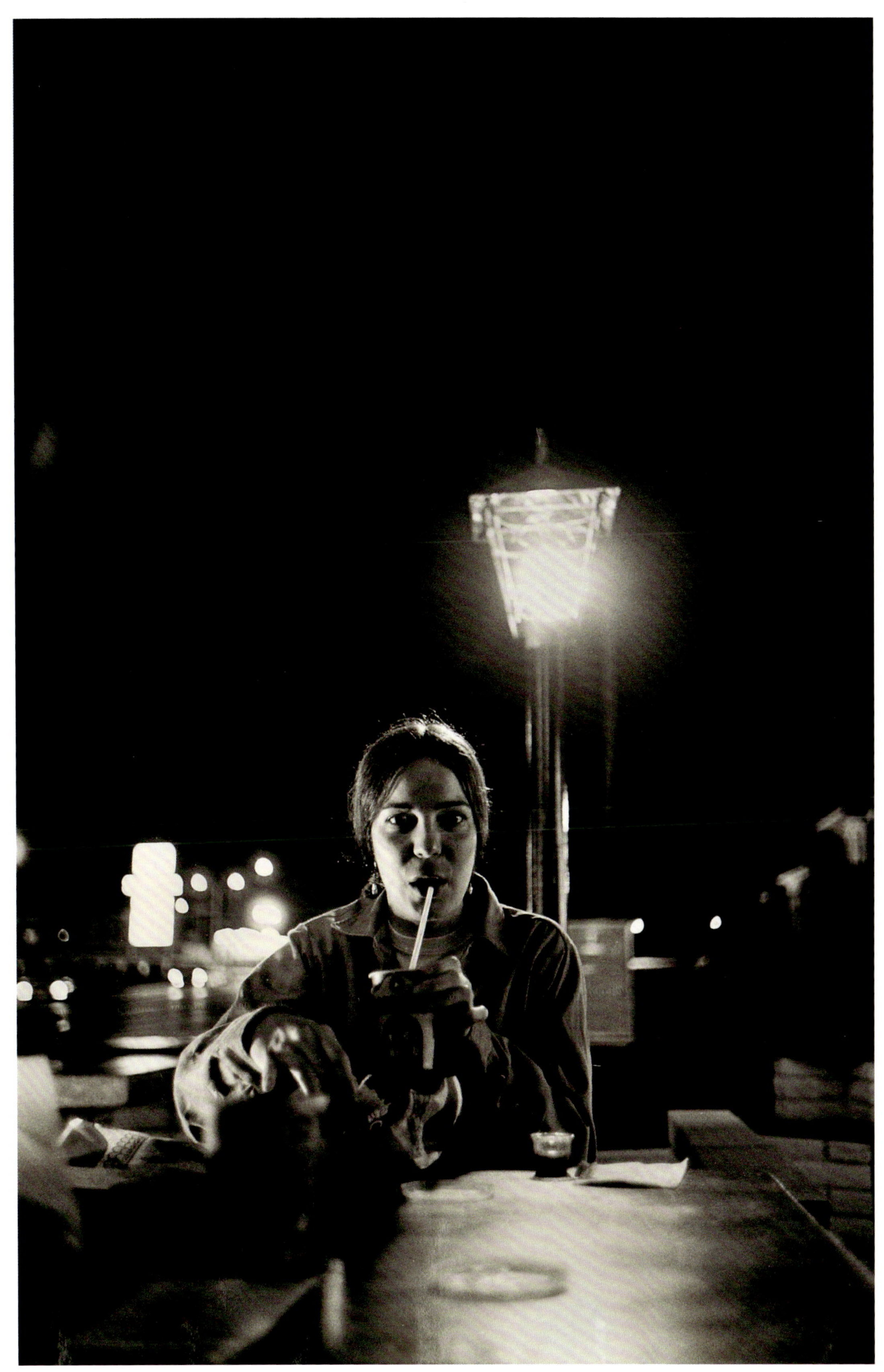

Untitled (Memphis, Tennessee), 1961.

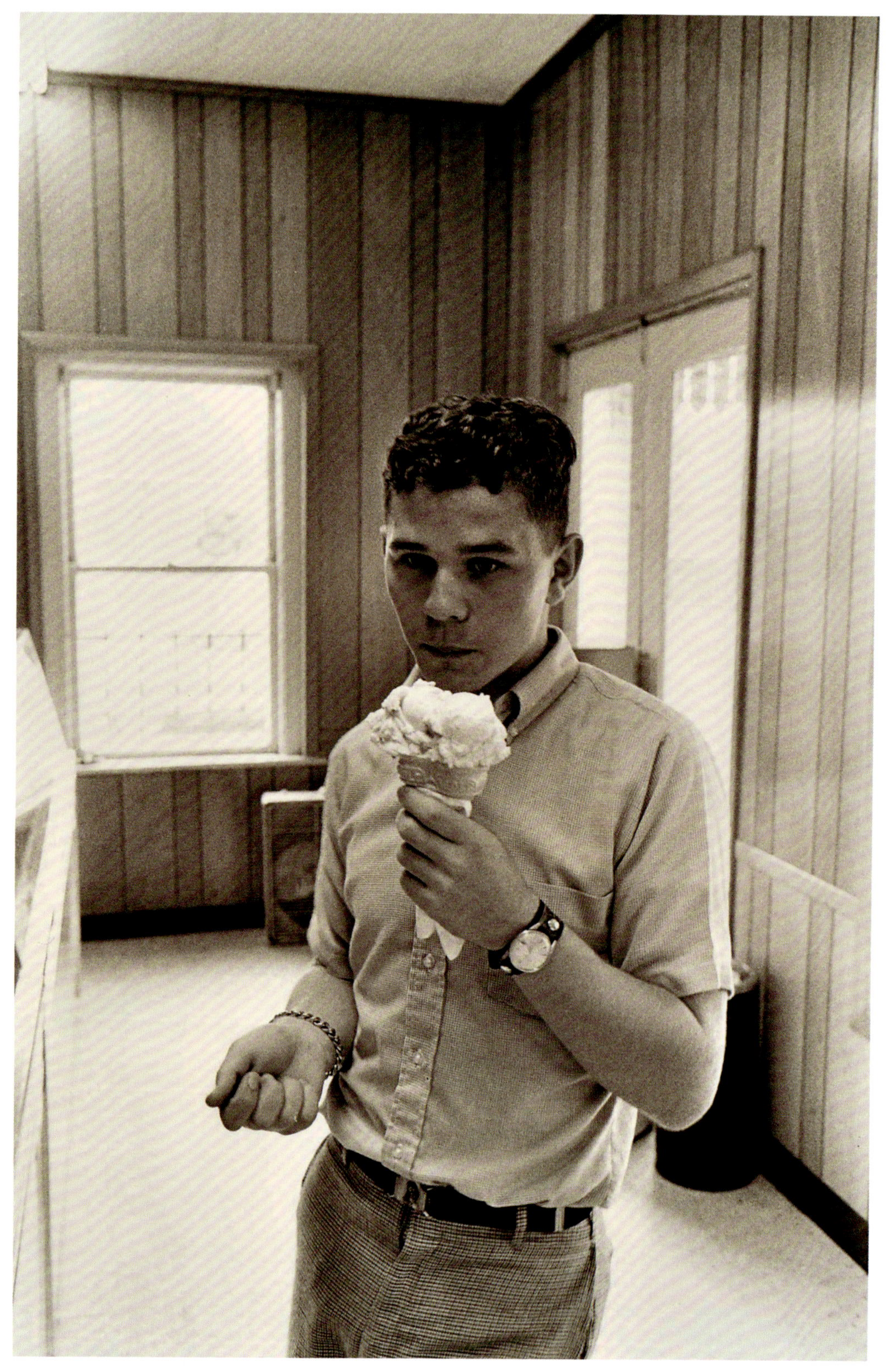

Untitled (Memphis, Tennessee), 1962.

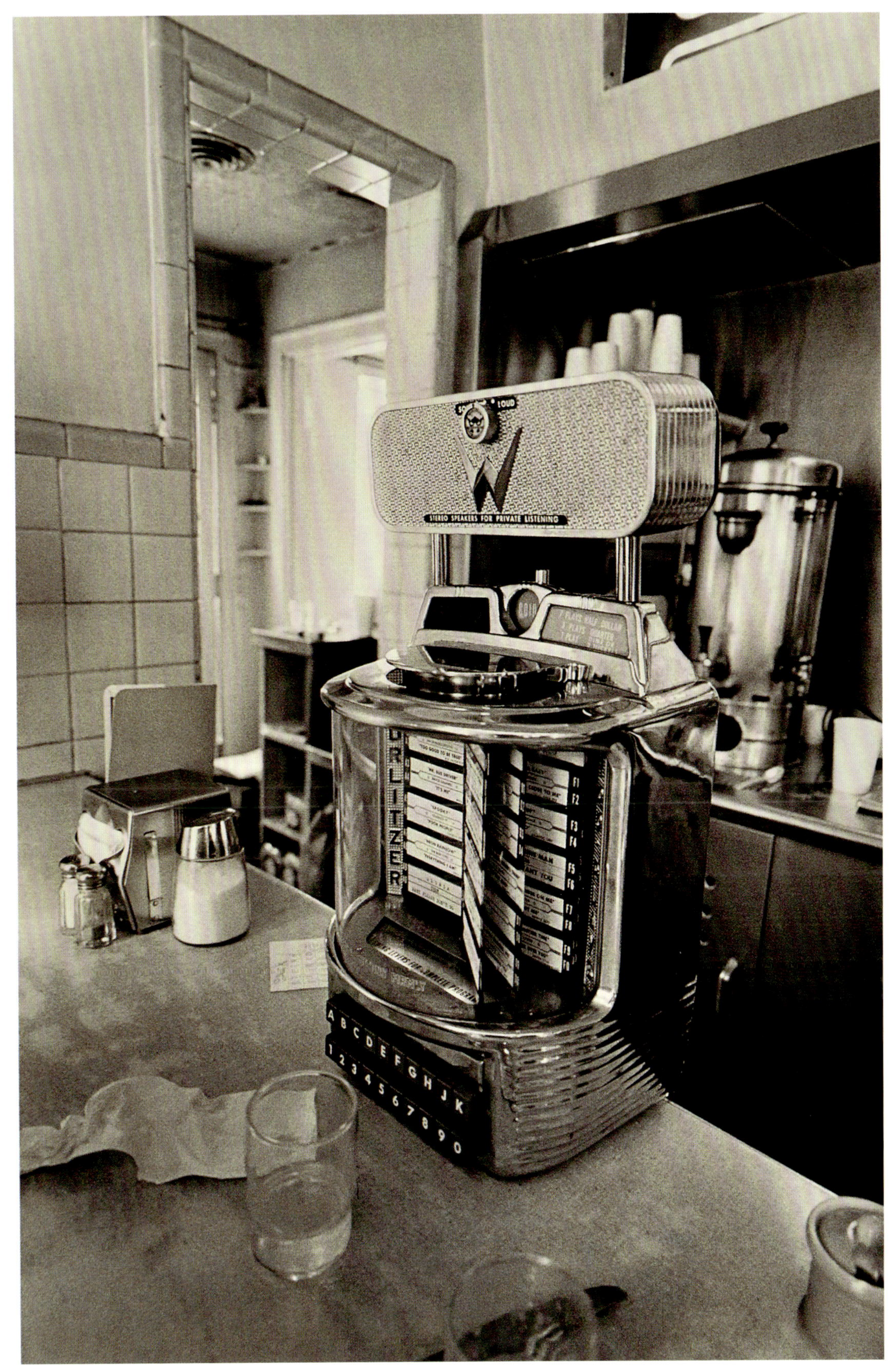

Untitled (diner, Memphis, Tennessee), 1963.

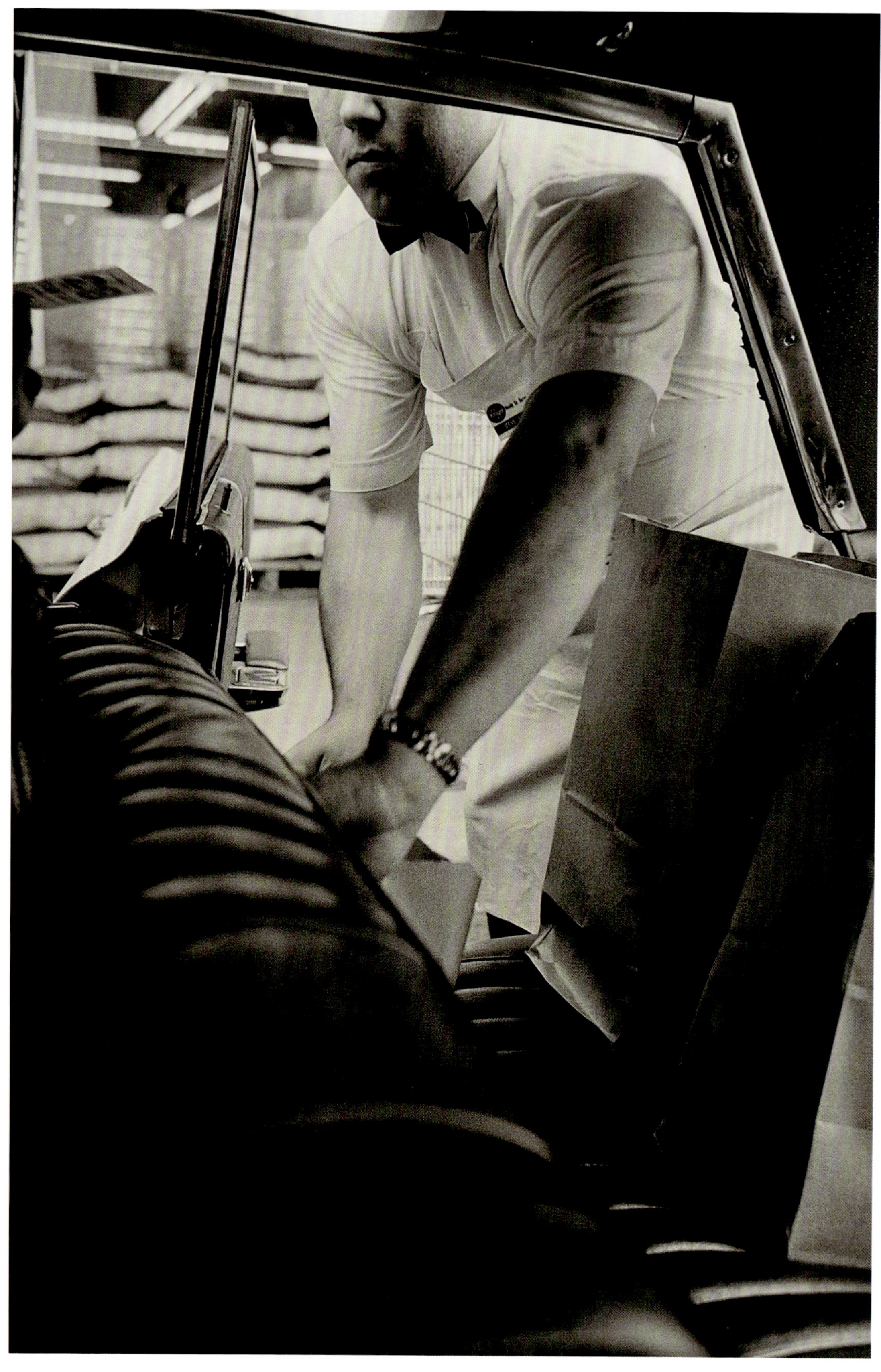

Untitled, 1964.

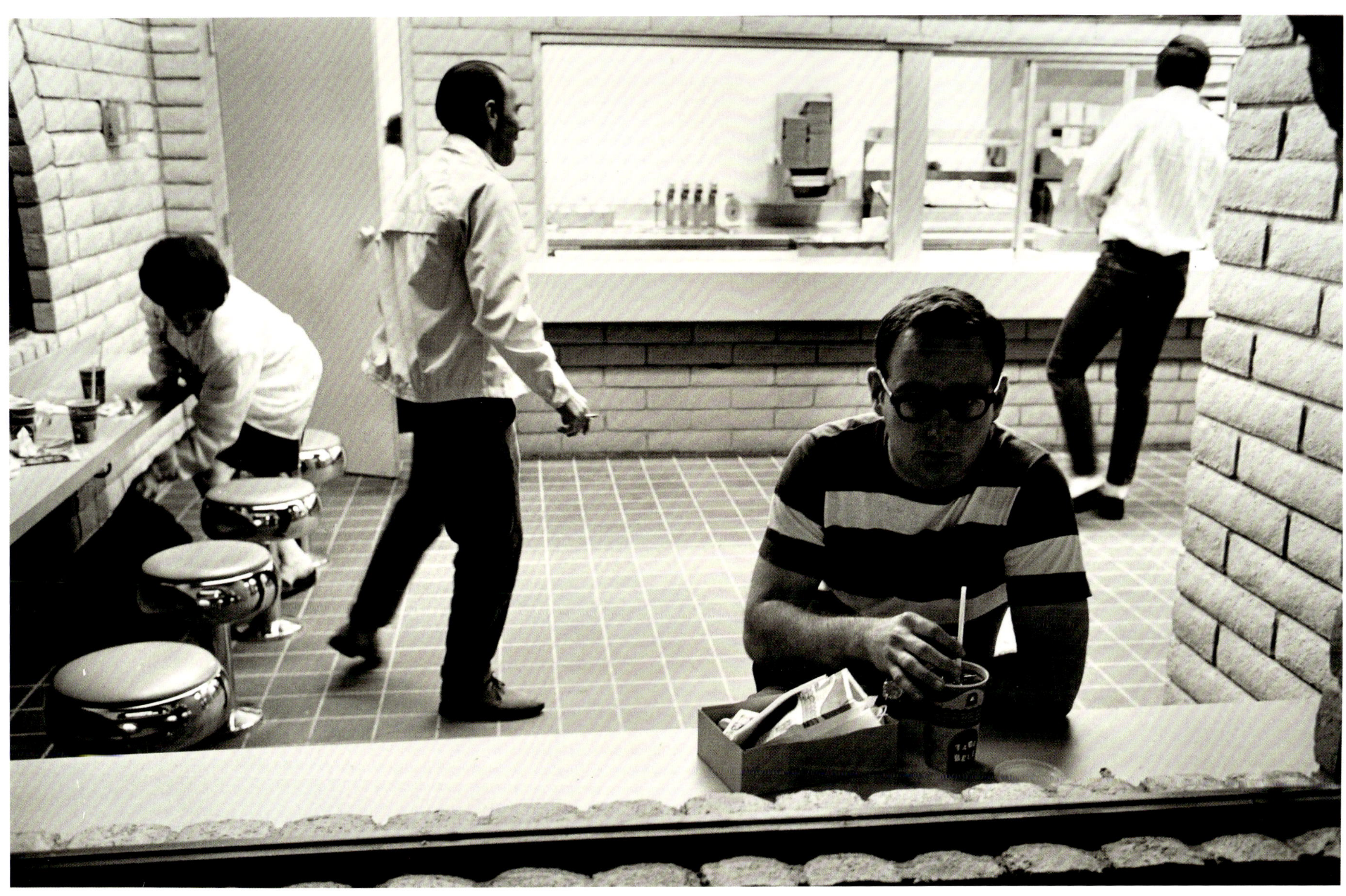

Untitled (Memphis, Tennessee), 1964–1965.

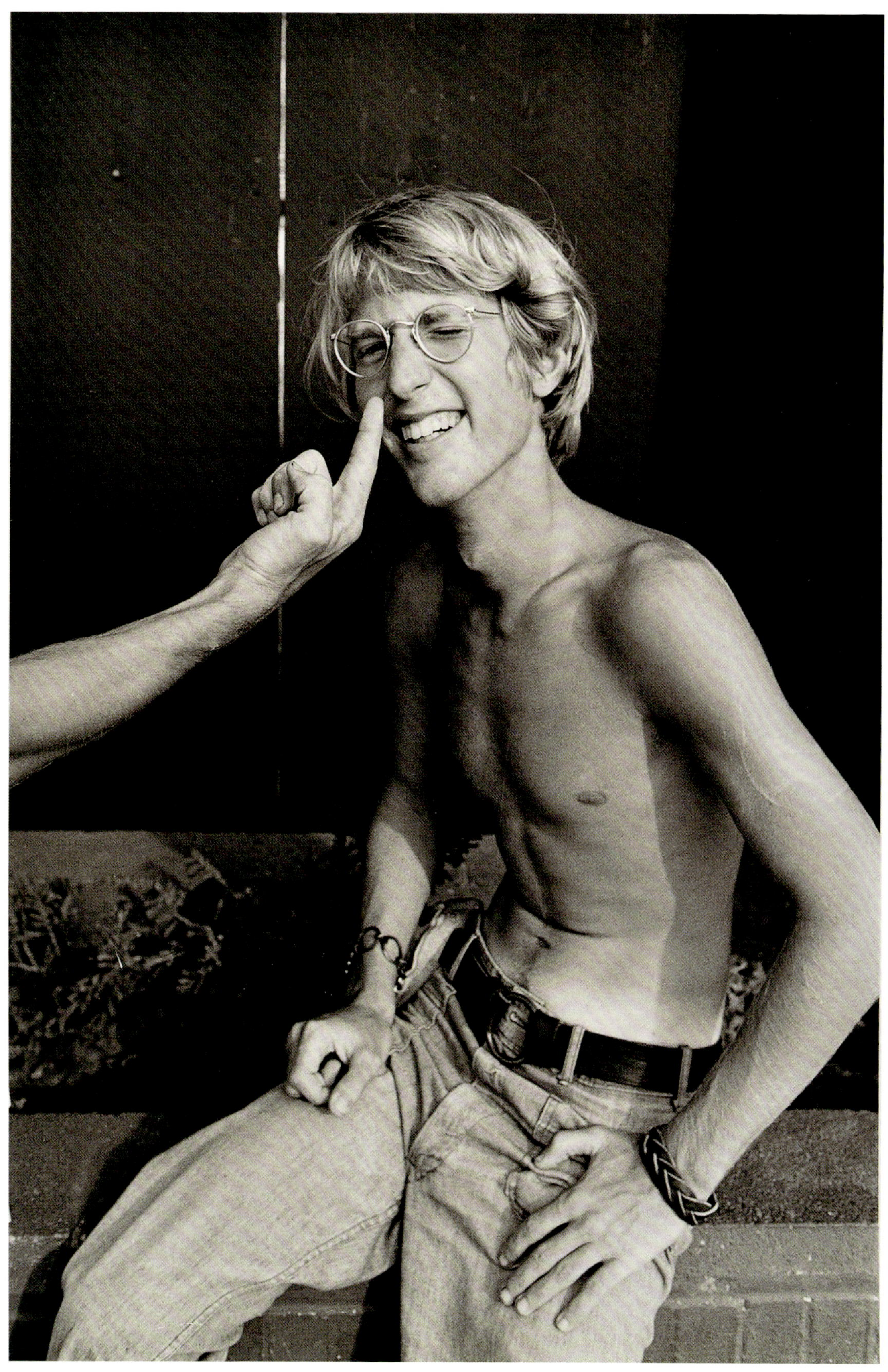

Untitled (Wrightsville Beach, North Carolina), 1968.

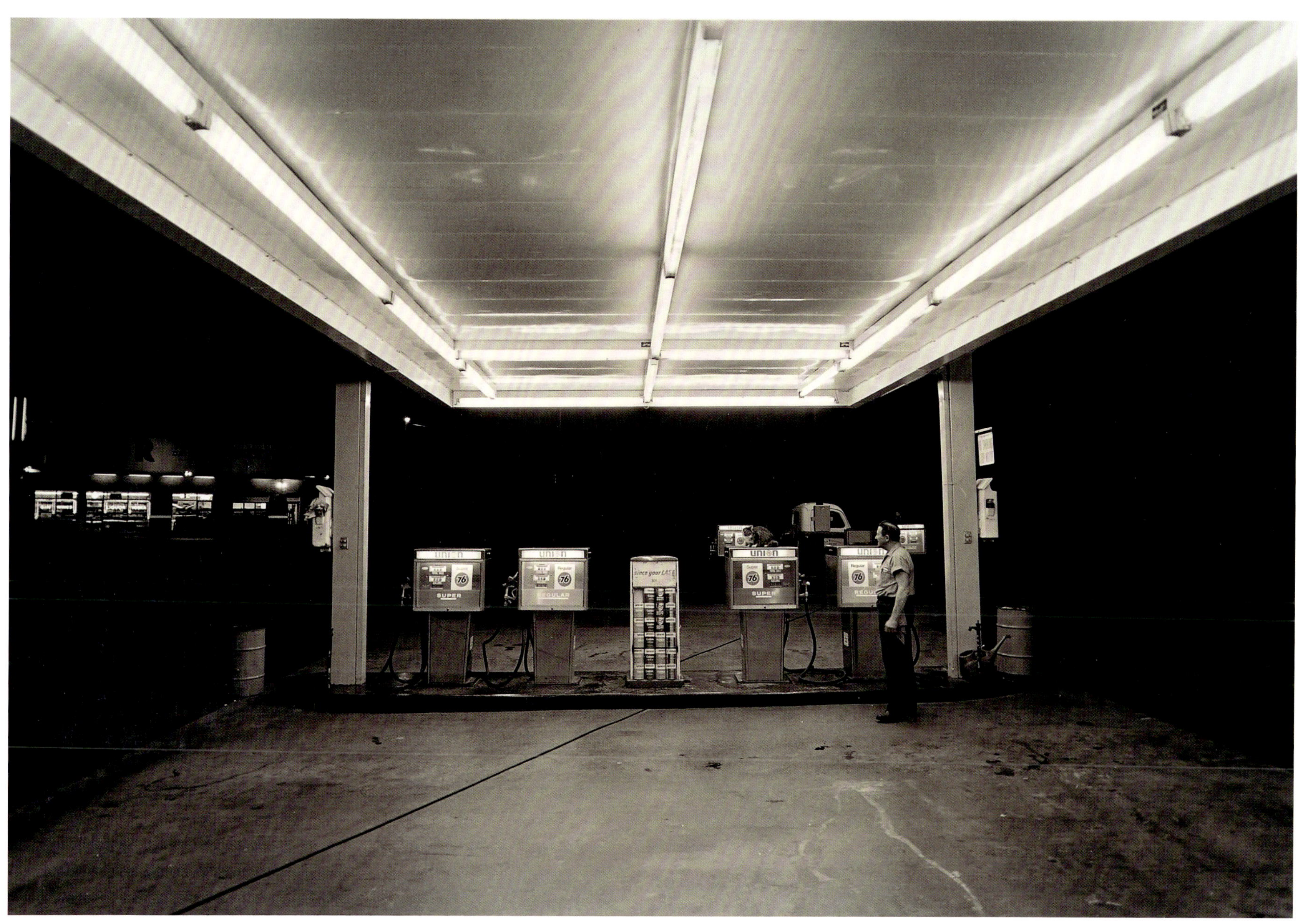

Untitled (Union Avenue, Memphis, Tennessee), 1969.

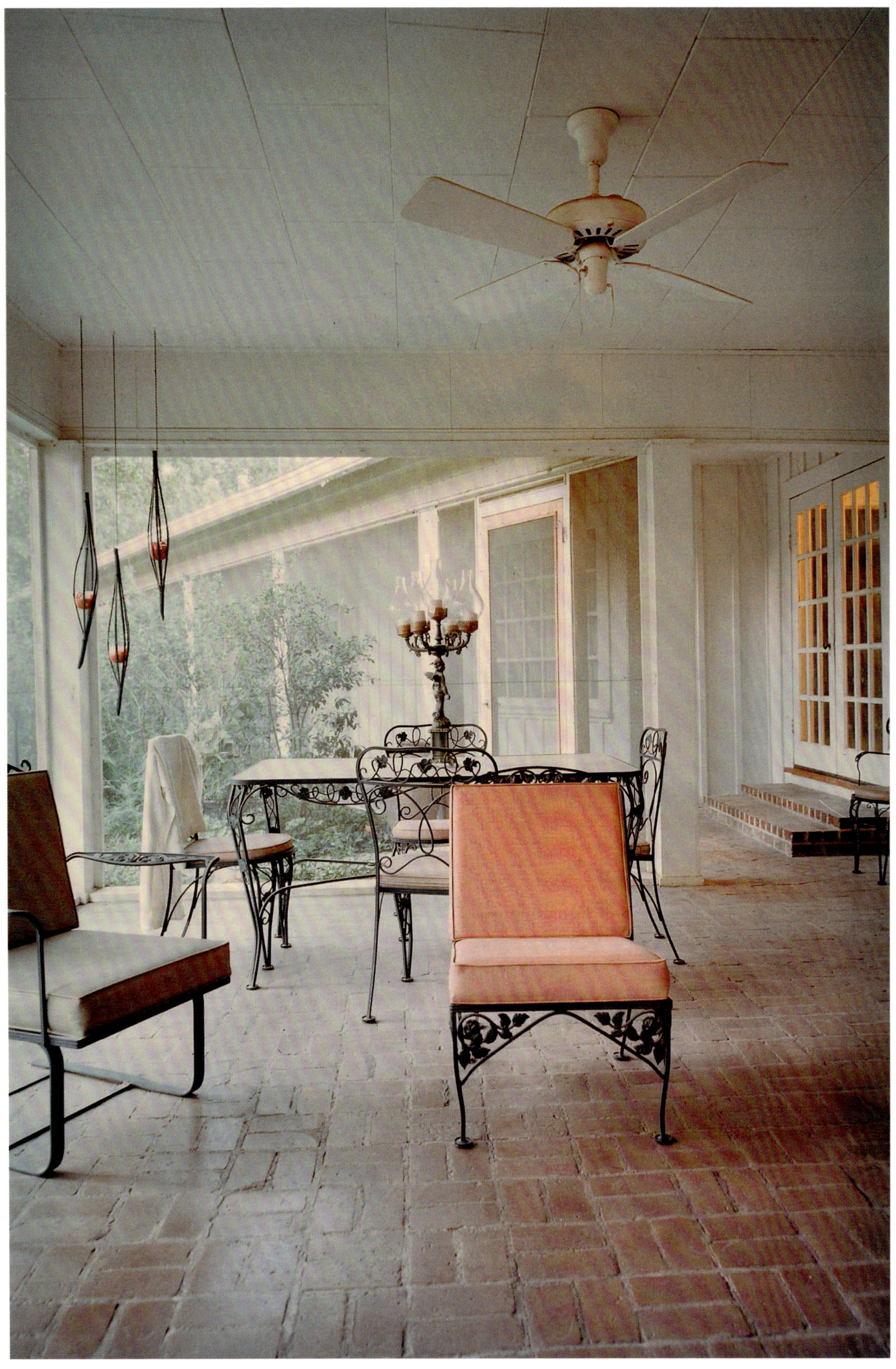

Untitled (Sid Selvidge's grandmother's home near Greenville, Mississippi), n.d.

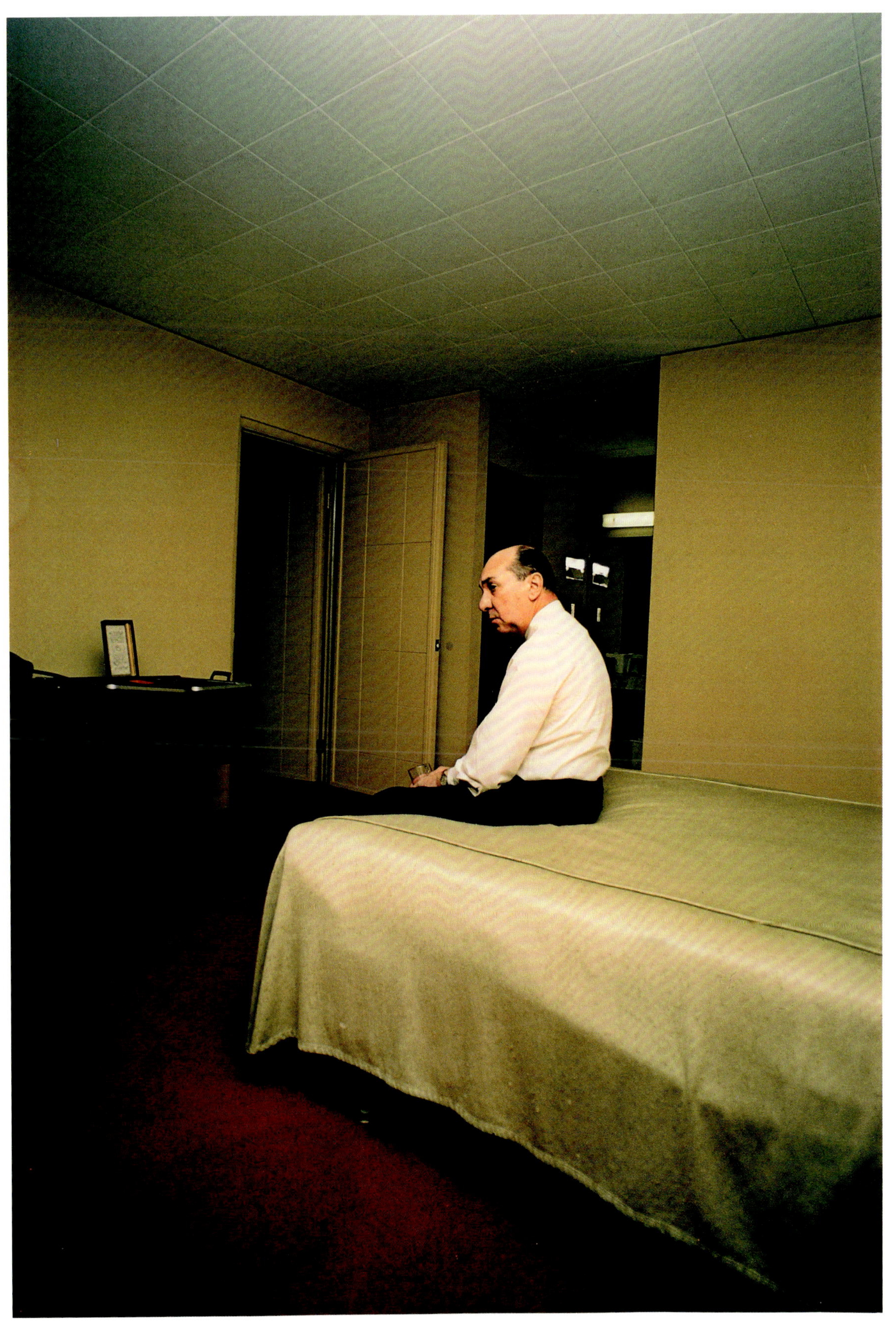

Untitled (Huntsville, Alabama), c. 1970.

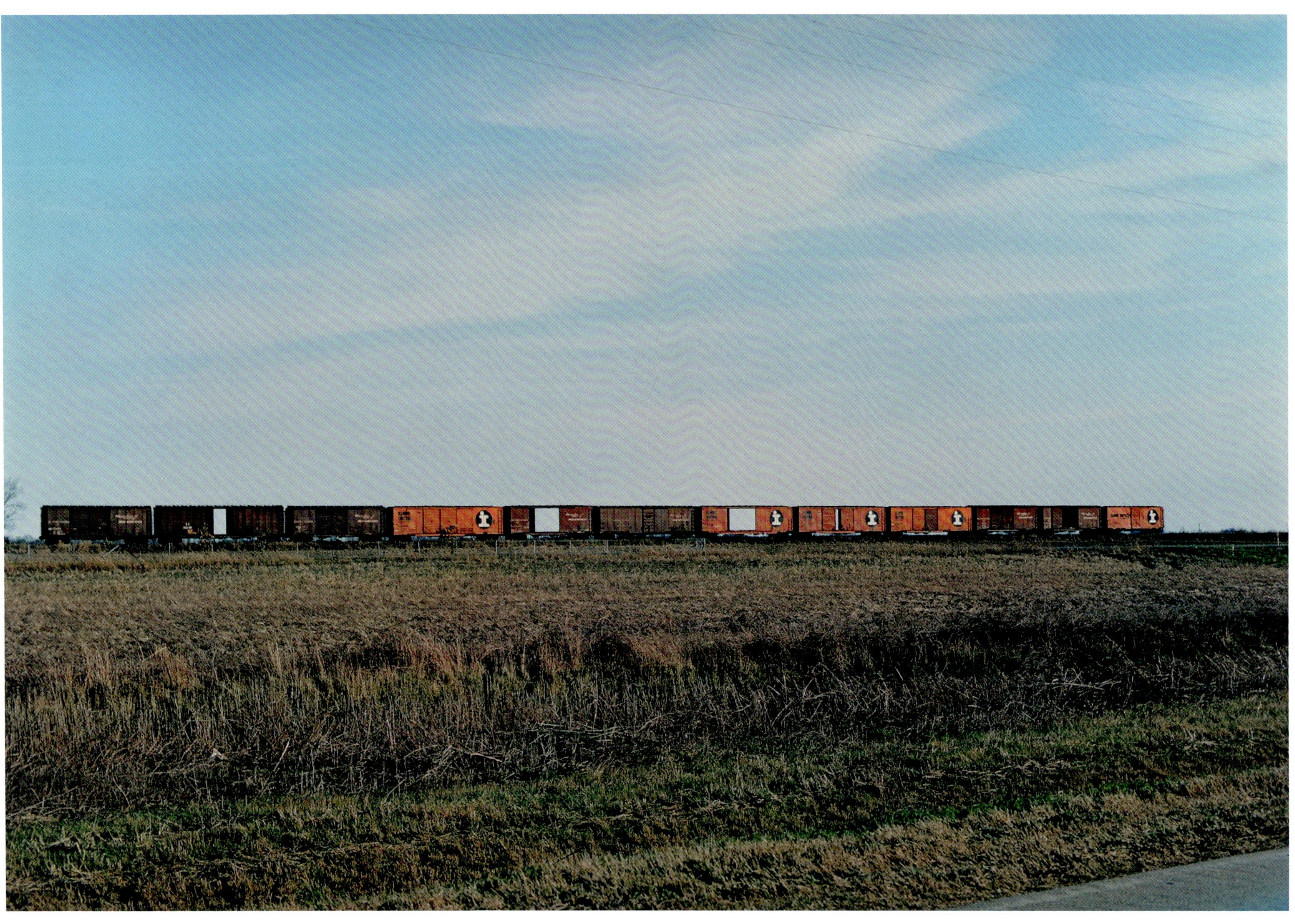

Untitled (near Marks, Mississippi), c. 1971.

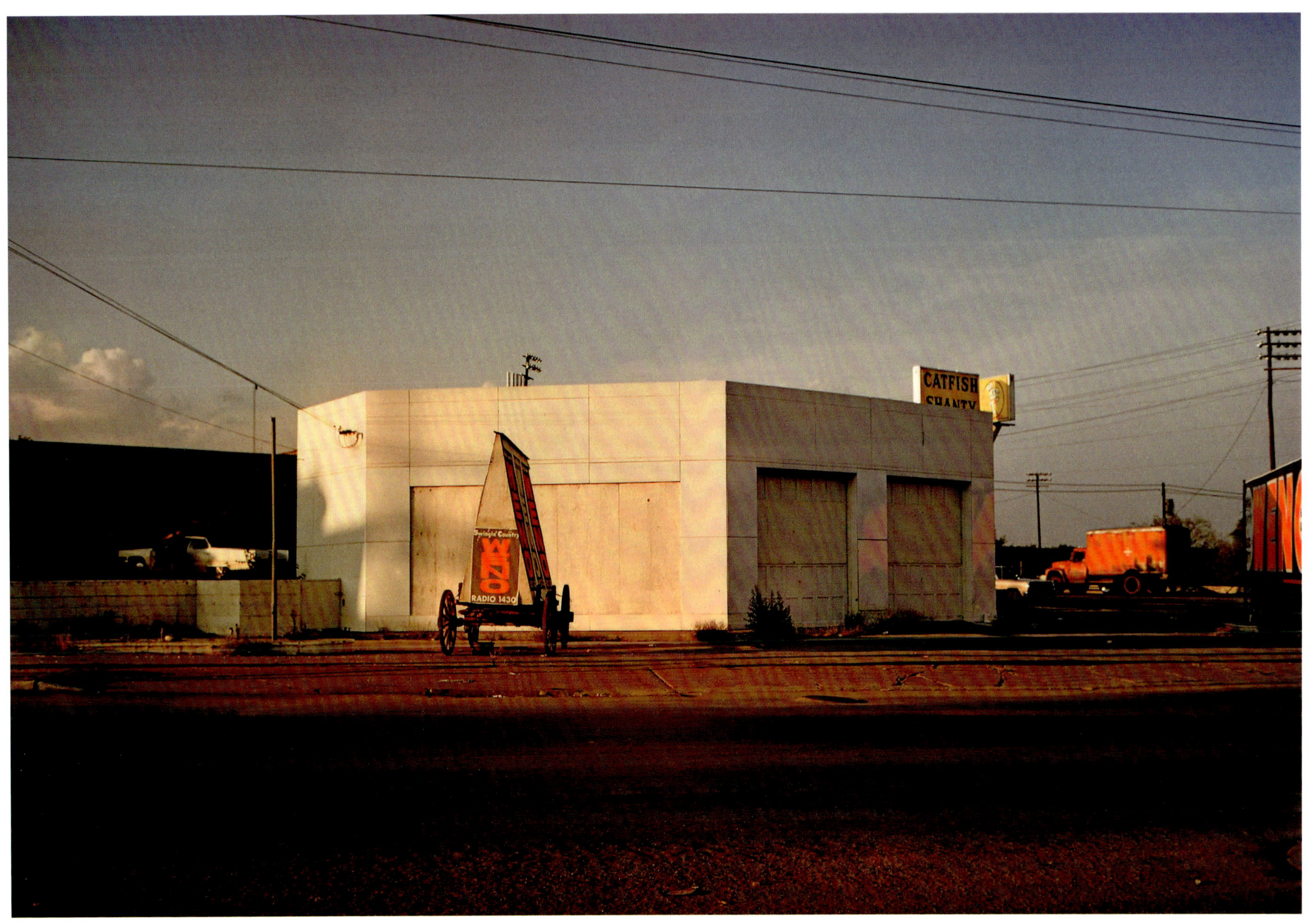

Untitled (Nashville, Tennessee), mid-summer 1971.

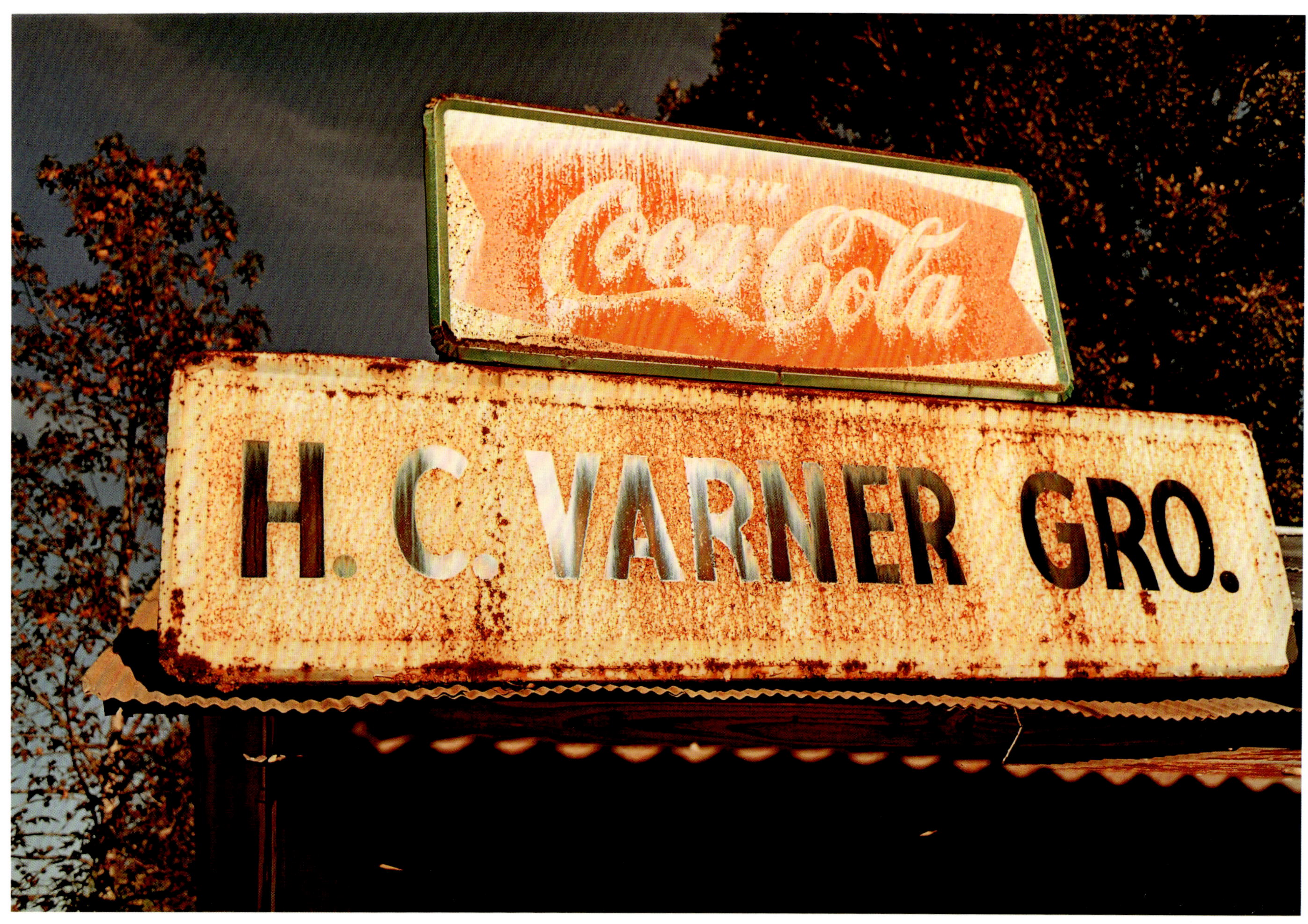

H. C. Varner Grocery, 1971.

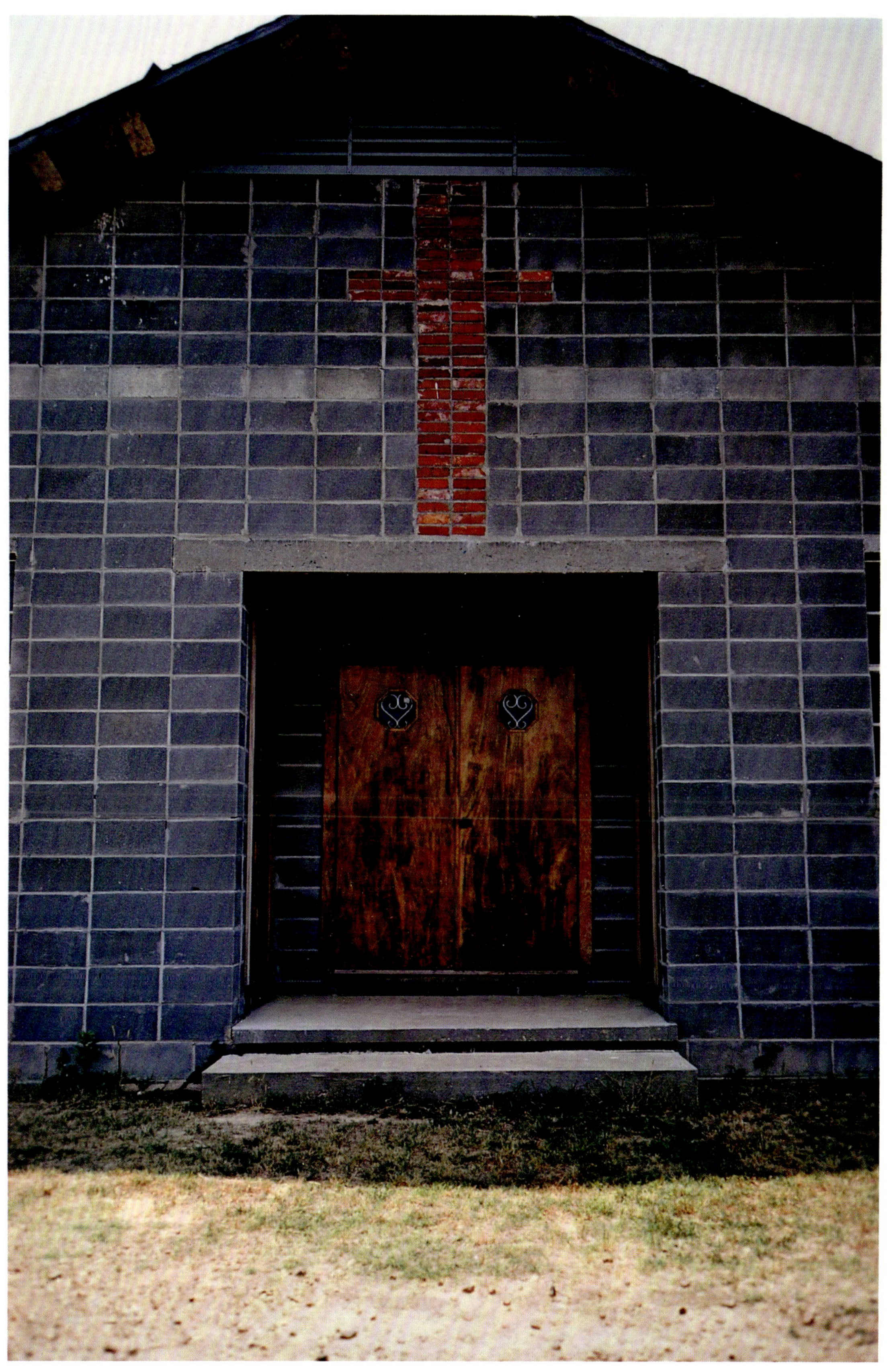

Untitled (rural Mississippi), 1972.

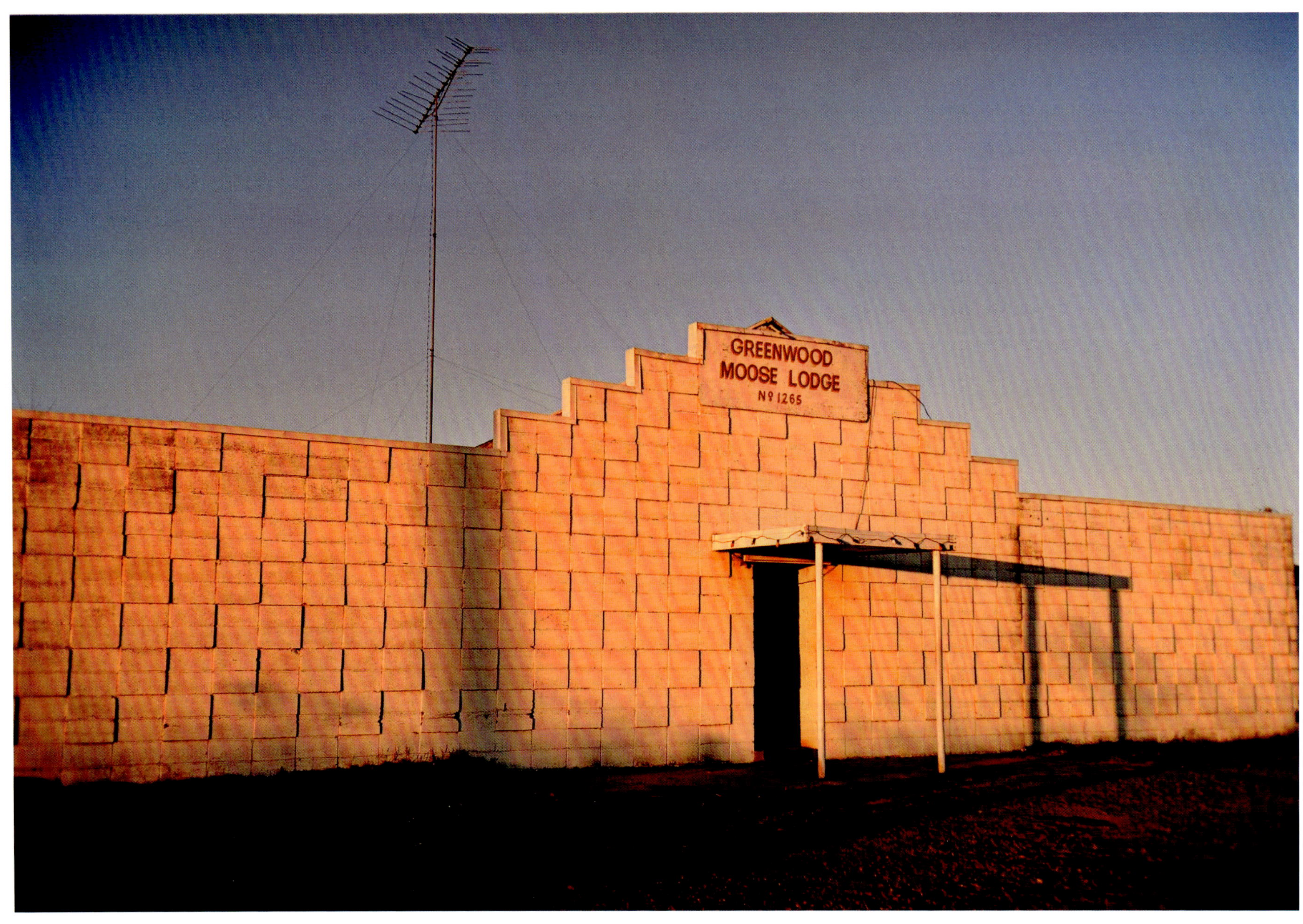

Moose Lodge (Greenwood, Mississippi), 1972.

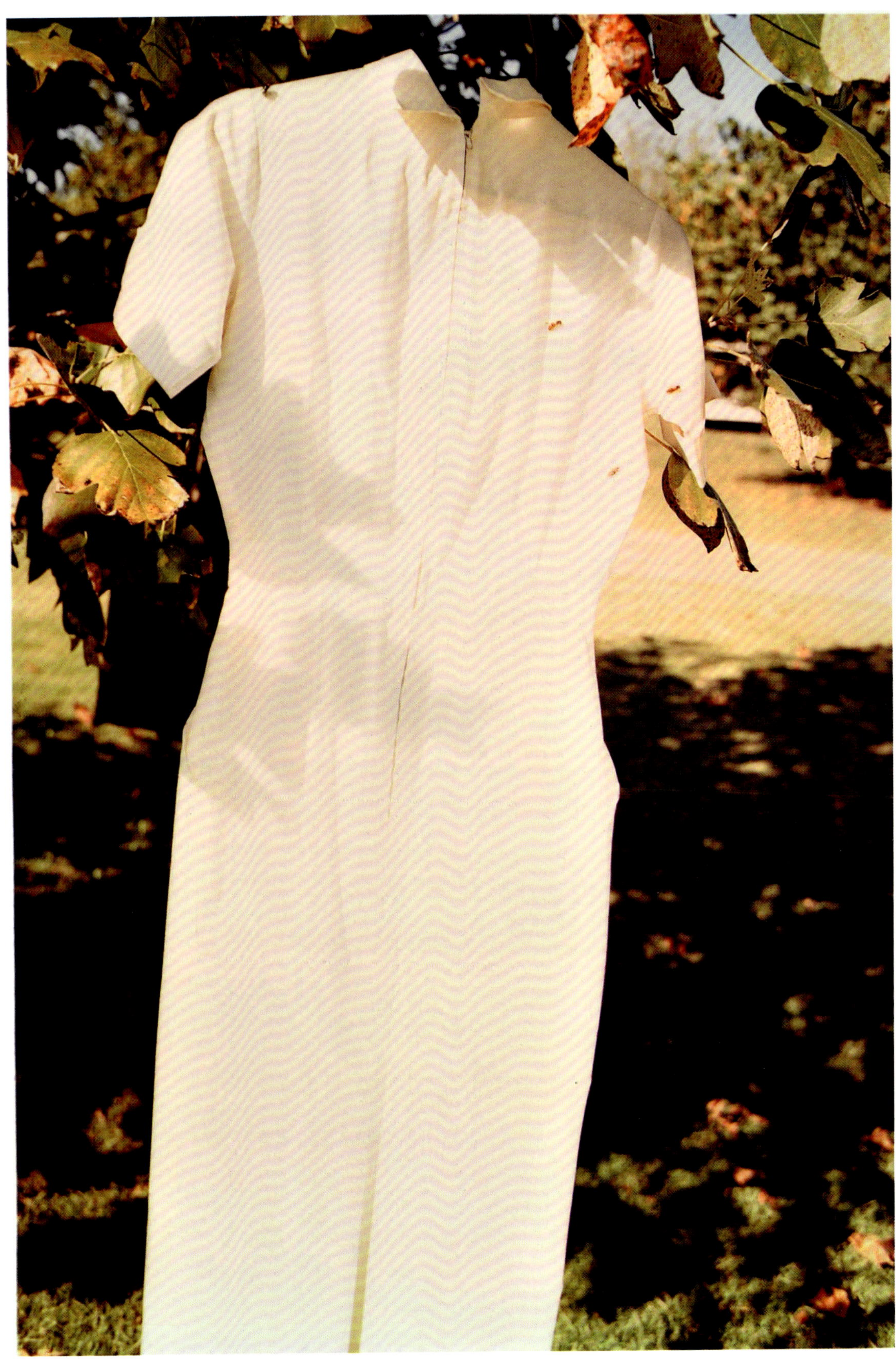

Maid's White Uniform with Bees (Memphis, Tennessee), 1972.

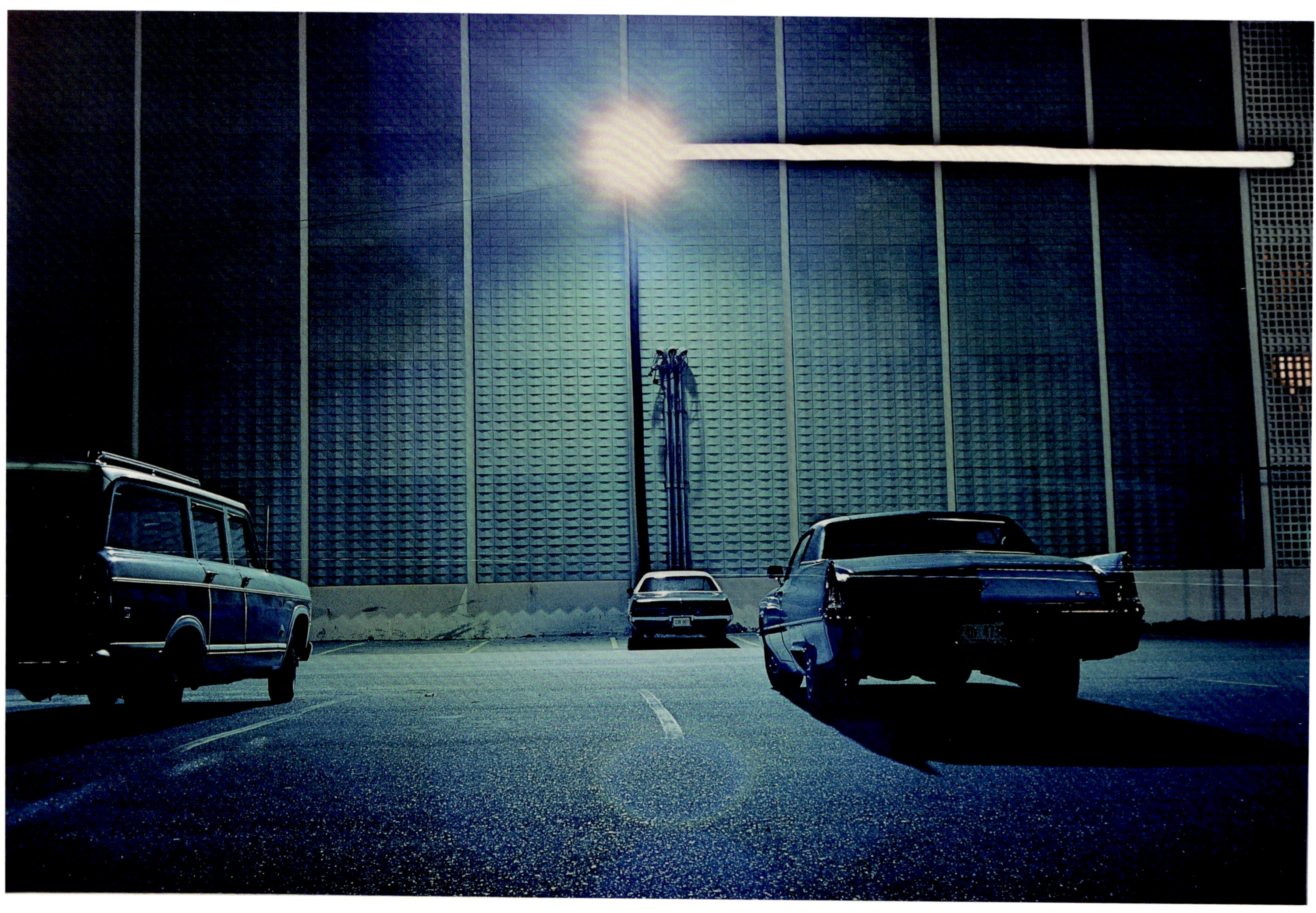

Untitled (Blue Parking Lot), 1973.

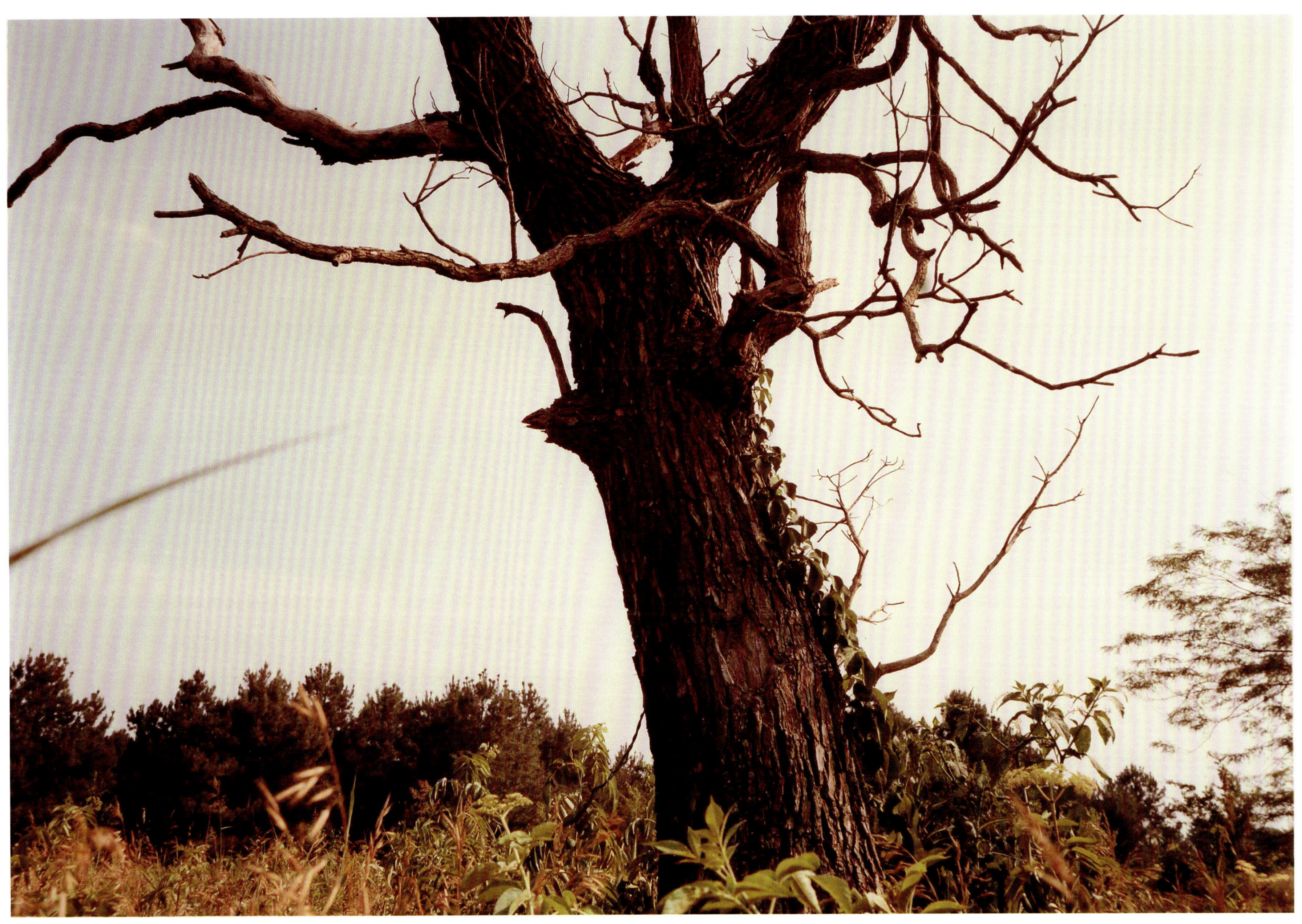

Untitled (near Plains, Georgia), 1976, from the series *Election Eve*.

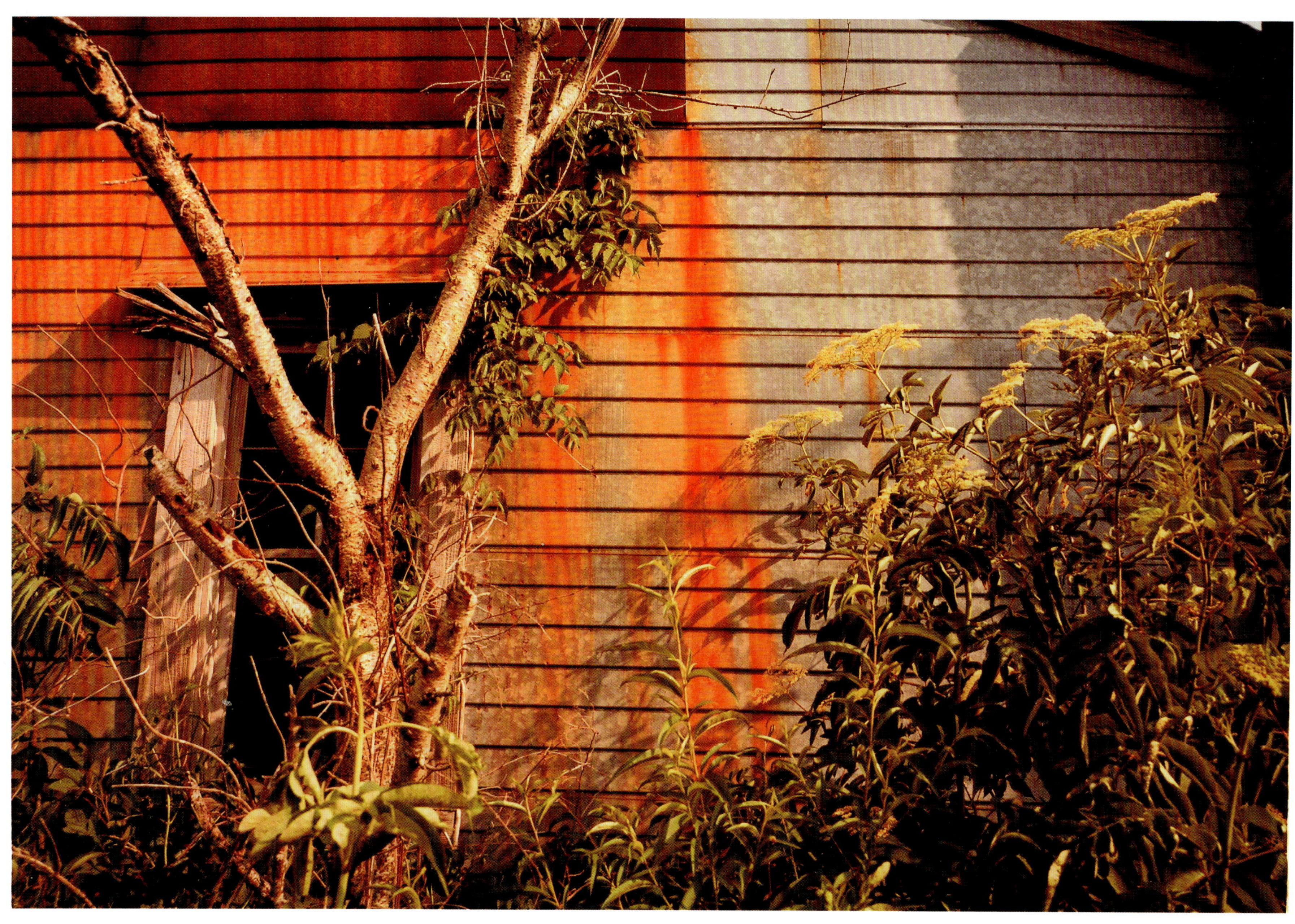

Untitled (near Plains, Georgia), 1976, from the series *Election Eve*.

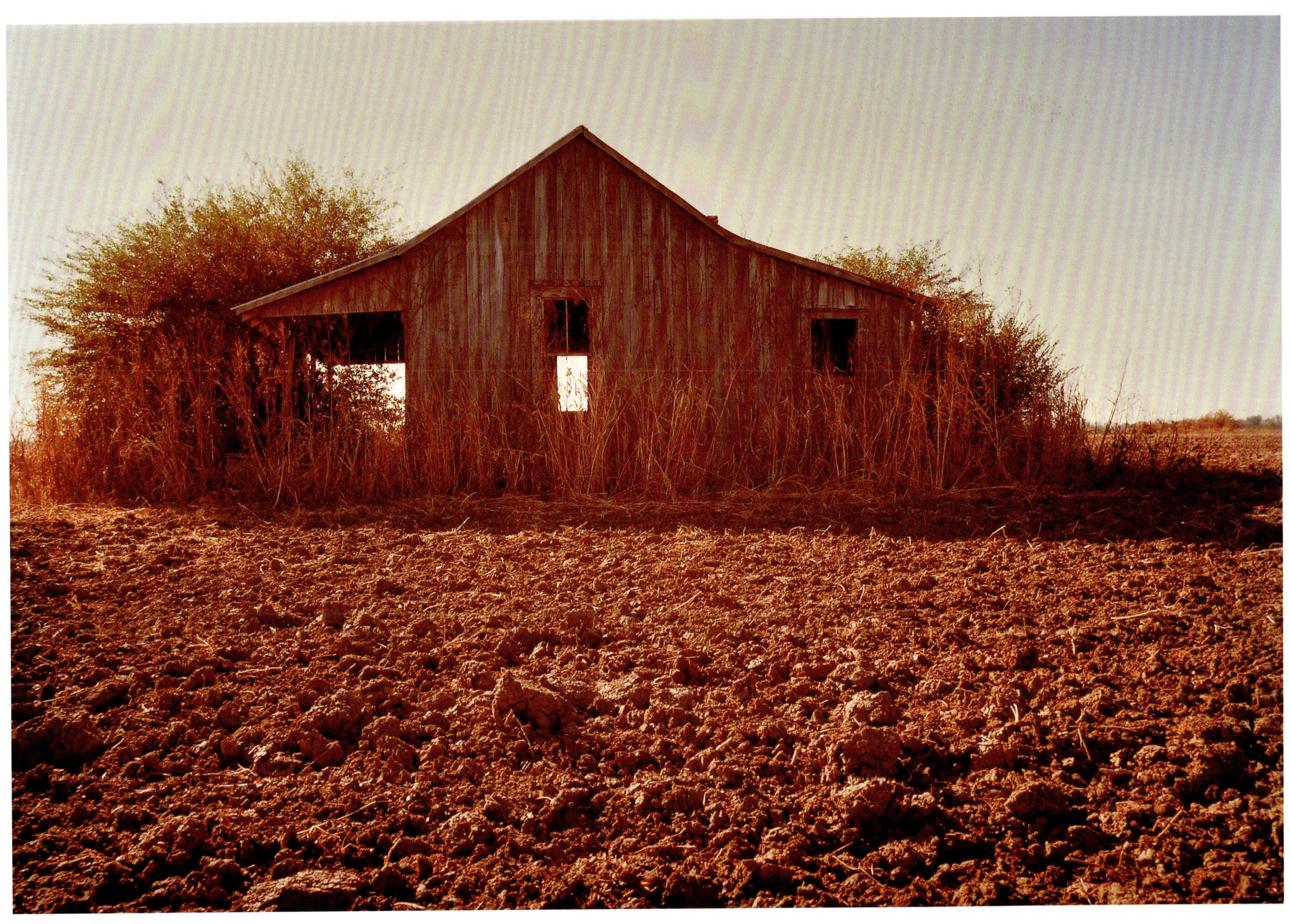

Untitled (near Plains, Georgia), 1976, from the series *Election Eve*.

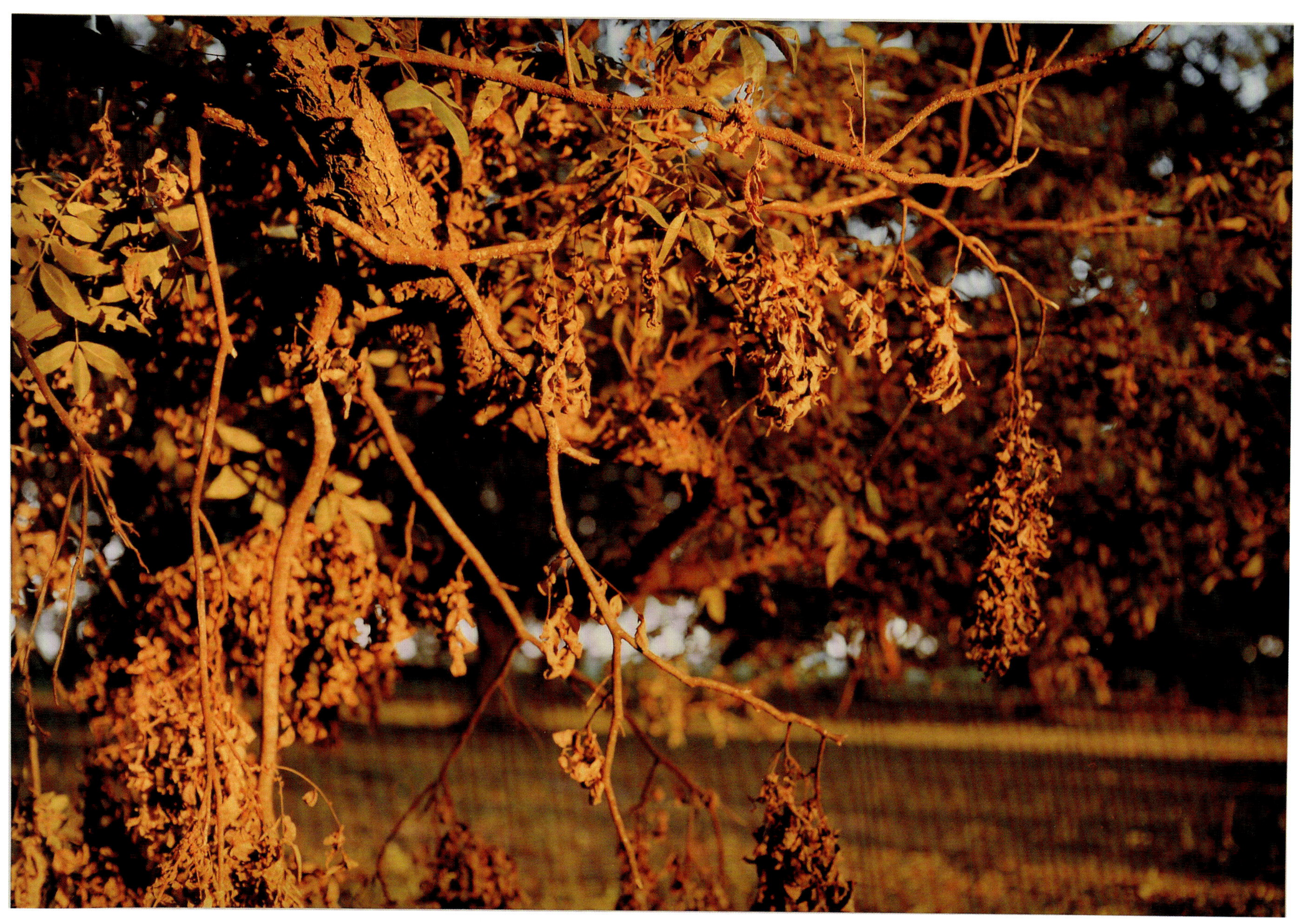

Untitled (near Plains, Georgia), 1976, from the series *Election Eve*.

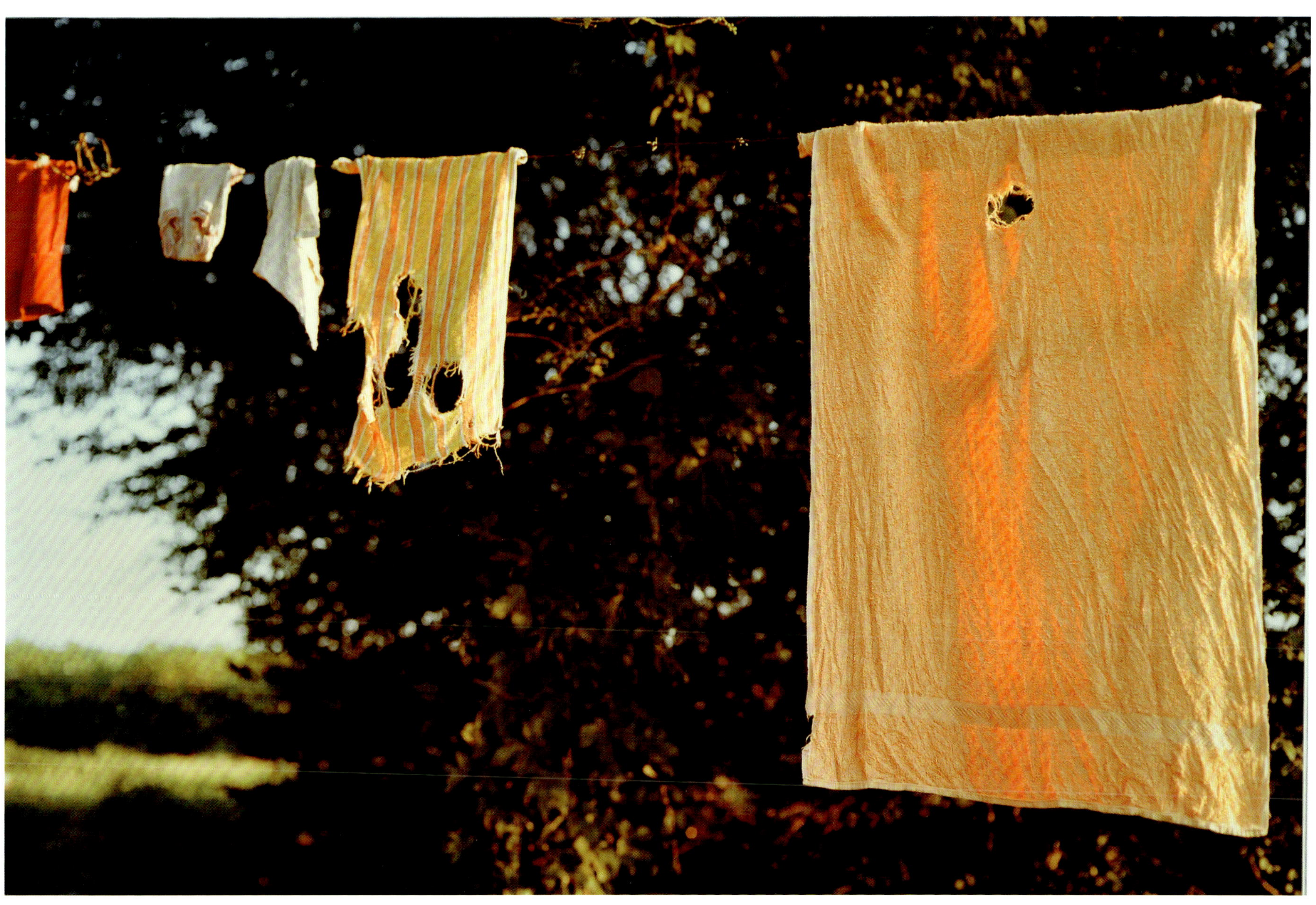

Untitled (near Plains, Georgia), 1976, from the series *Election Eve*.

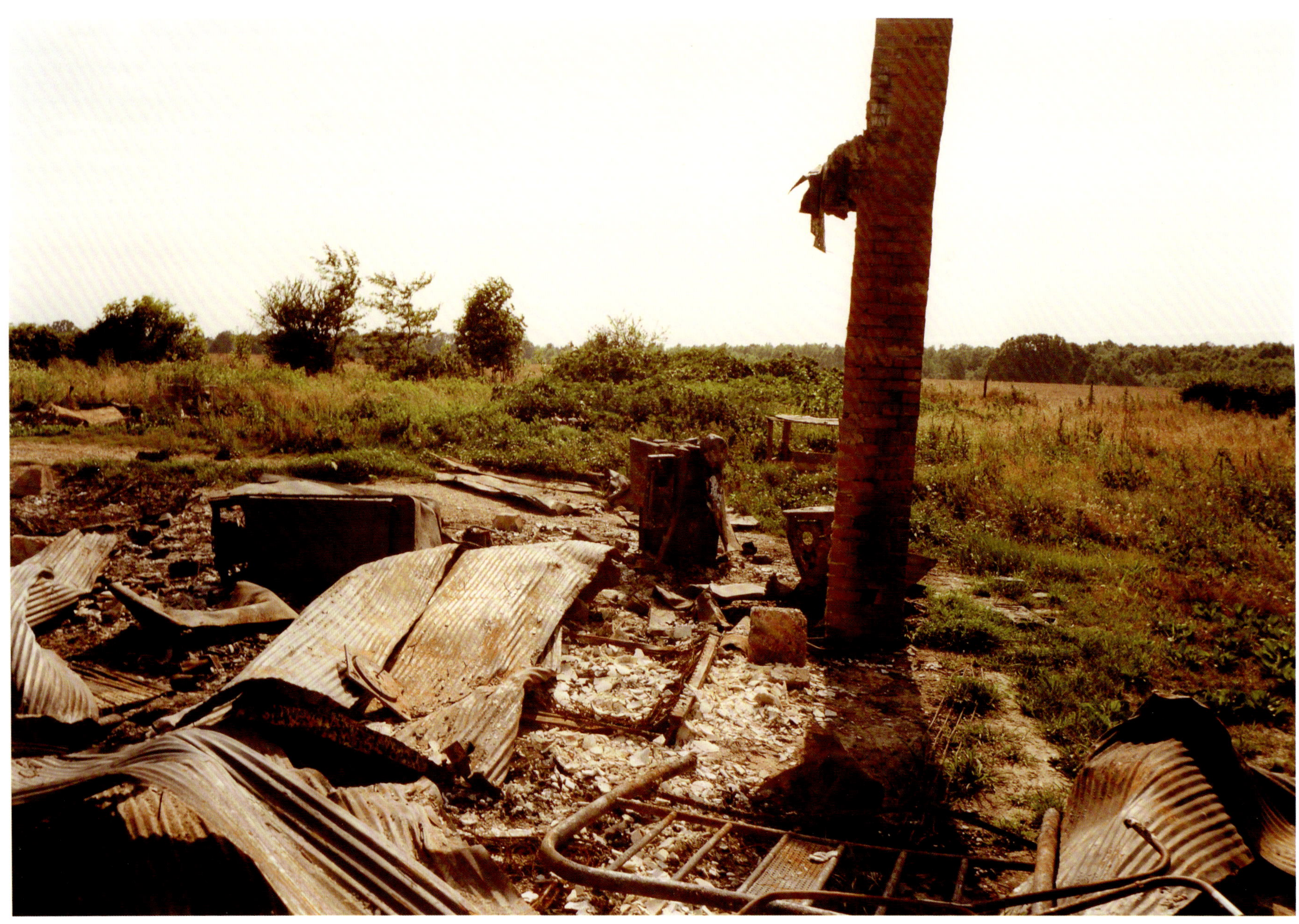

Untitled (near Plains, Georgia), 1976, from the series *Election Eve*.

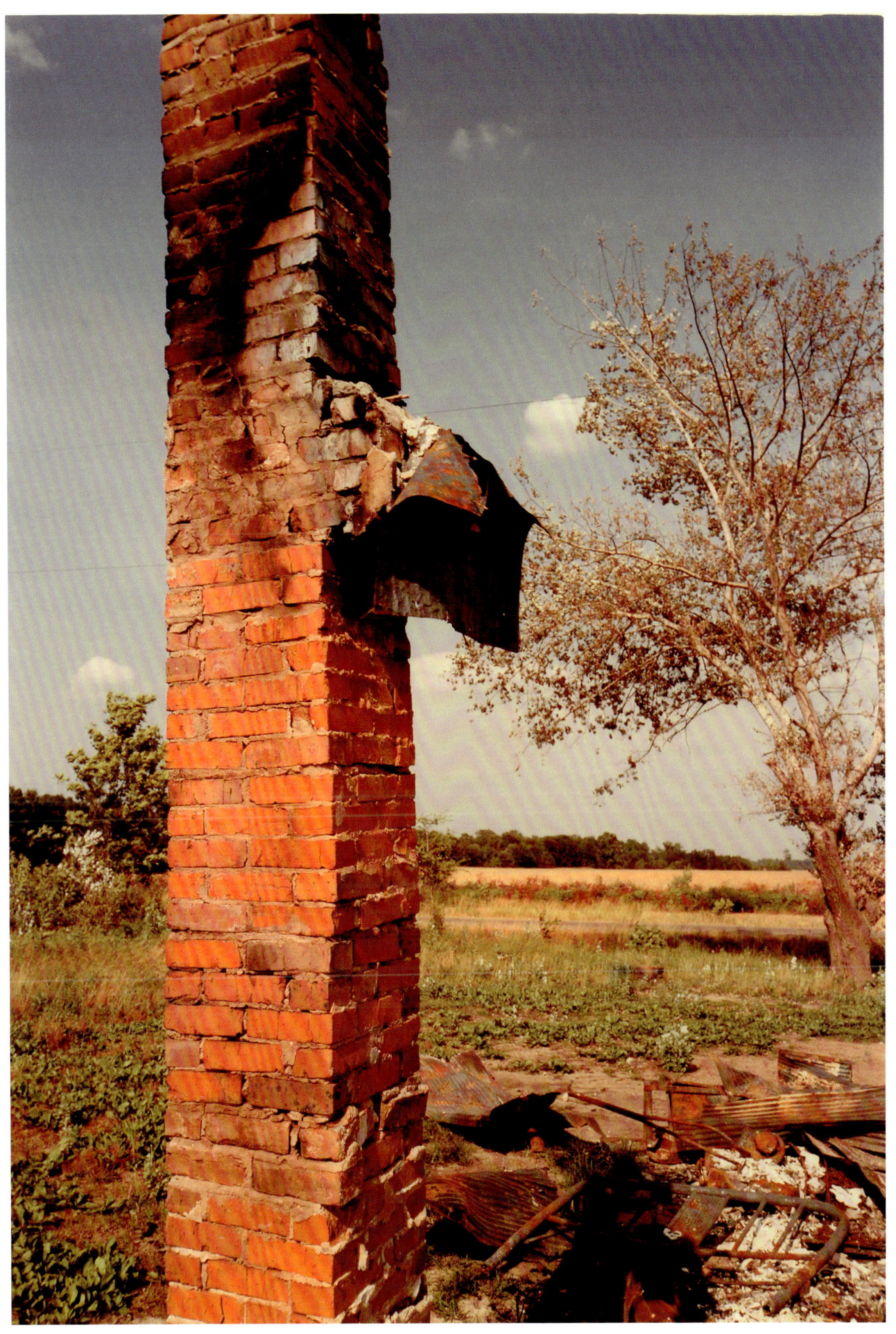

Untitled (near Plains, Georgia), 1976, from the series *Election Eve*.

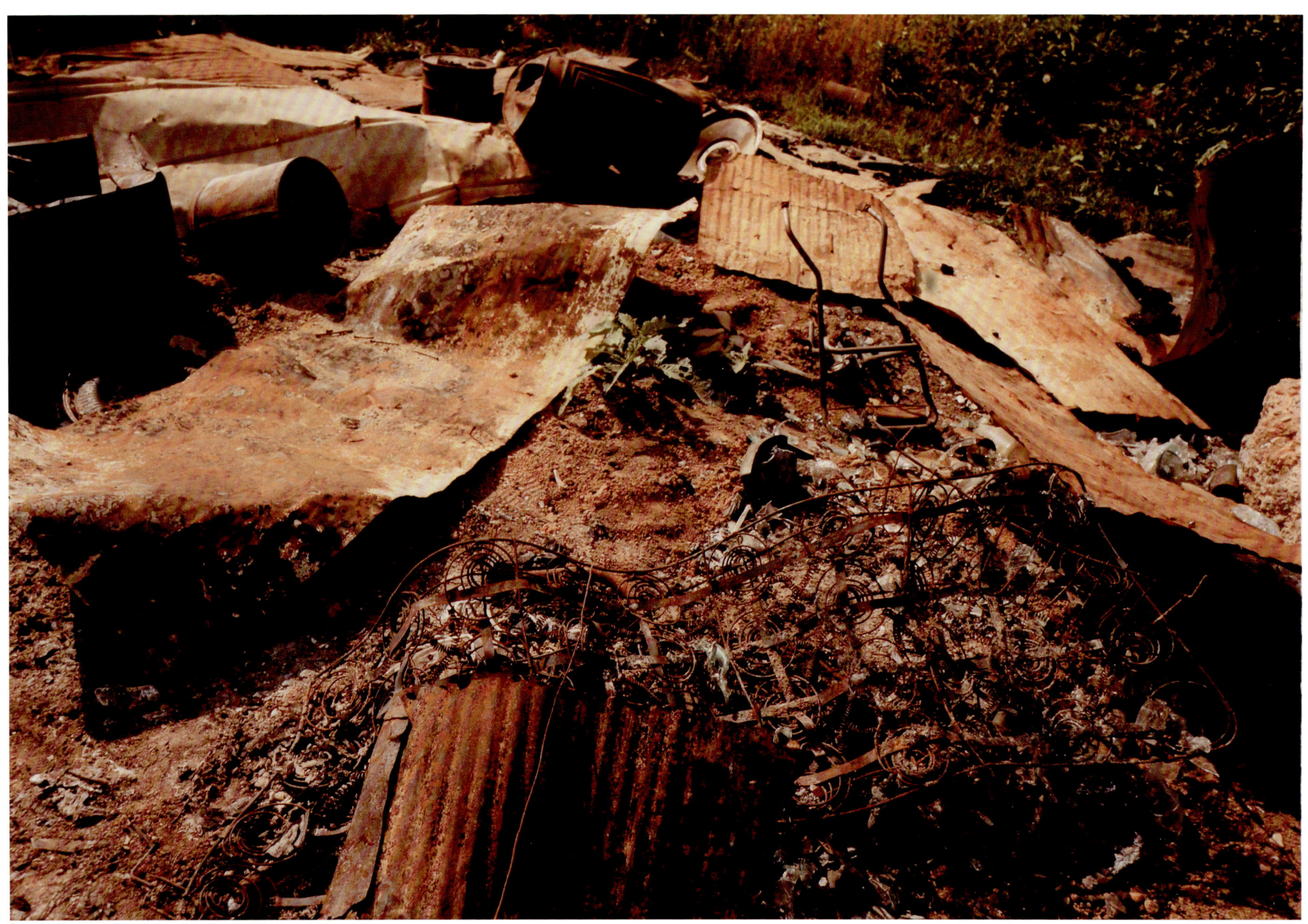

Untitled (near Plains, Georgia), 1976, from the series *Election Eve*.

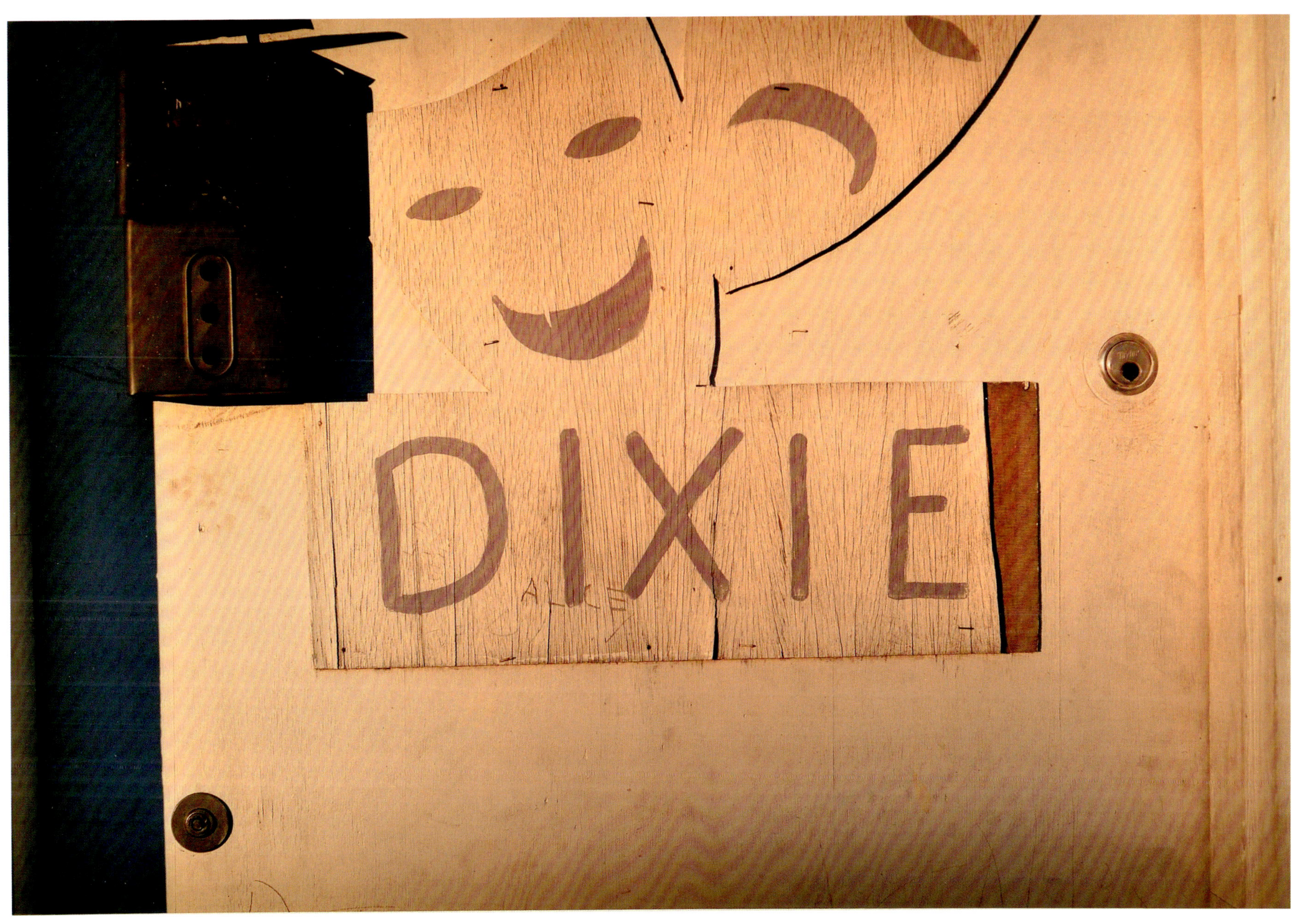

Untitled, 1981, from *The Louisiana Project*.

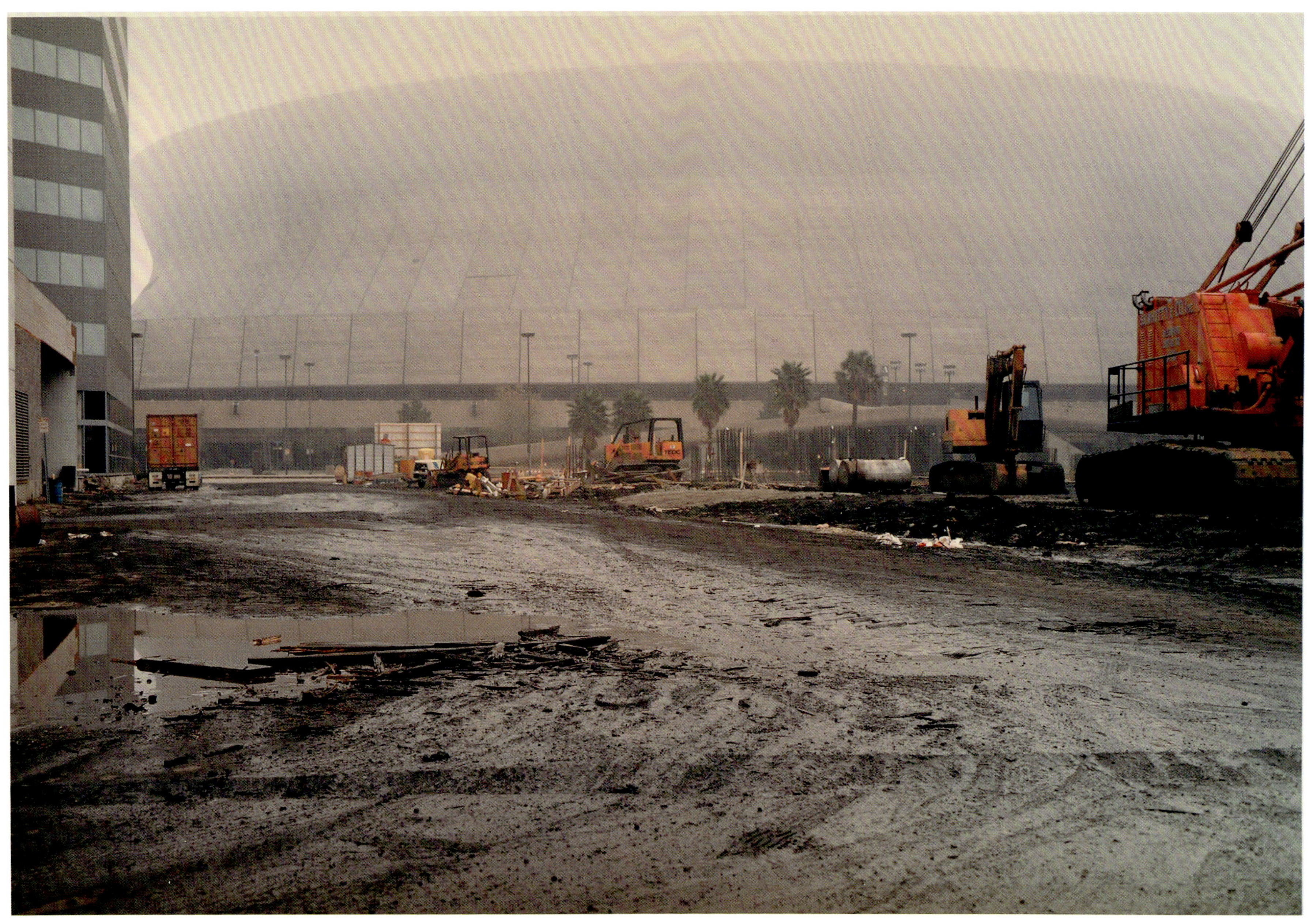

A Good View, 1981, from *The Louisiana Project*

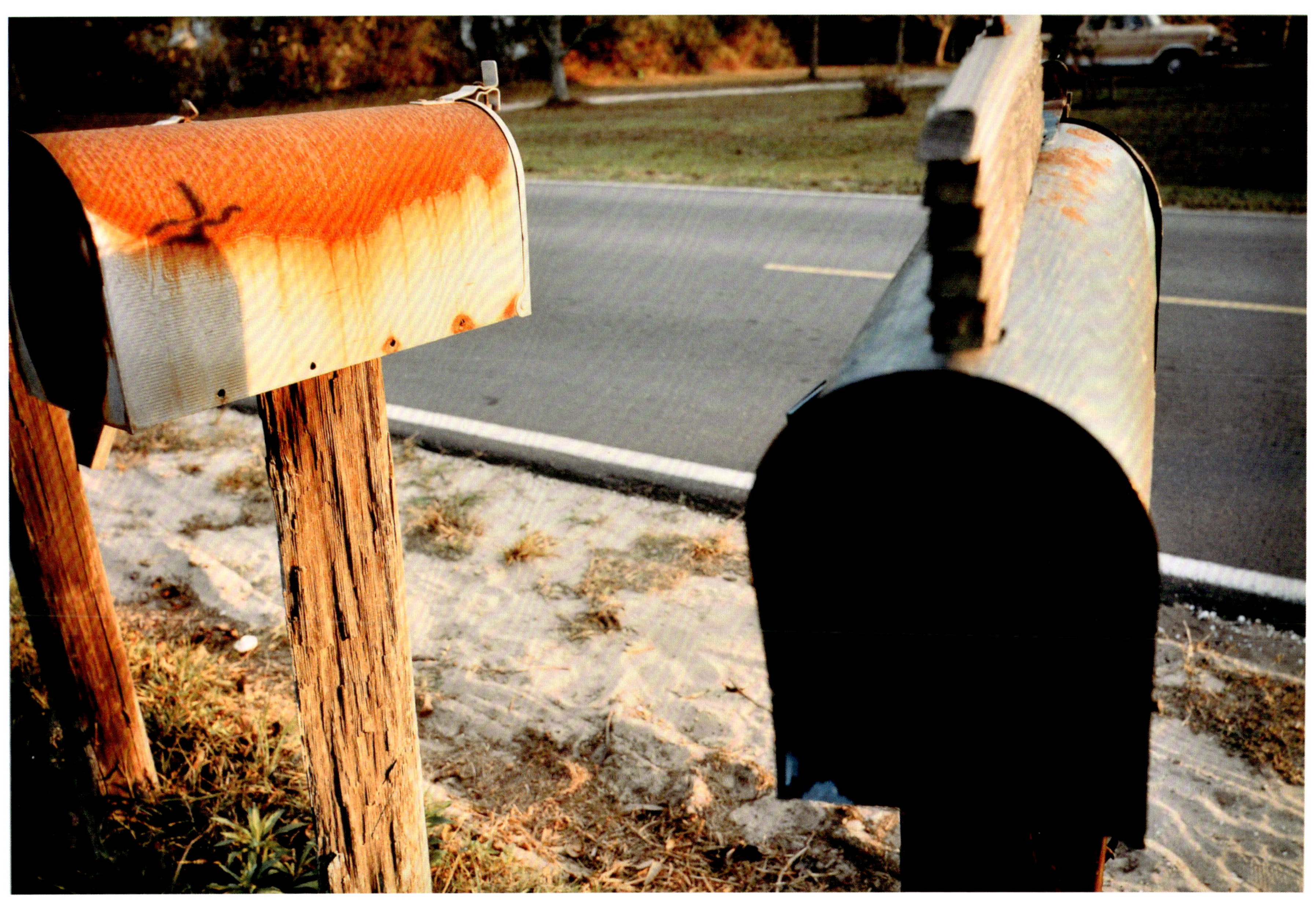

Oh, No! (Oxford, Mississippi), 1981.

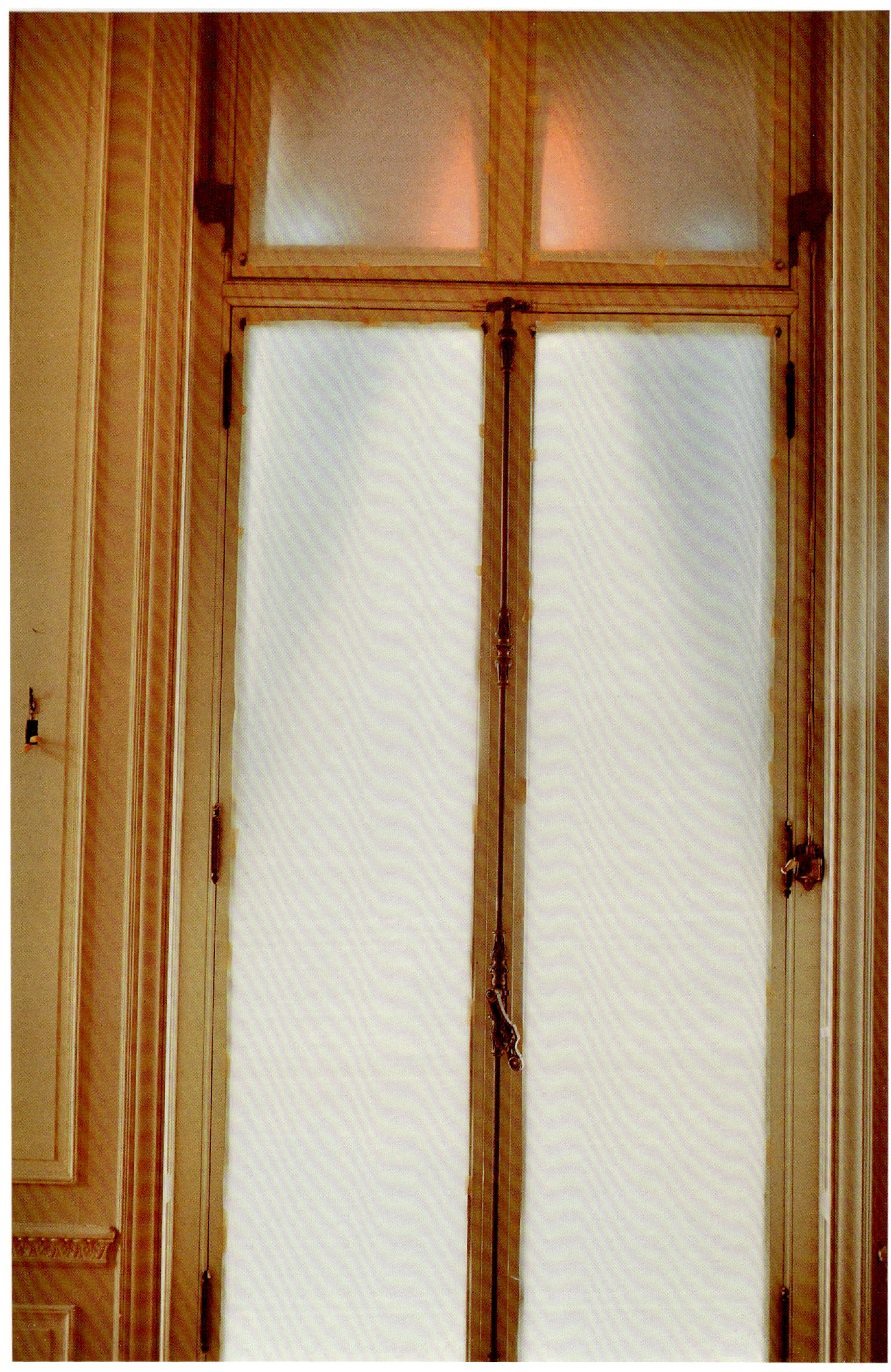

Untitled (Monmouth College, West Long Branch, New Jersey), 1982, from the assignment *Annie*.

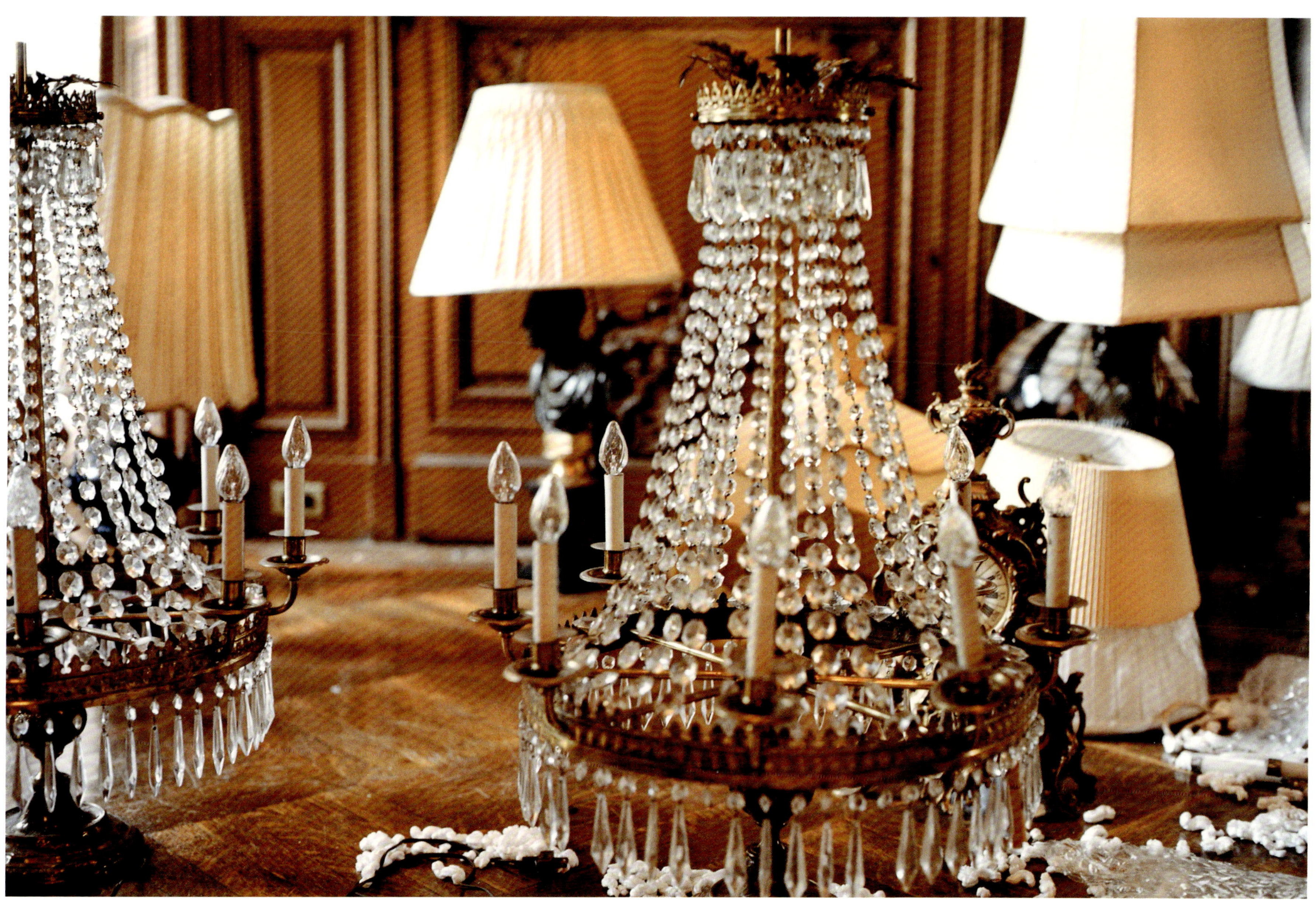

Untitled (Monmouth College, West Long Branch, New Jersey), 1982, from the assignment *Annie*.

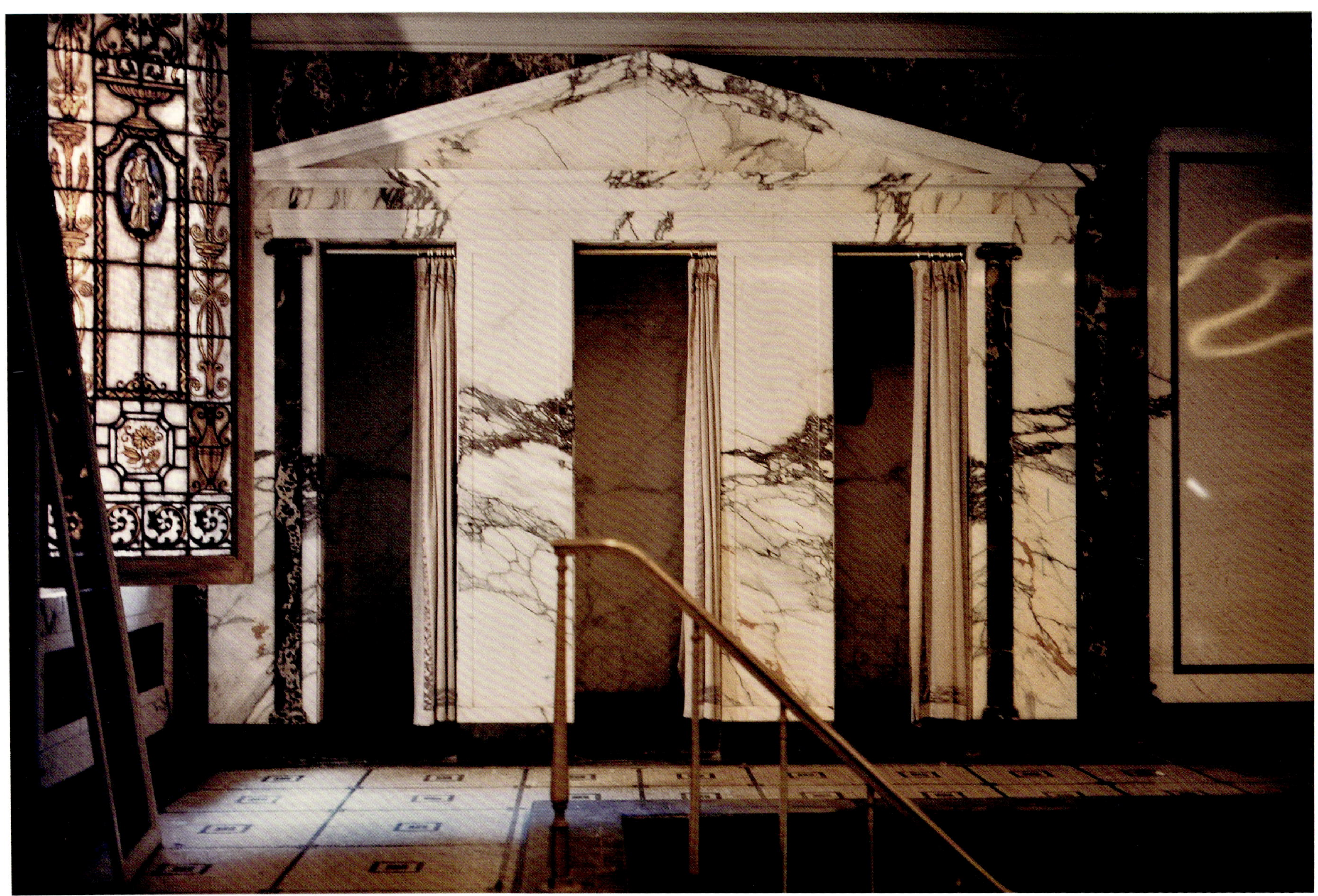

Untitled (Monmouth College, West Long Branch, New Jersey), 1982, from the assignment *Annie*.

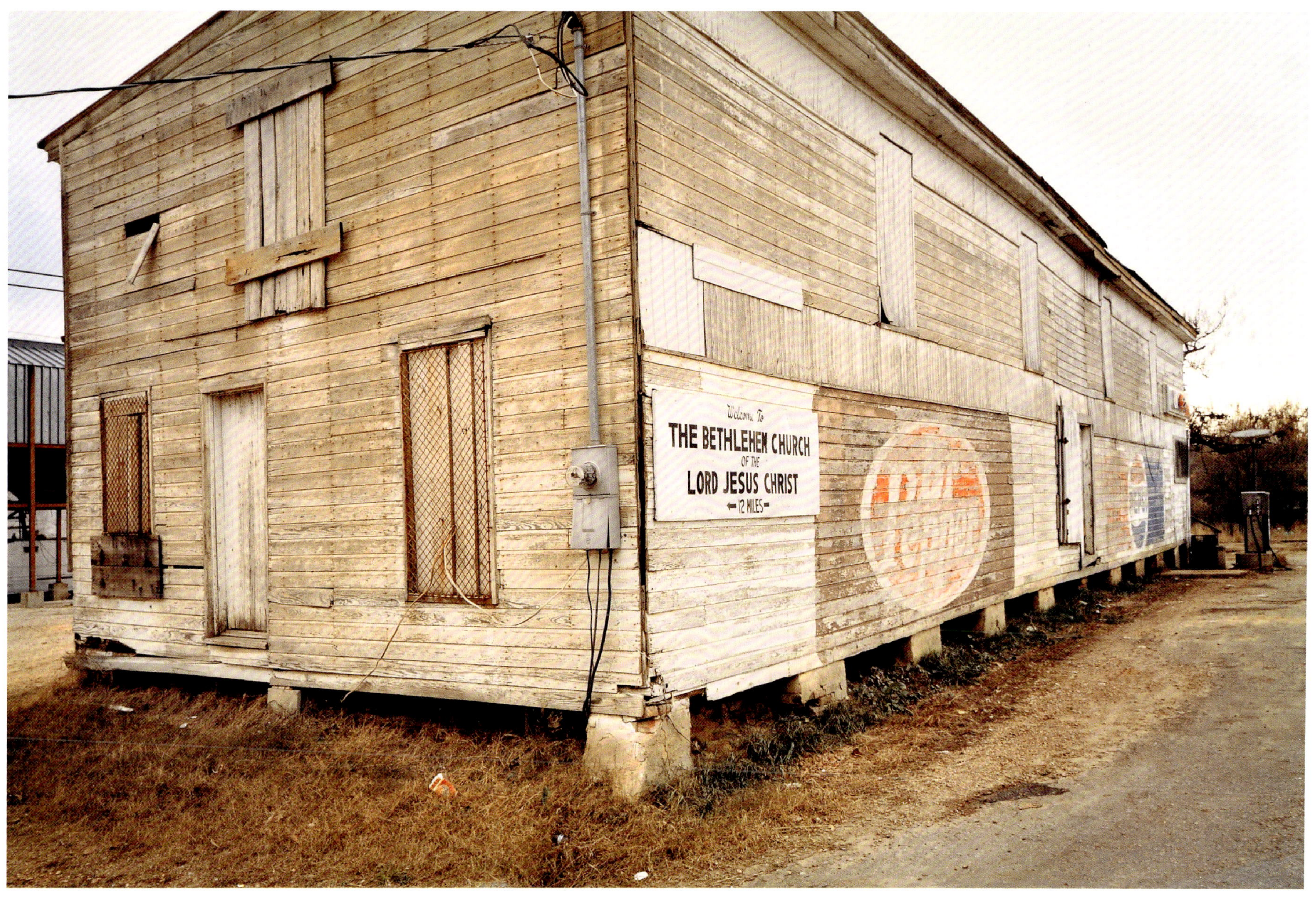

Holly Springs Road at Waterford, Mississippi, 1982.

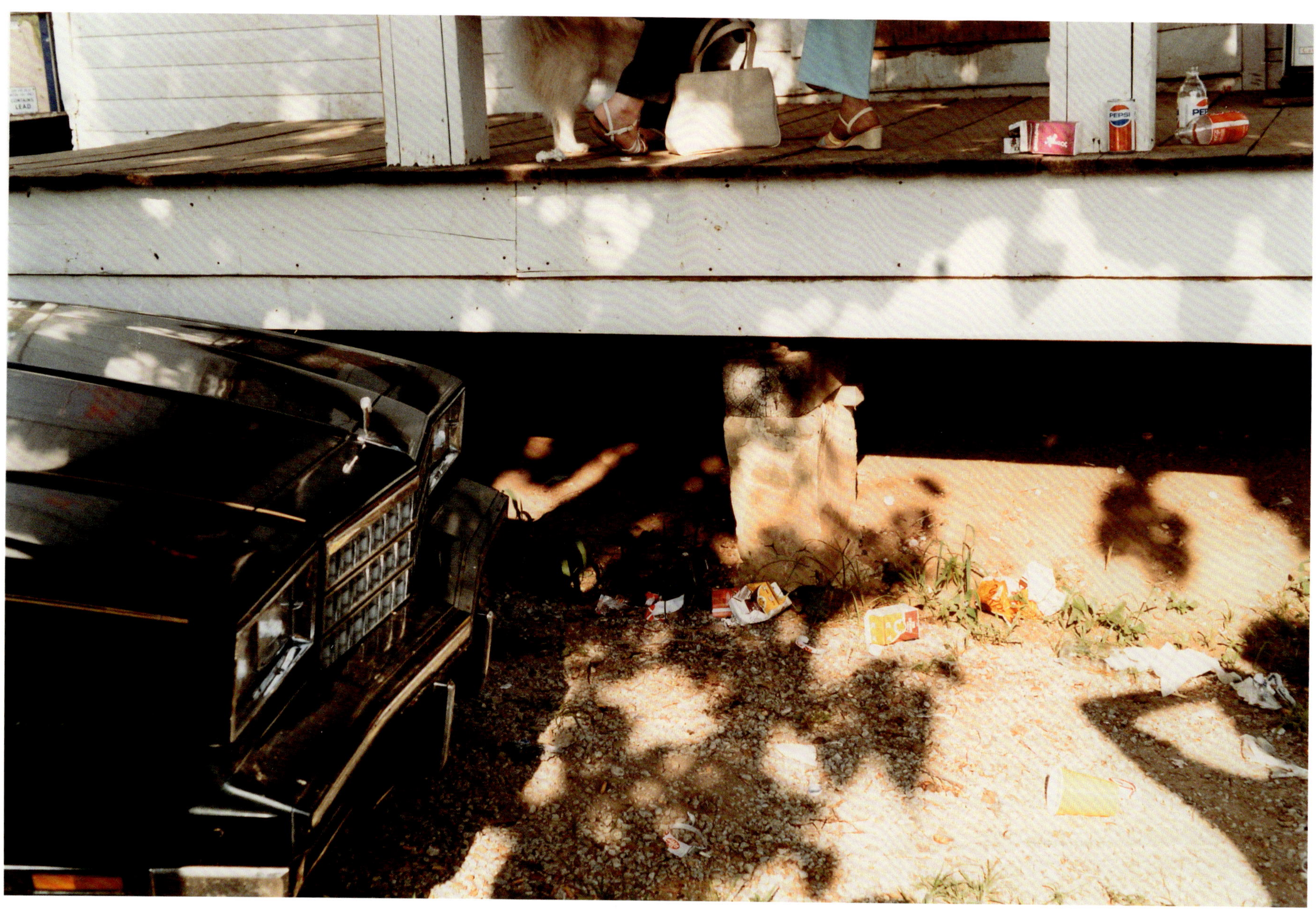

Untitled (Waterford, Mississippi), 1983.

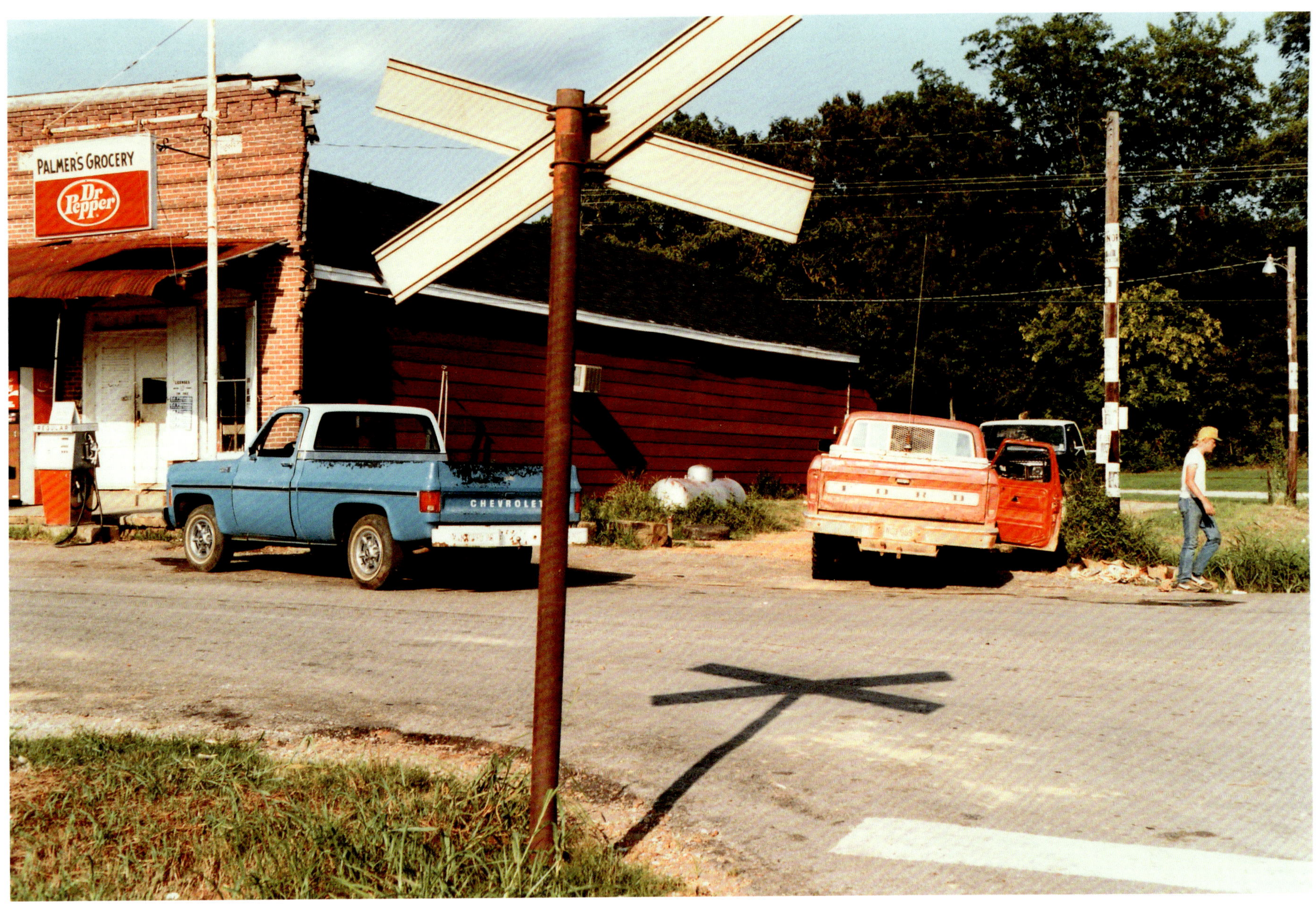

Untitled (Palmer's Grocery, Waterford, Mississippi), 1983.

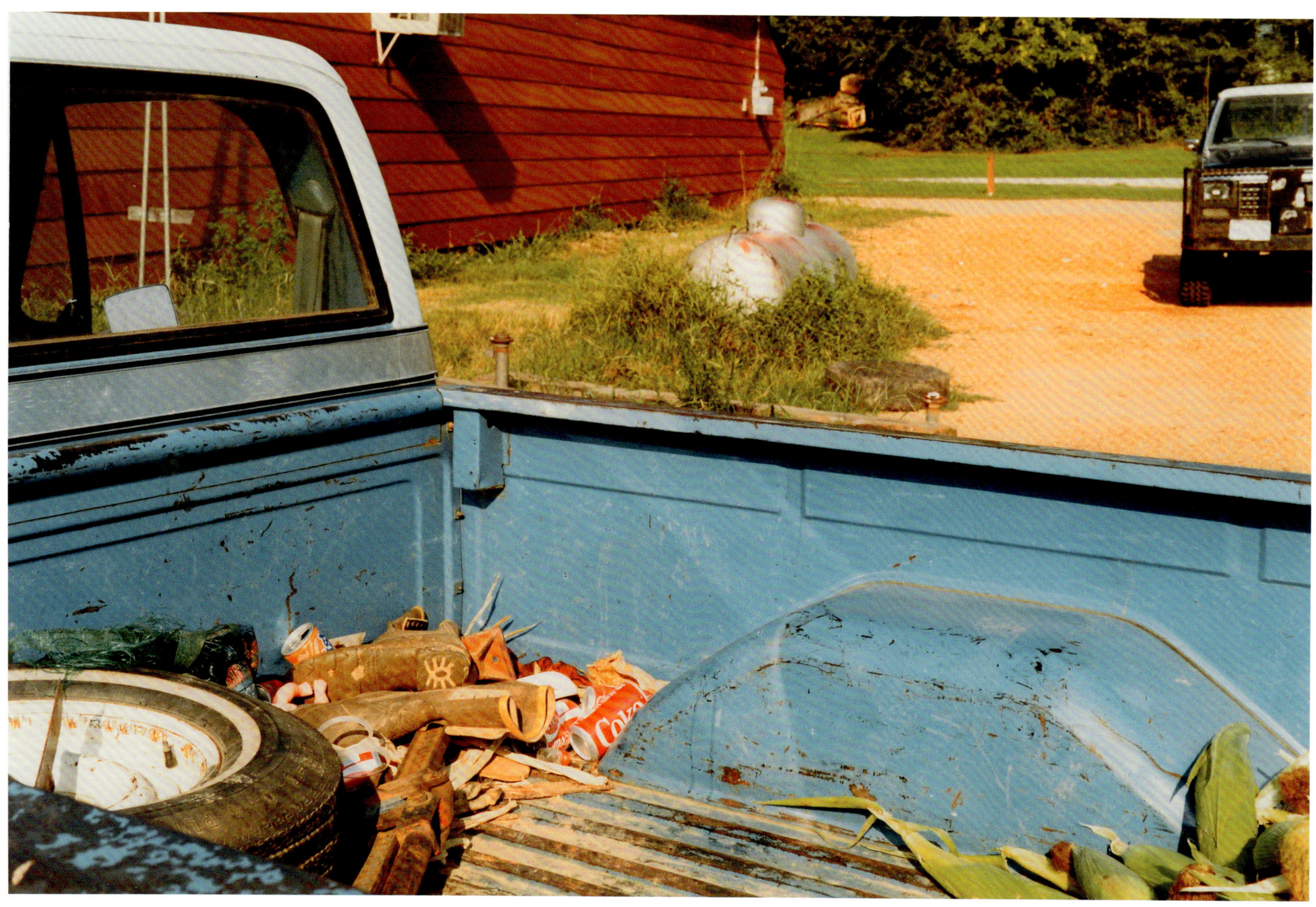

Untitled (Waterford, Mississippi), 1983.

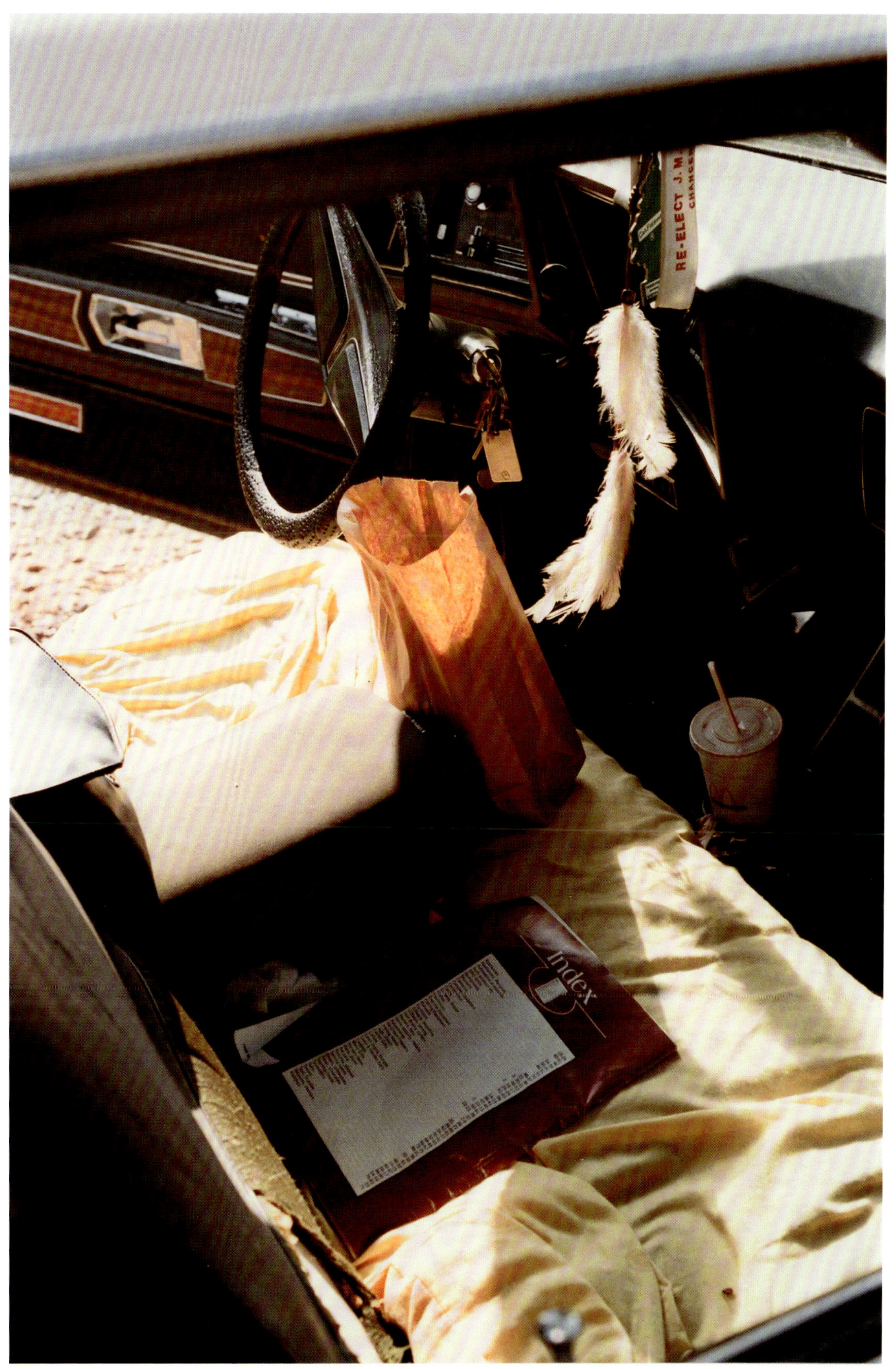

Untitled (Waterford, Mississippi), 1983.

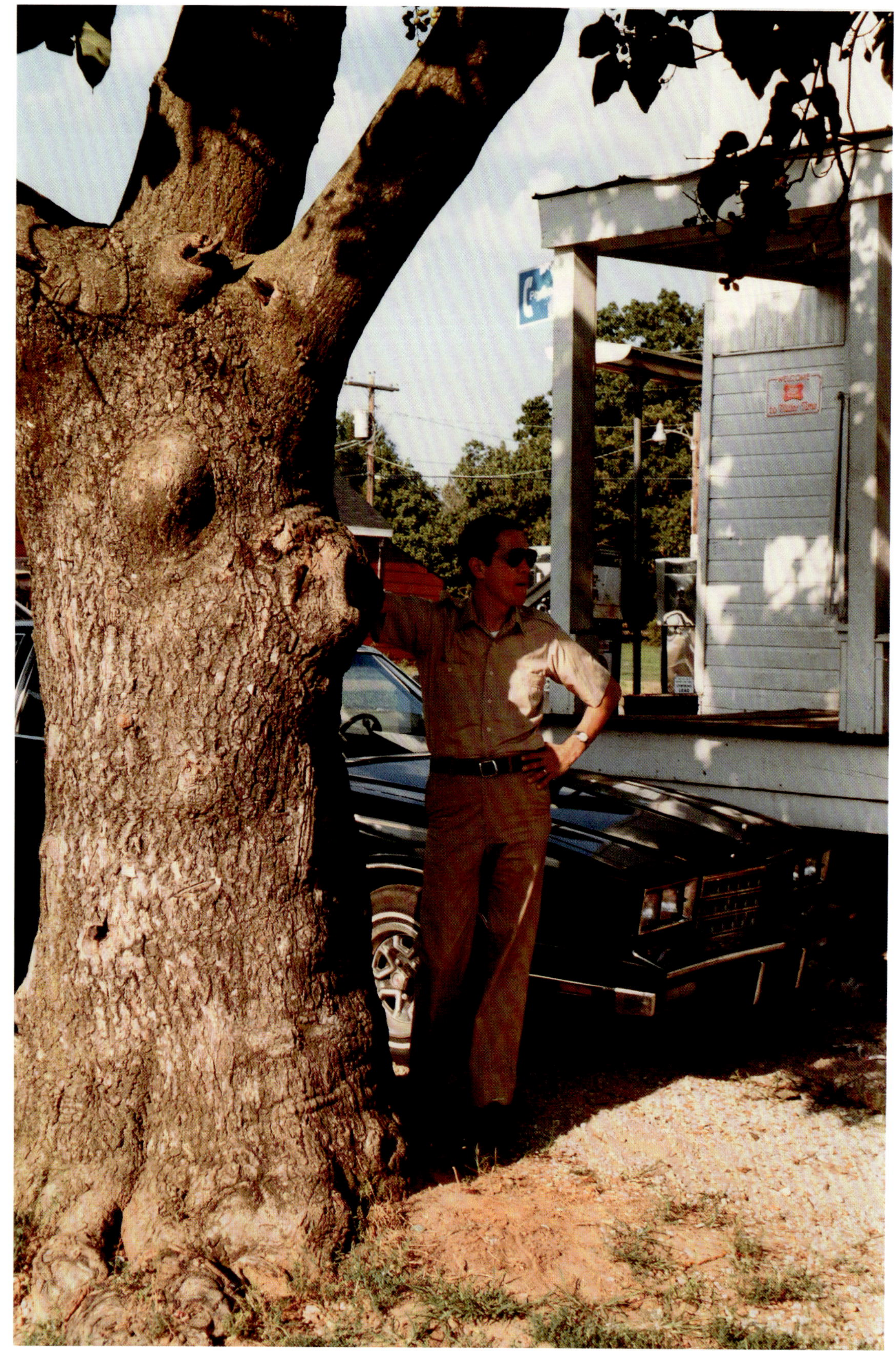

Untitled (Waterford, Mississippi), 1983.

Additional Eggleston Photographs in the Ferris Collection

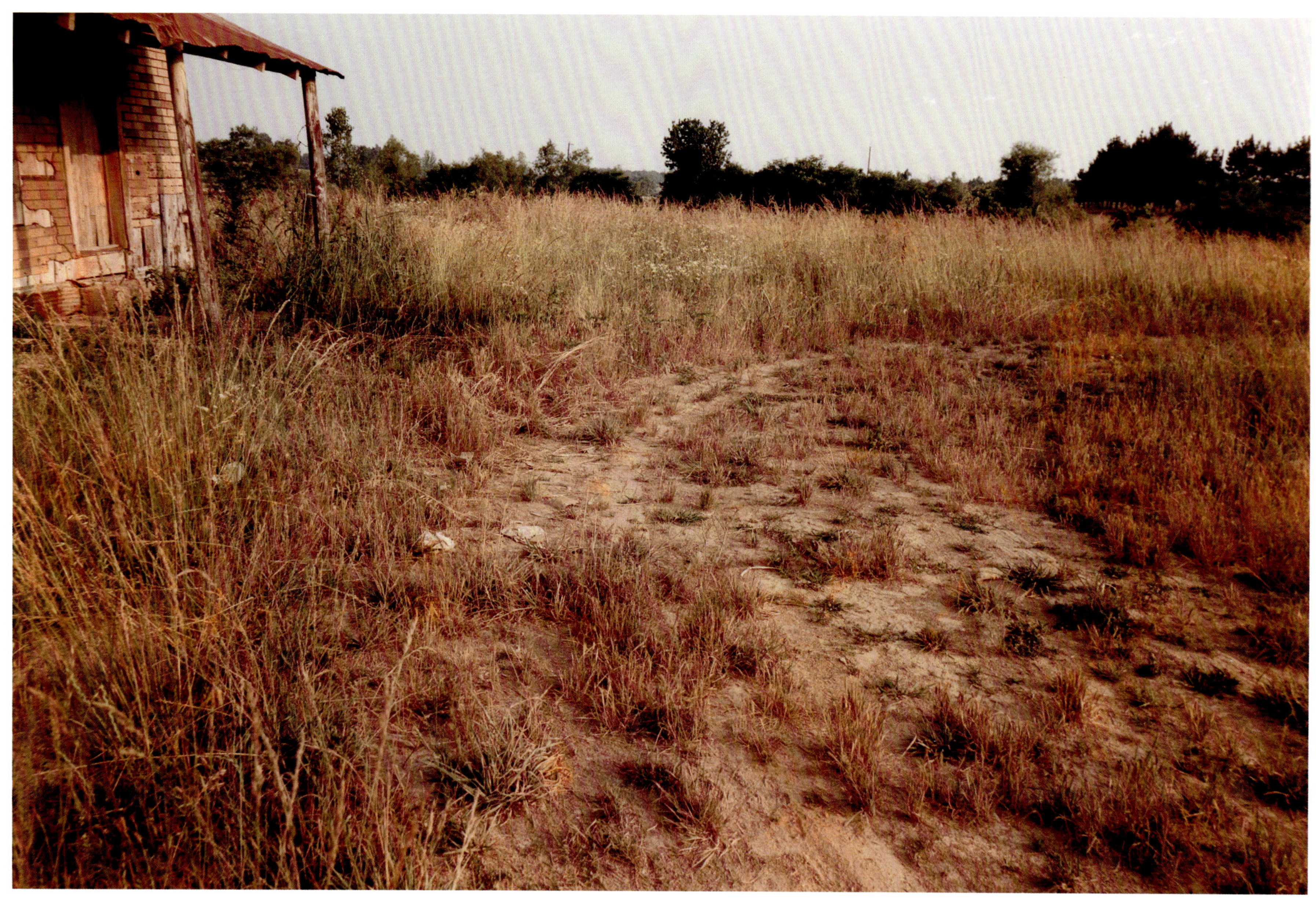

Untitled (near Plains, Georgia), 1976, from the series *Election Eve*. Resin-coated photograph, 1988.5.11.

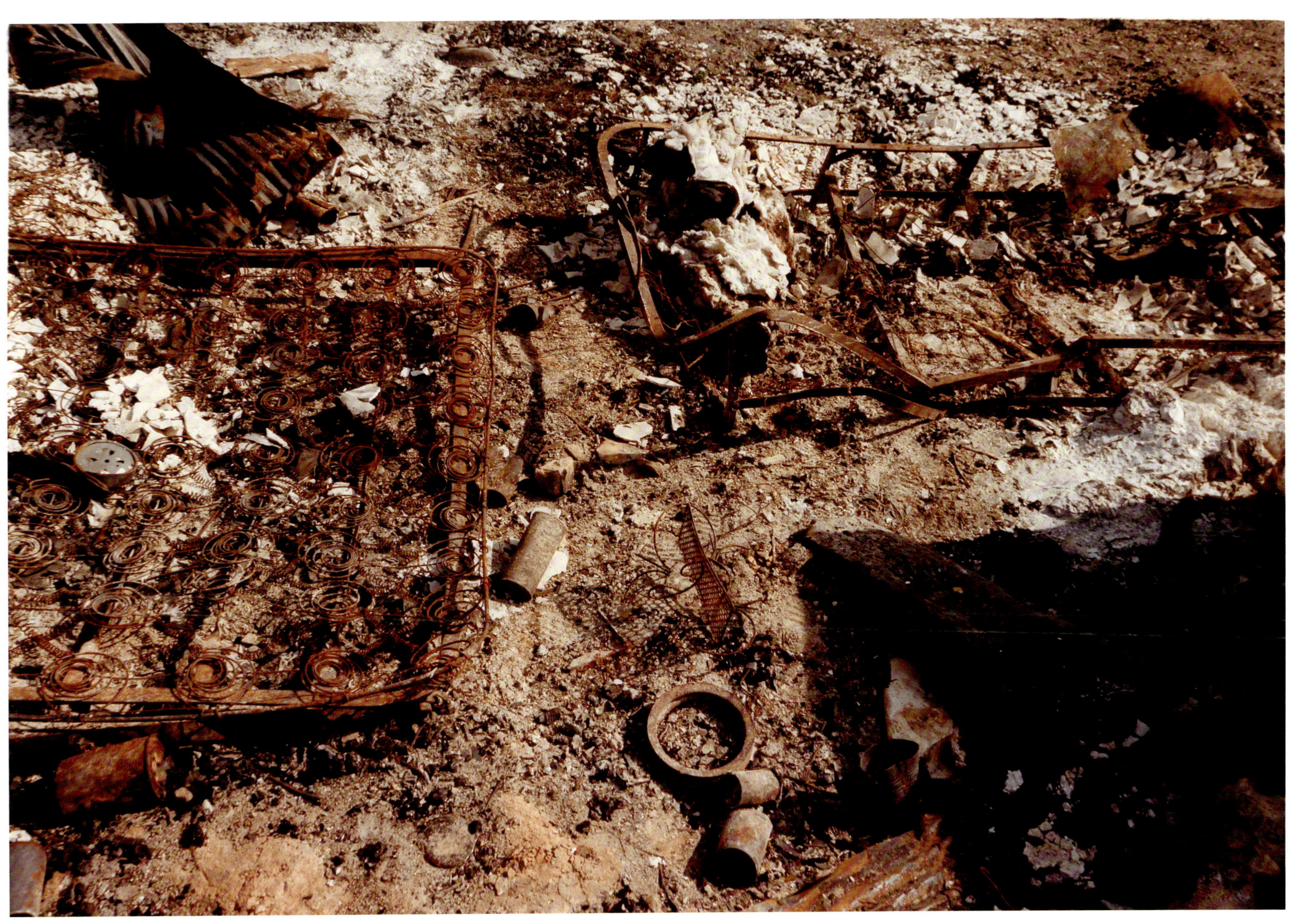

Untitled (near Plains, Georgia), 1976, from the series *Election Eve*. Resin-coated photograph, 1988.5.43.

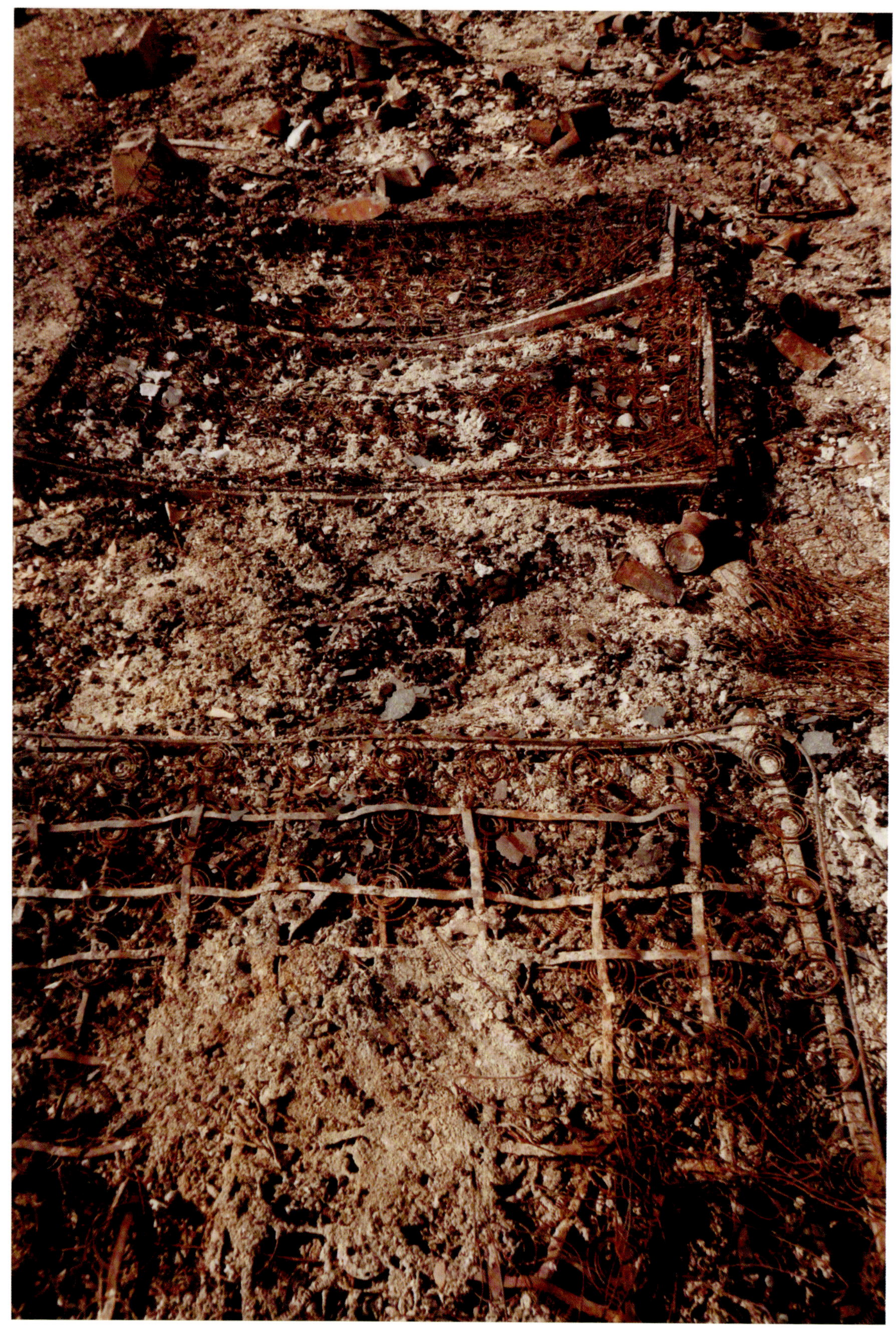

Untitled (near Plains, Georgia), 1976, from the series *Election Eve*. Resin-coated photograph, 1988.5.44.

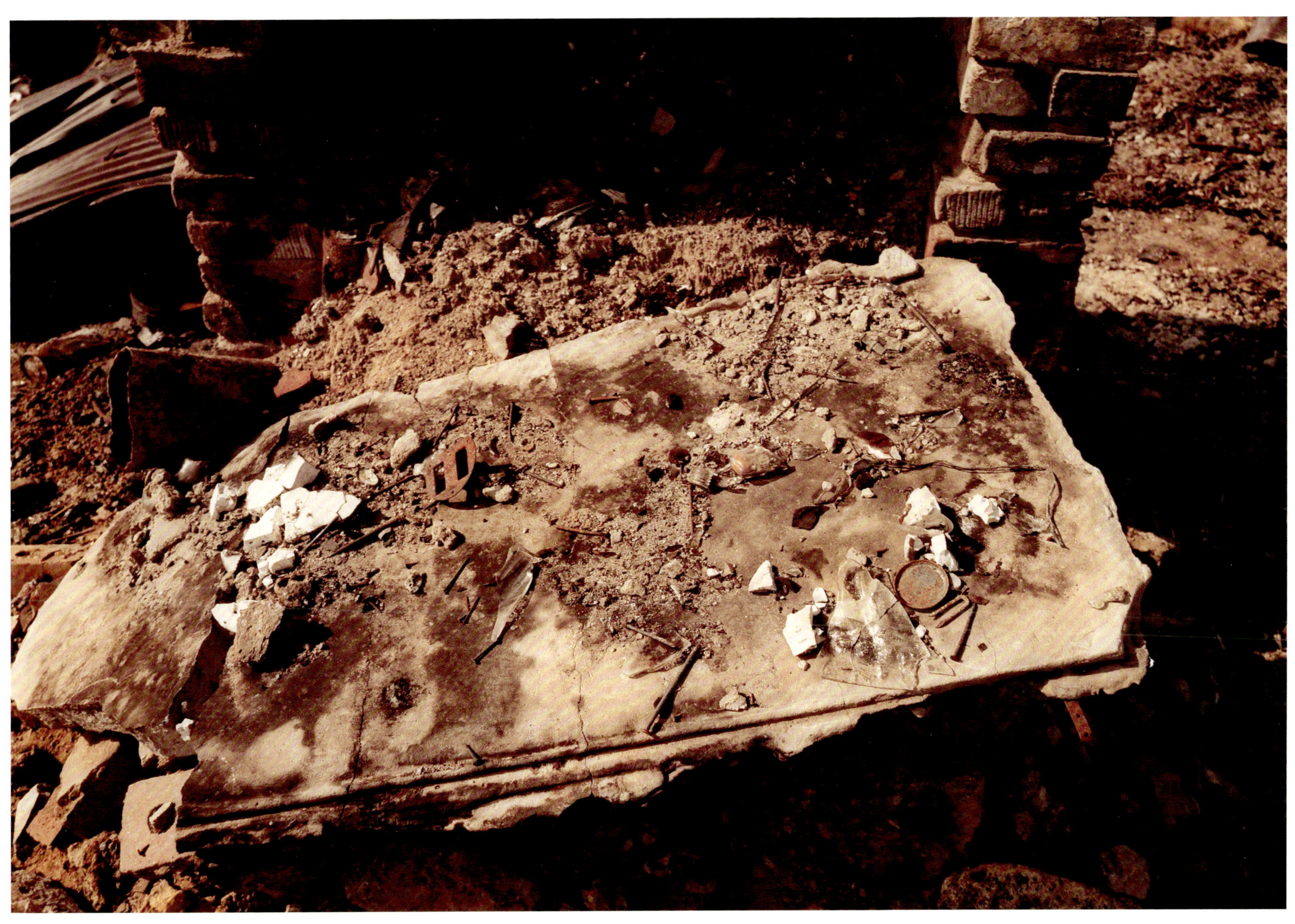

Untitled (near Plains, Georgia), 1976, from the series *Election Eve*. Resin-coated photograph. 1988.5.59.

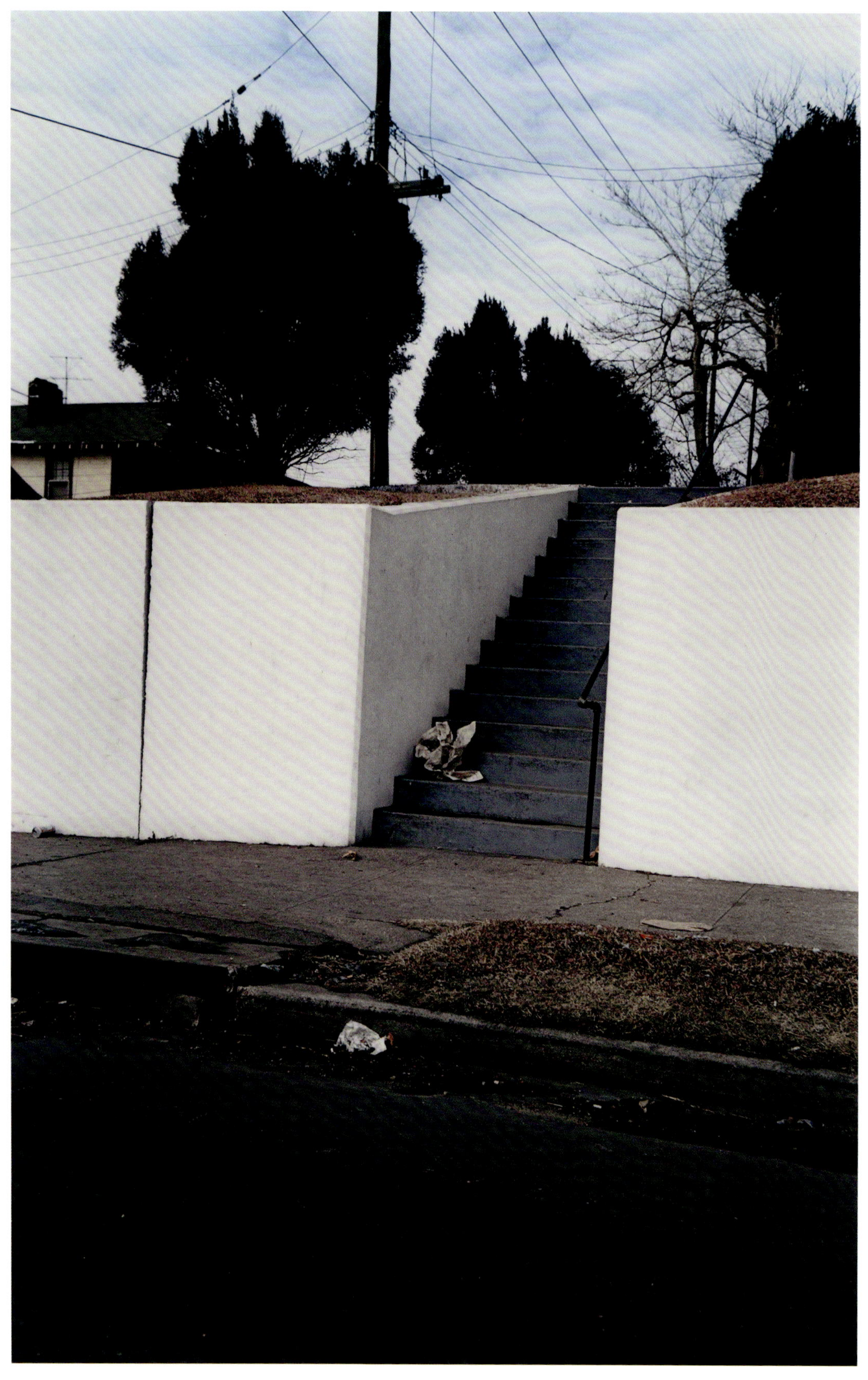

Untitled, n.d. (Memphis, Tennessee, 1969–1970). Resin-coated photograph. 1982.1.5.

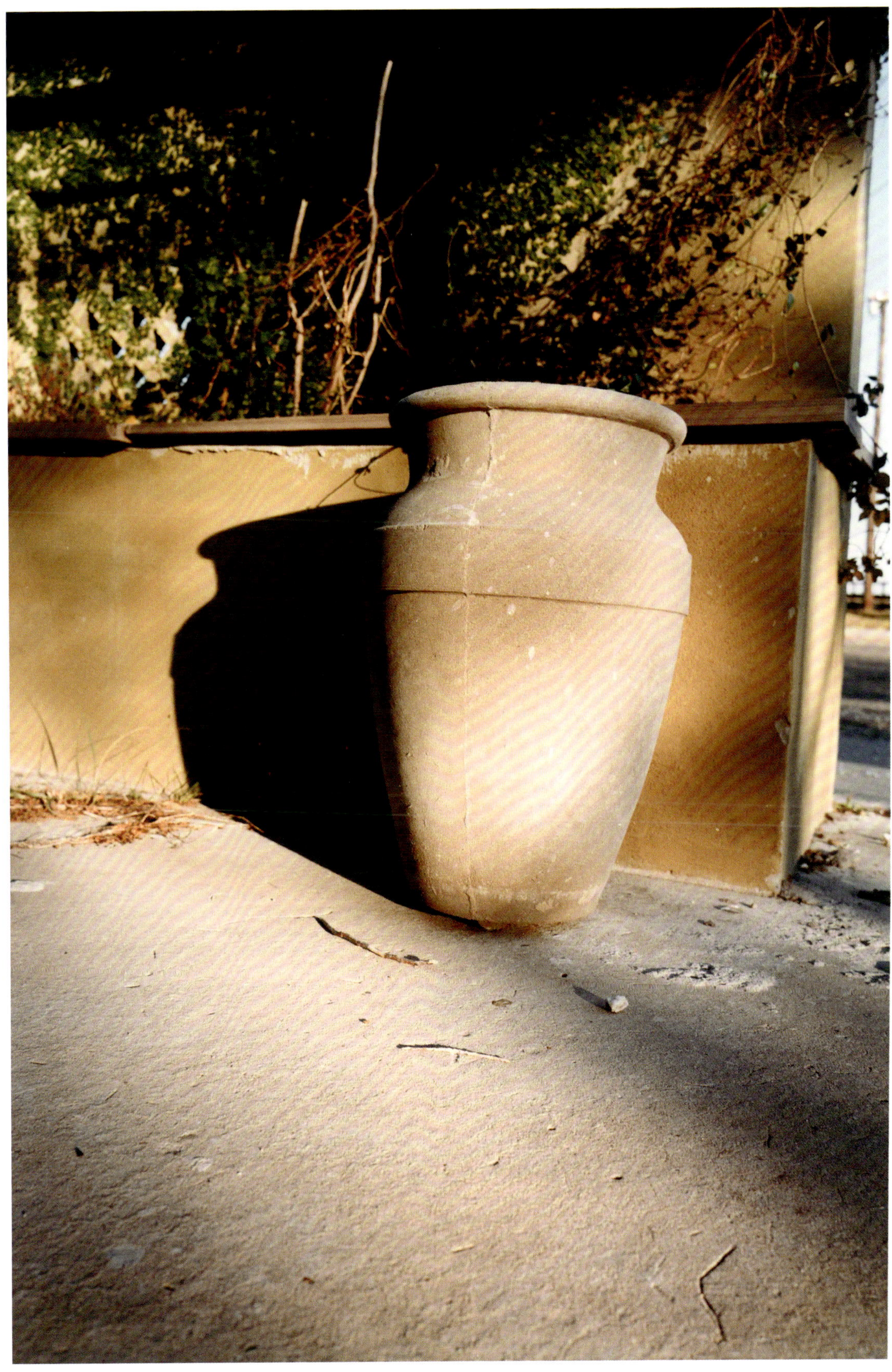

Untitled, 1982. Resin-coated photograph. "For Bill Ferris Oxford 6/82" on front. "For B.F. Hope you can live with it. Love B. Eggleston 1982" on verso. 1988.5.5.

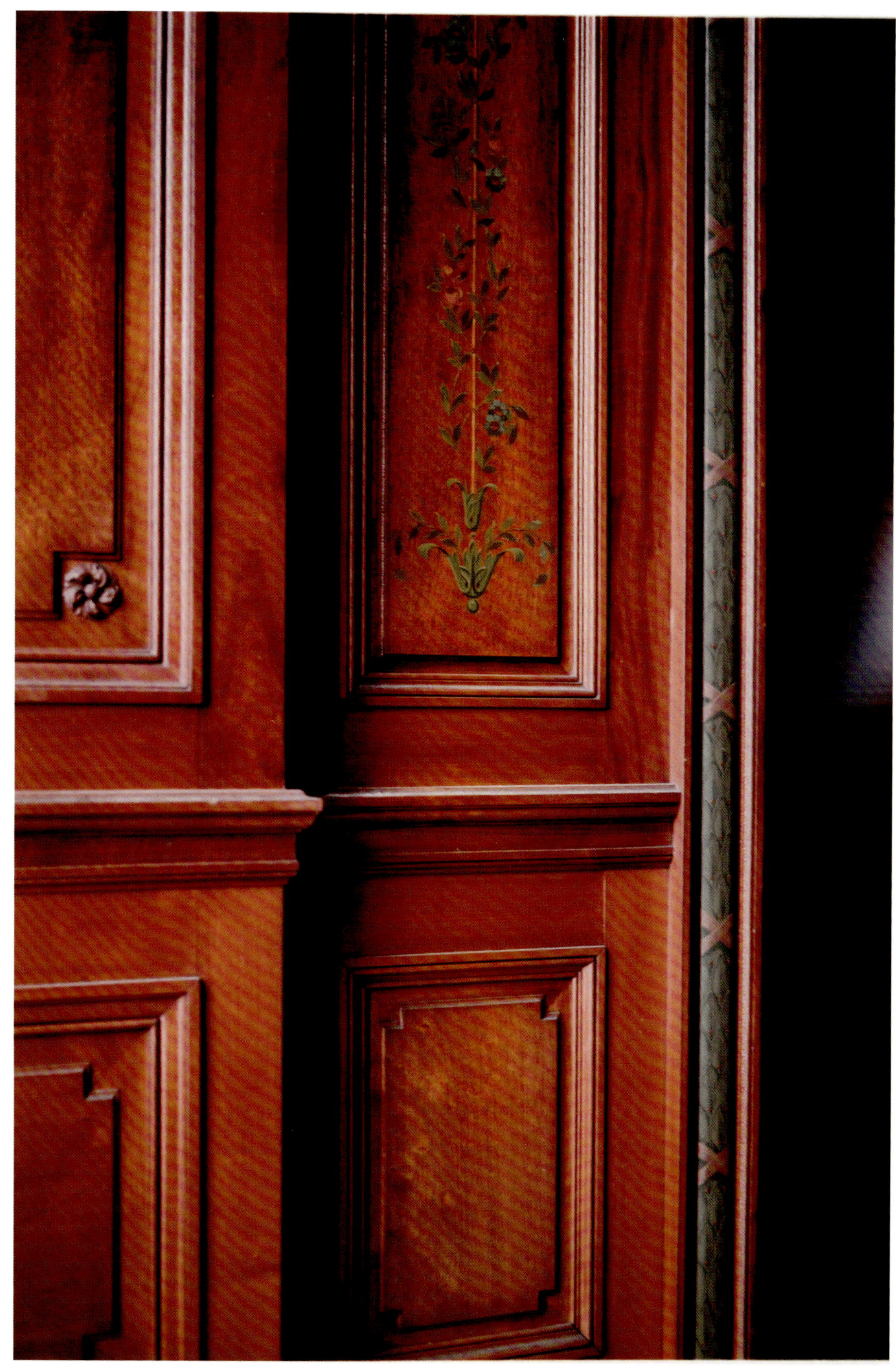

Untitled (Monmouth College, West Long Branch, New Jersey), 1982, from the assignment *Annie*. Resin-coated photograph. 1988.5.27.

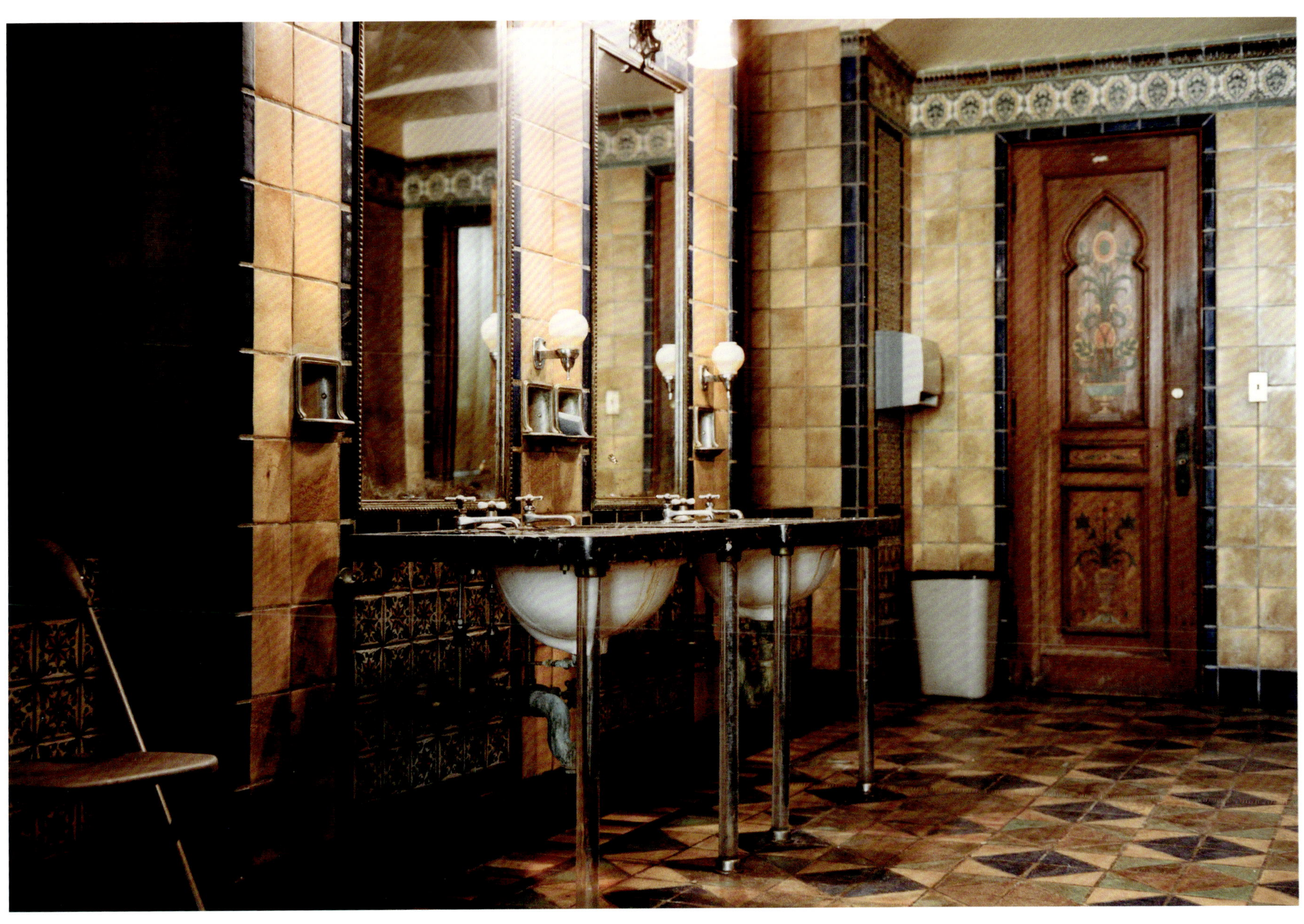

Untitled (Monmouth College, West Long Branch, New Jersey), 1982, from the assignment *Annie*. Resin-coated photograph. 1988.5.28.

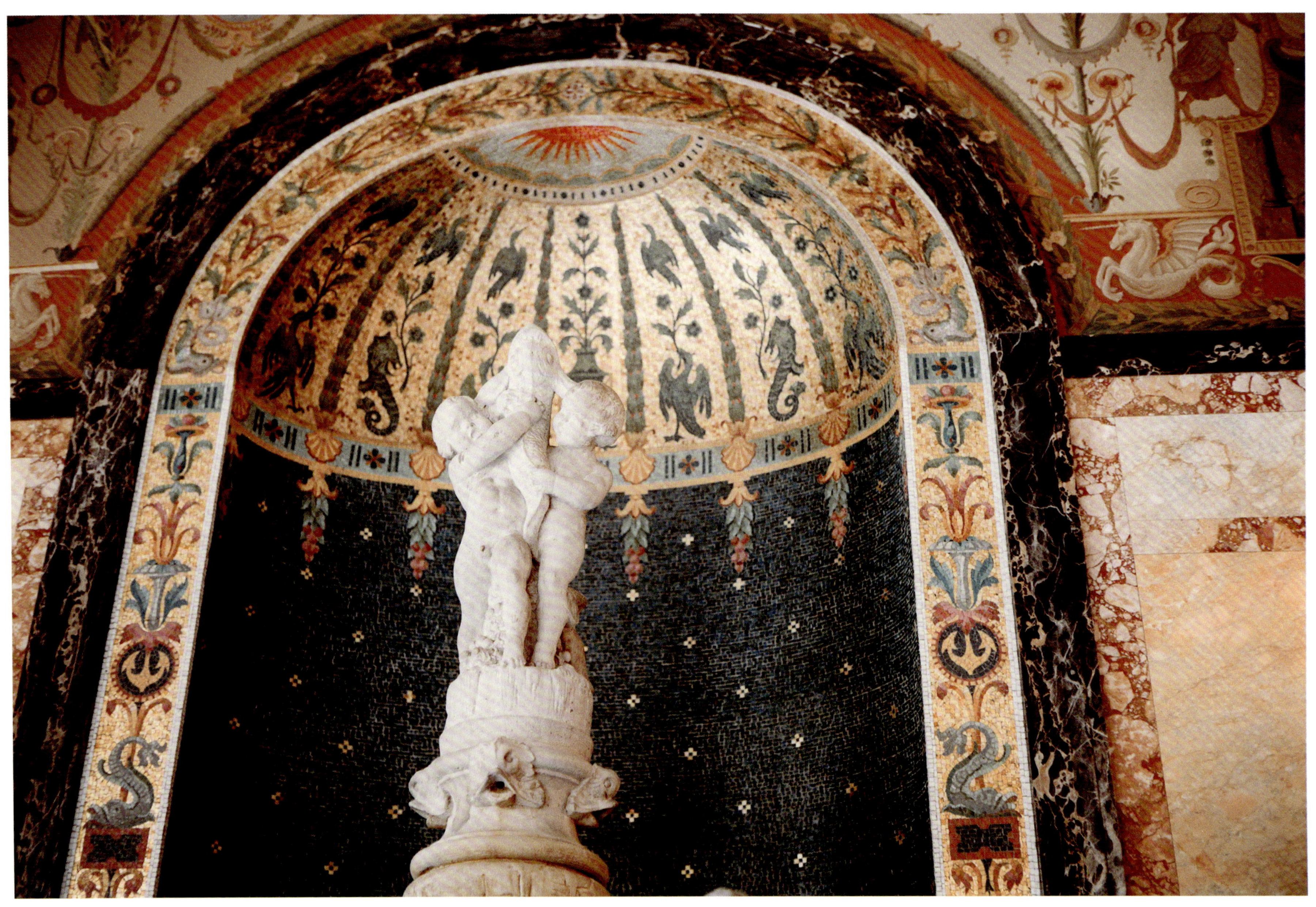

Untitled (Monmouth College, West Long Branch, New Jersey), 1982, from the assignment *Annie*. Resin-coated photograph. 1988.5.29.

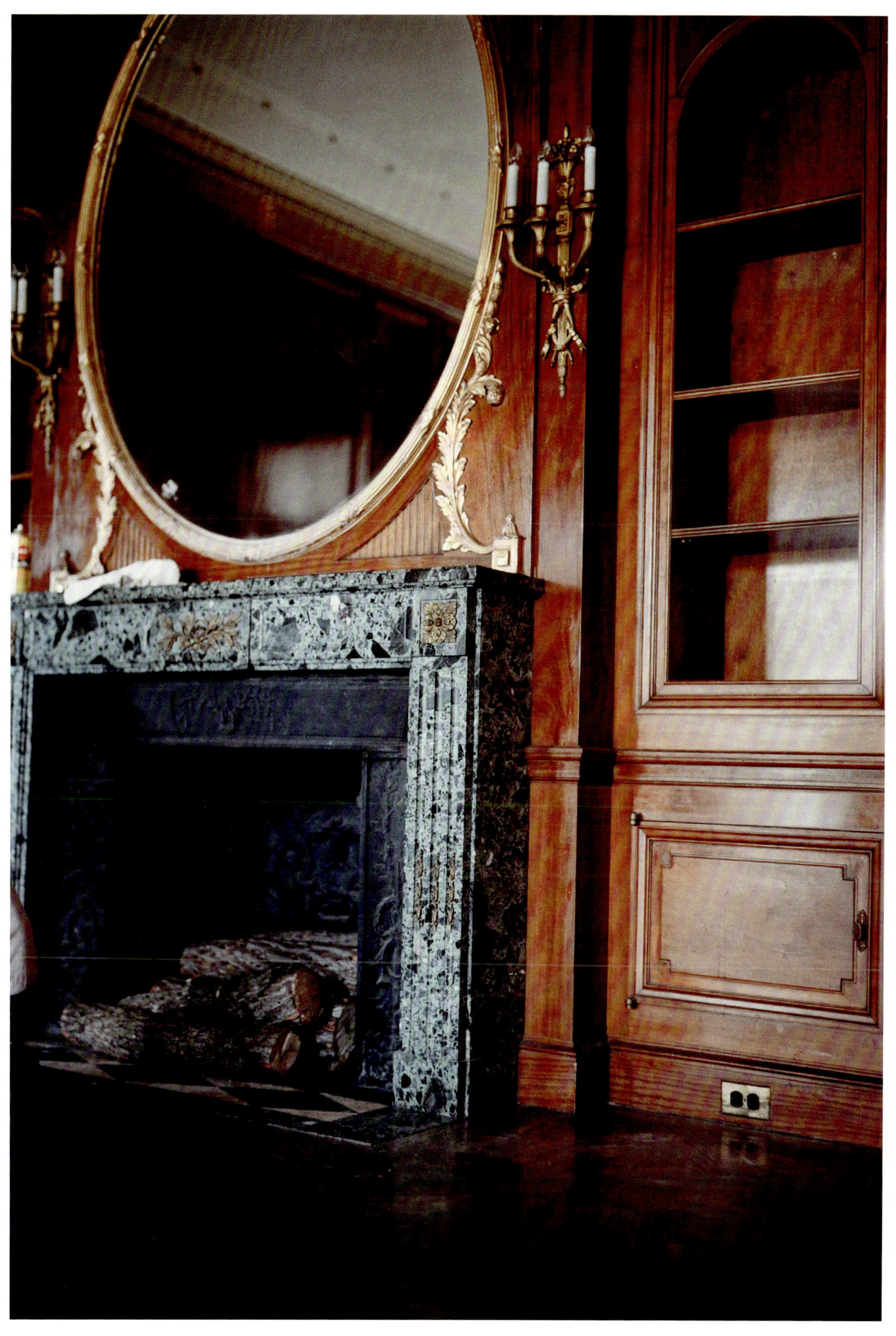

Untitled (Monmouth College, West Long Branch, New Jersey), 1982, from the assignment *Annie*. Resin-coated photograph. 1988.5.31.

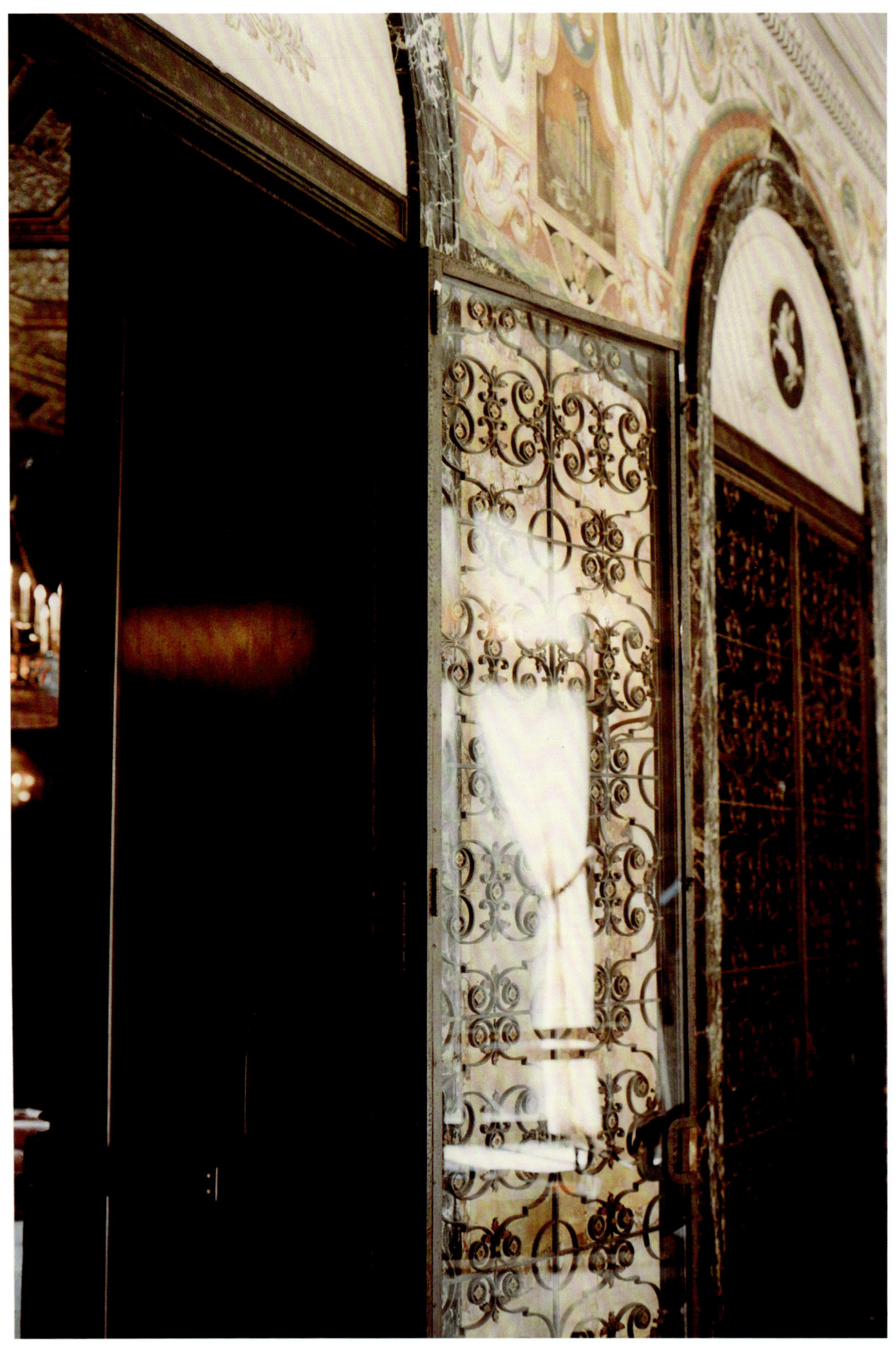

Untitled (Monmouth College, West Long Branch, New Jersey), 1982, from the assignment *Annie*. Resin-coated photograph. 1988.5.32.

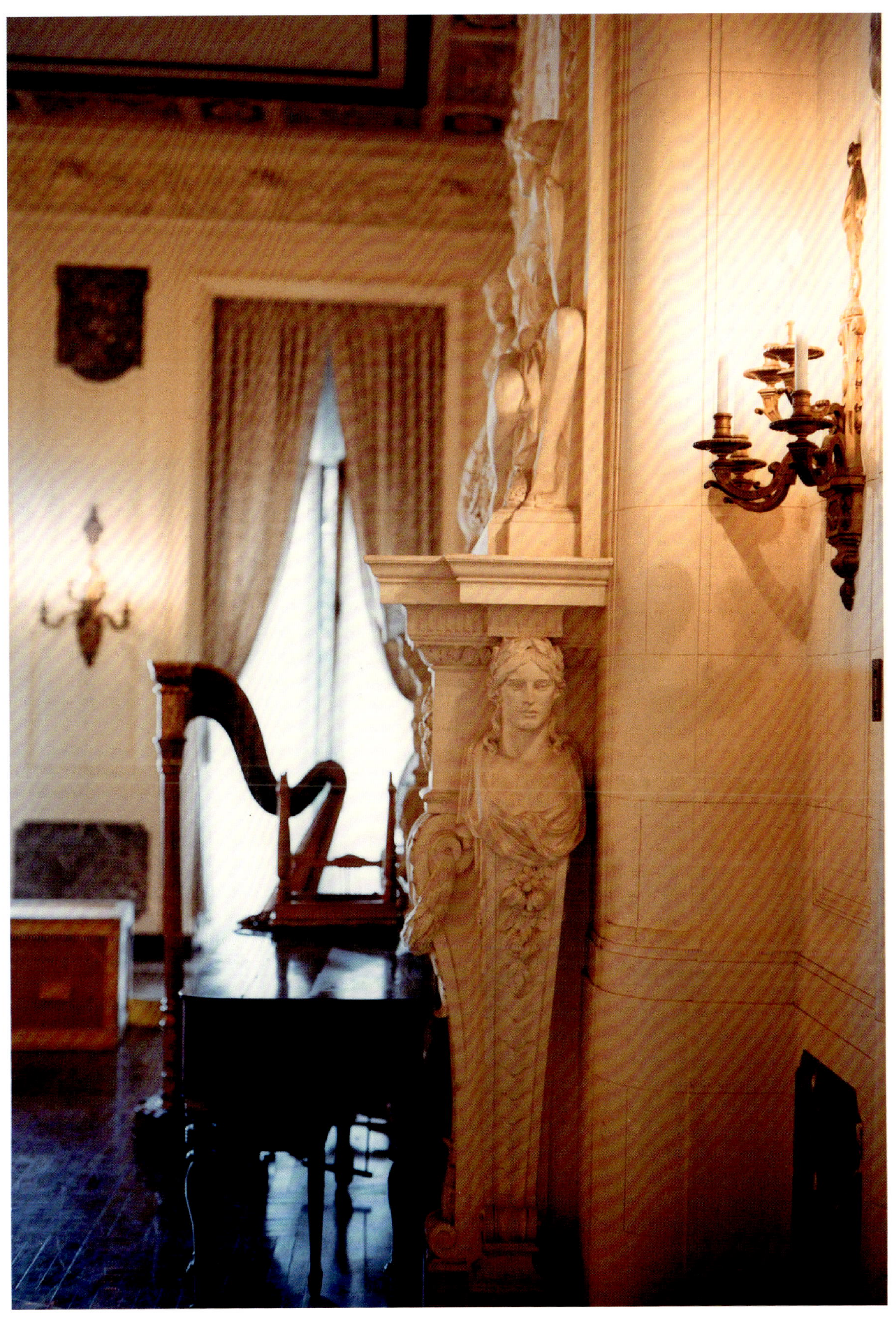

Untitled (Monmouth College, West Long Branch, New Jersey), 1982, from the assignment *Annie*. Resin-coated photograph. 1988.5.33.

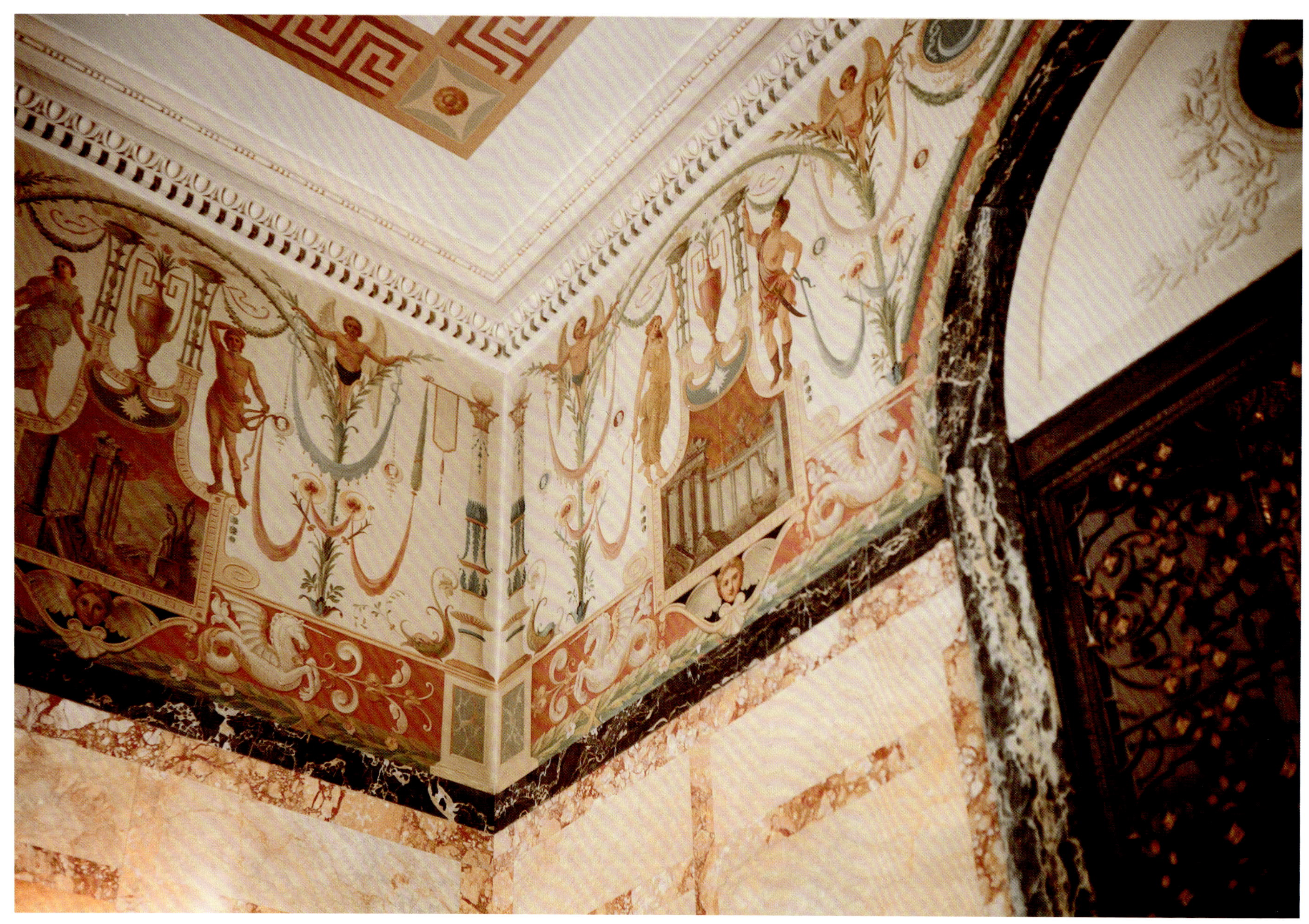

Untitled (Monmouth College, West Long Branch, New Jersey), 1982, from the assignment *Annie*. Resin-coated photograph. 1988.5.34.

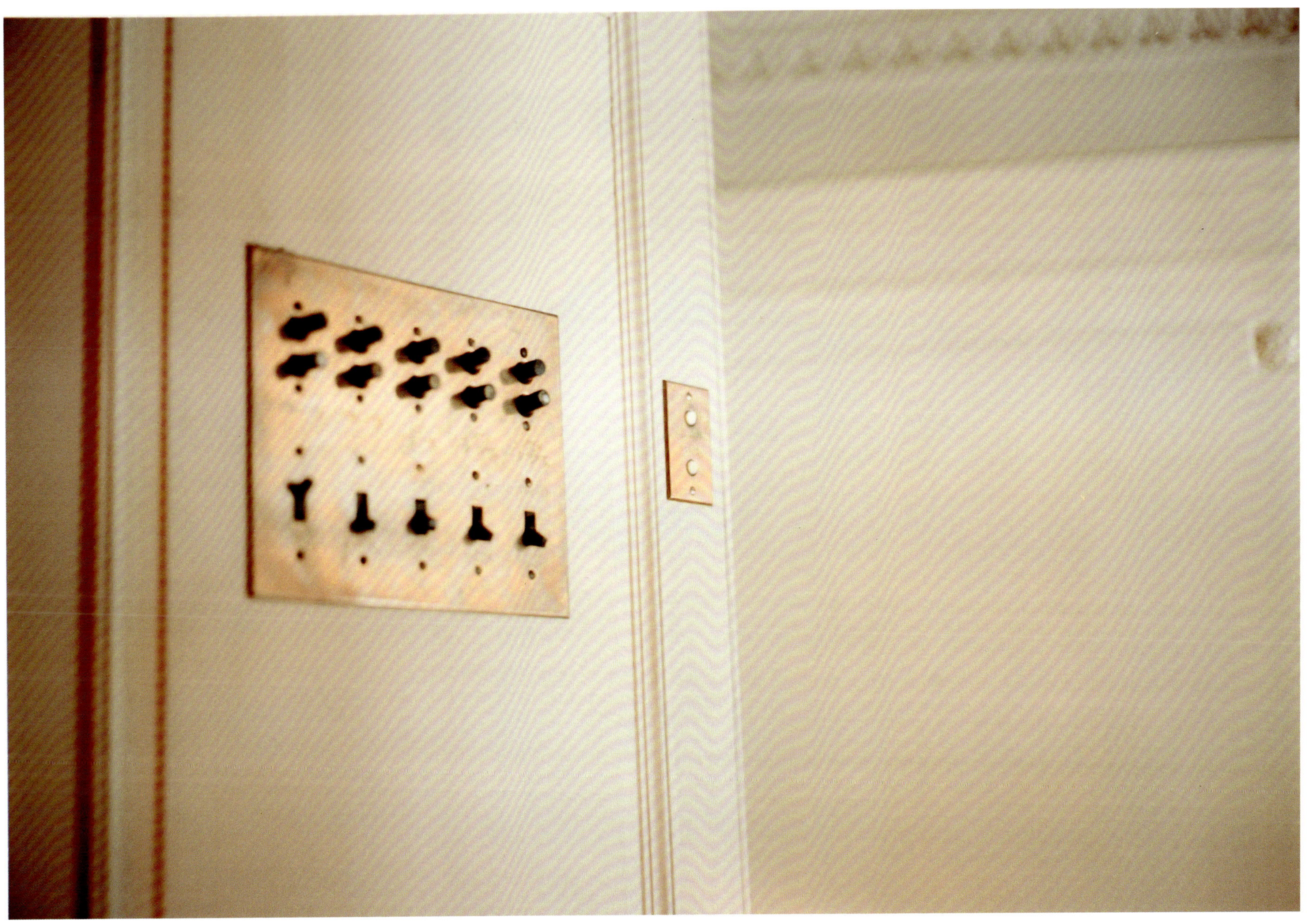

Untitled (Monmouth College, West Long Branch, New Jersey), 1982, from the assignment *Annie*. Resin-coated photograph. 1988.5.35.

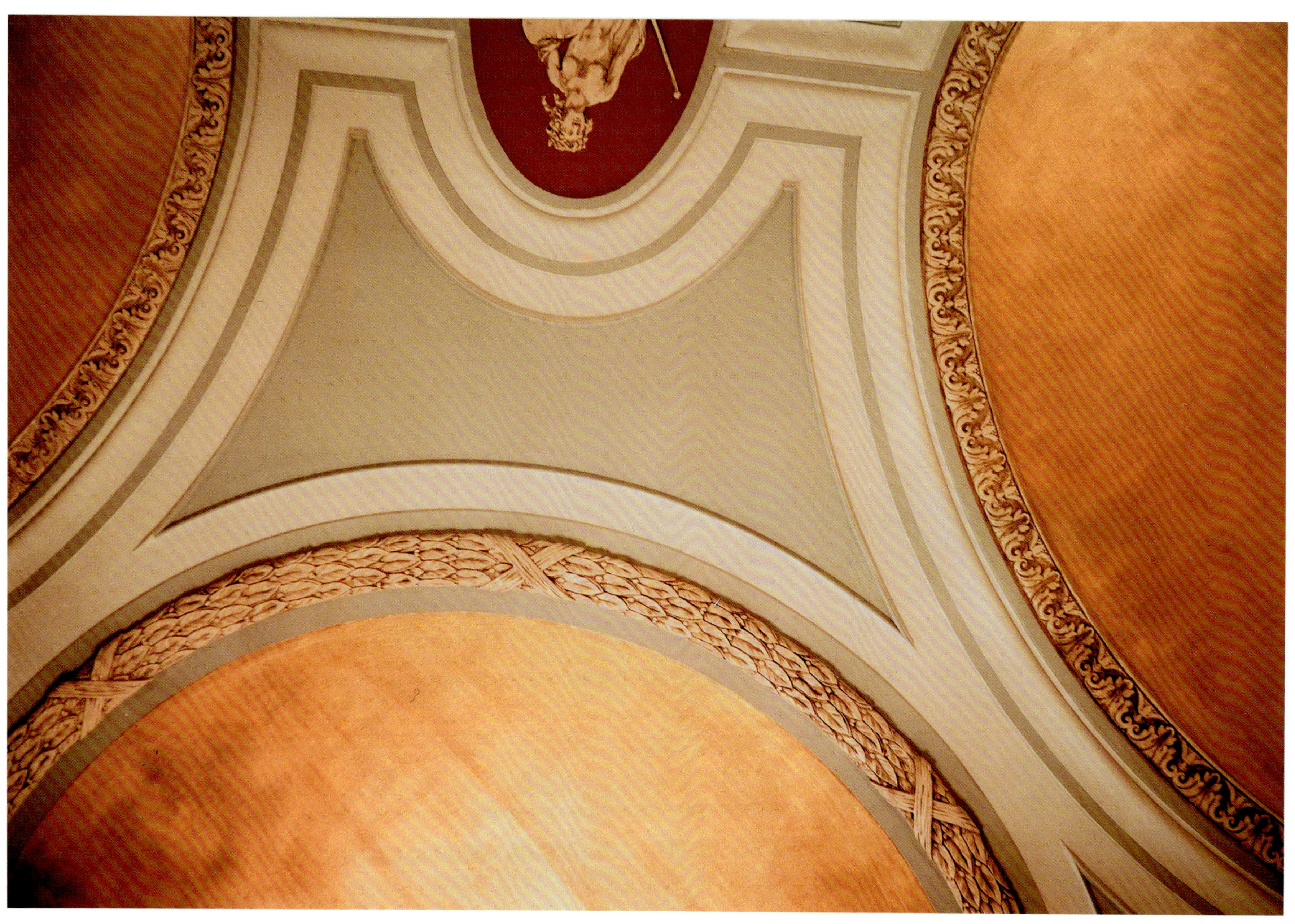

Untitled (Monmouth College, West Long Branch, New Jersey), 1982, from the assignment *Annie*. Resin-coated photograph. 1988.5.36.

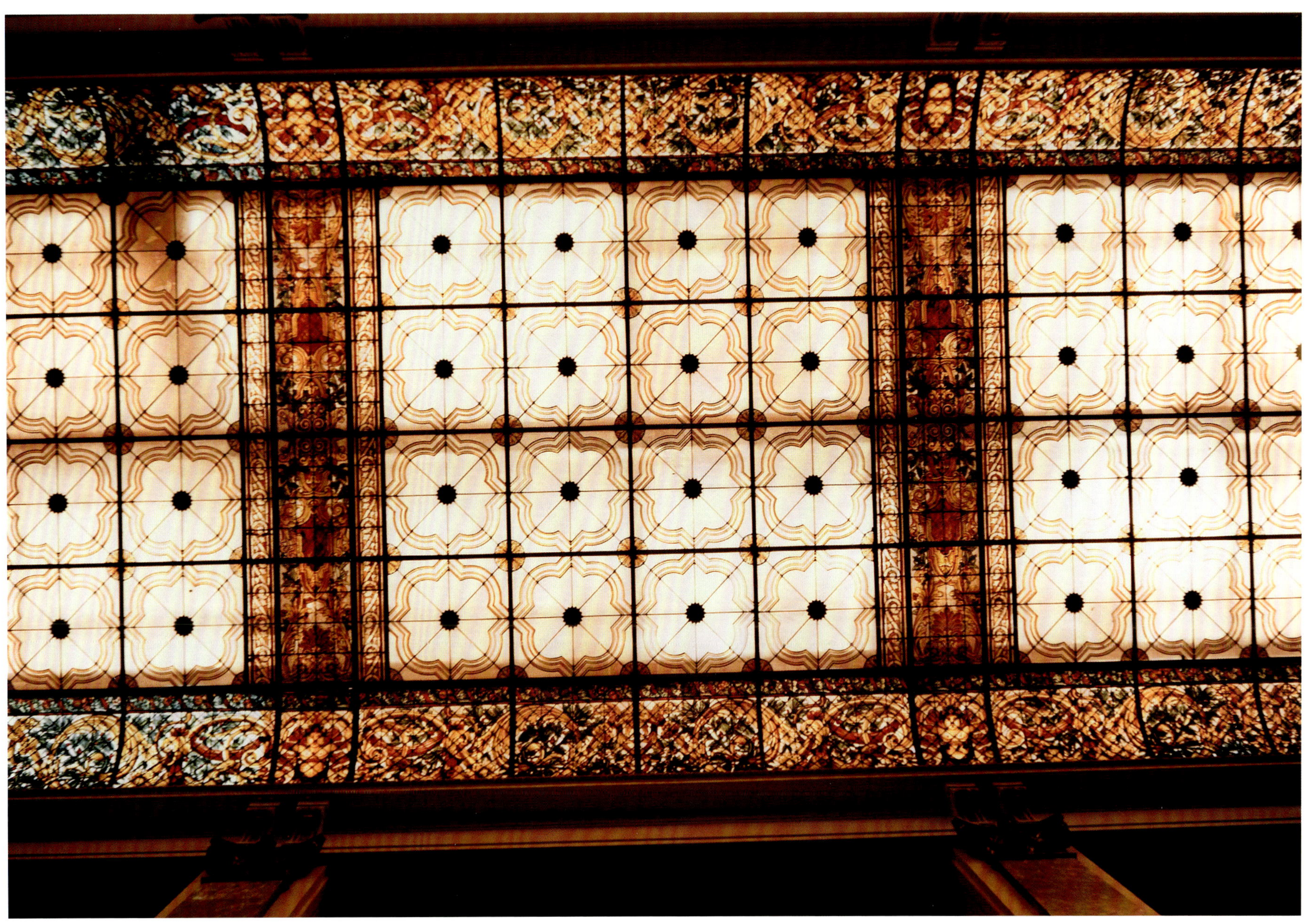

Untitled (Monmouth College, West Long Branch, New Jersey), 1982, from the assignment *Annie*. Resin-coated photograph. 1988.5.37.

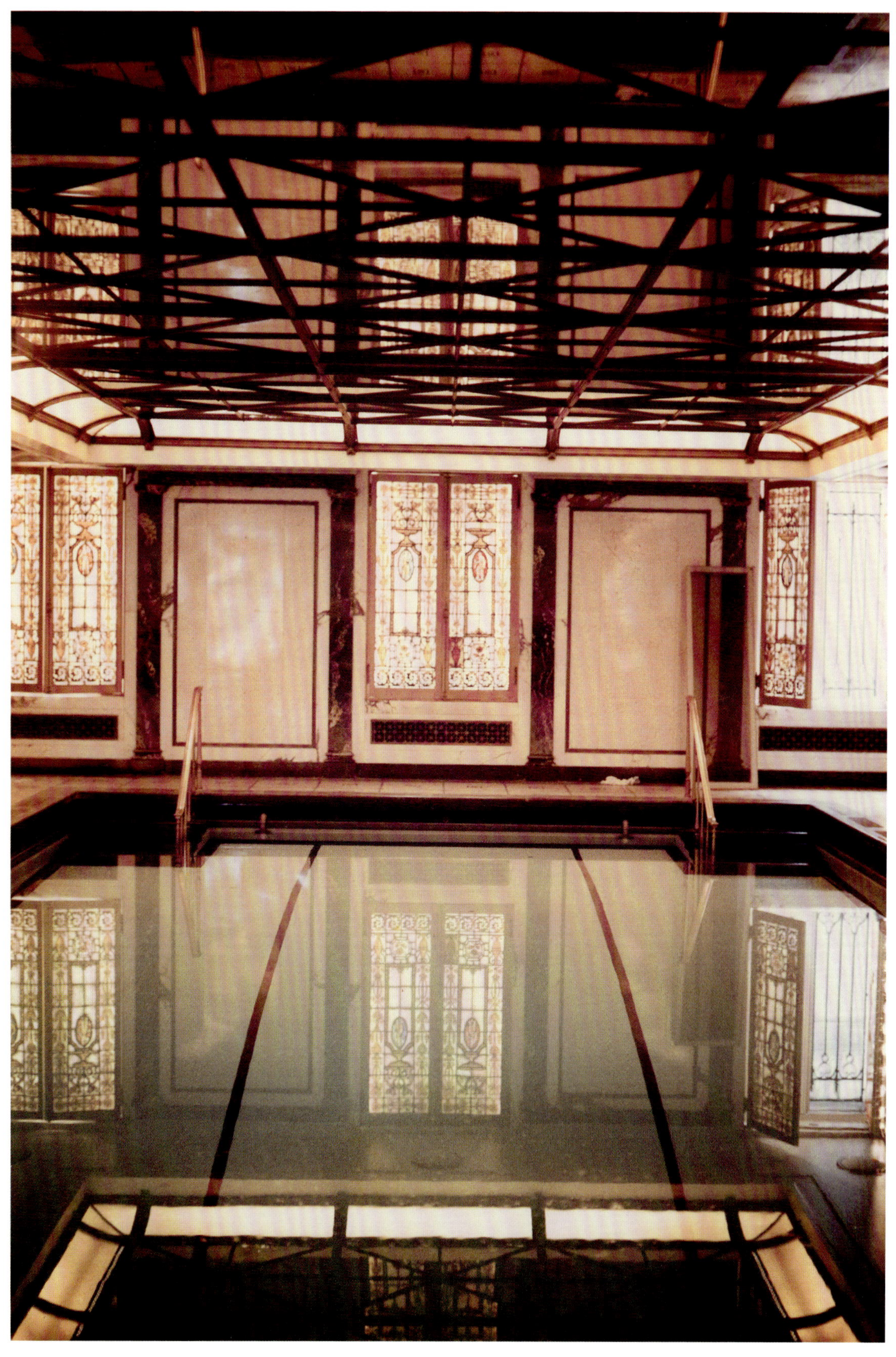

Untitled (Monmouth College, West Long Branch, New Jersey), 1982, from the assignment *Annie*. Resin-coated photograph. 1988.5.38.

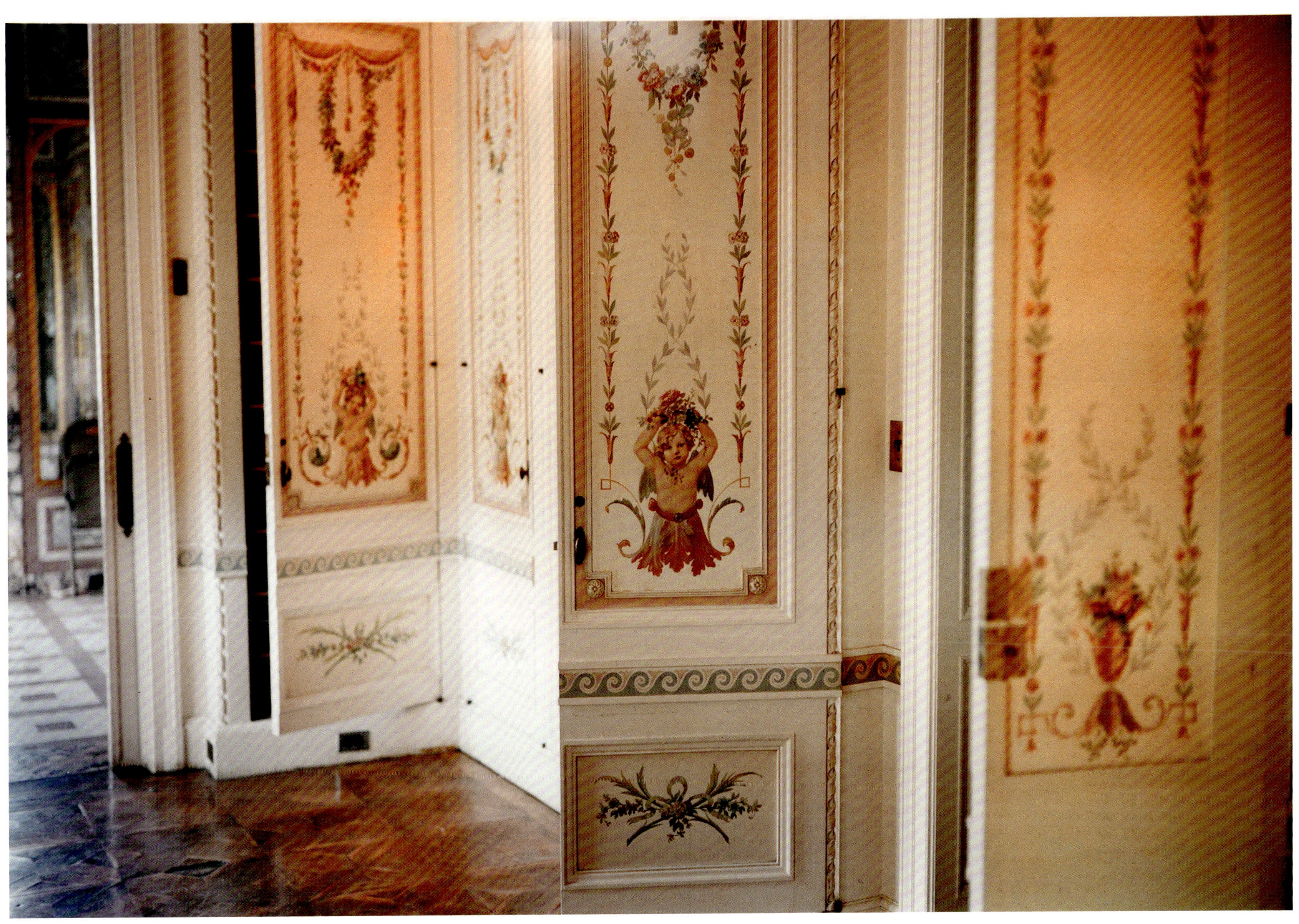

Untitled (Monmouth College, West Long Branch, New Jersey), 1982, from the assignment *Annie*. Resin-coated photograph. 1988.5.40.

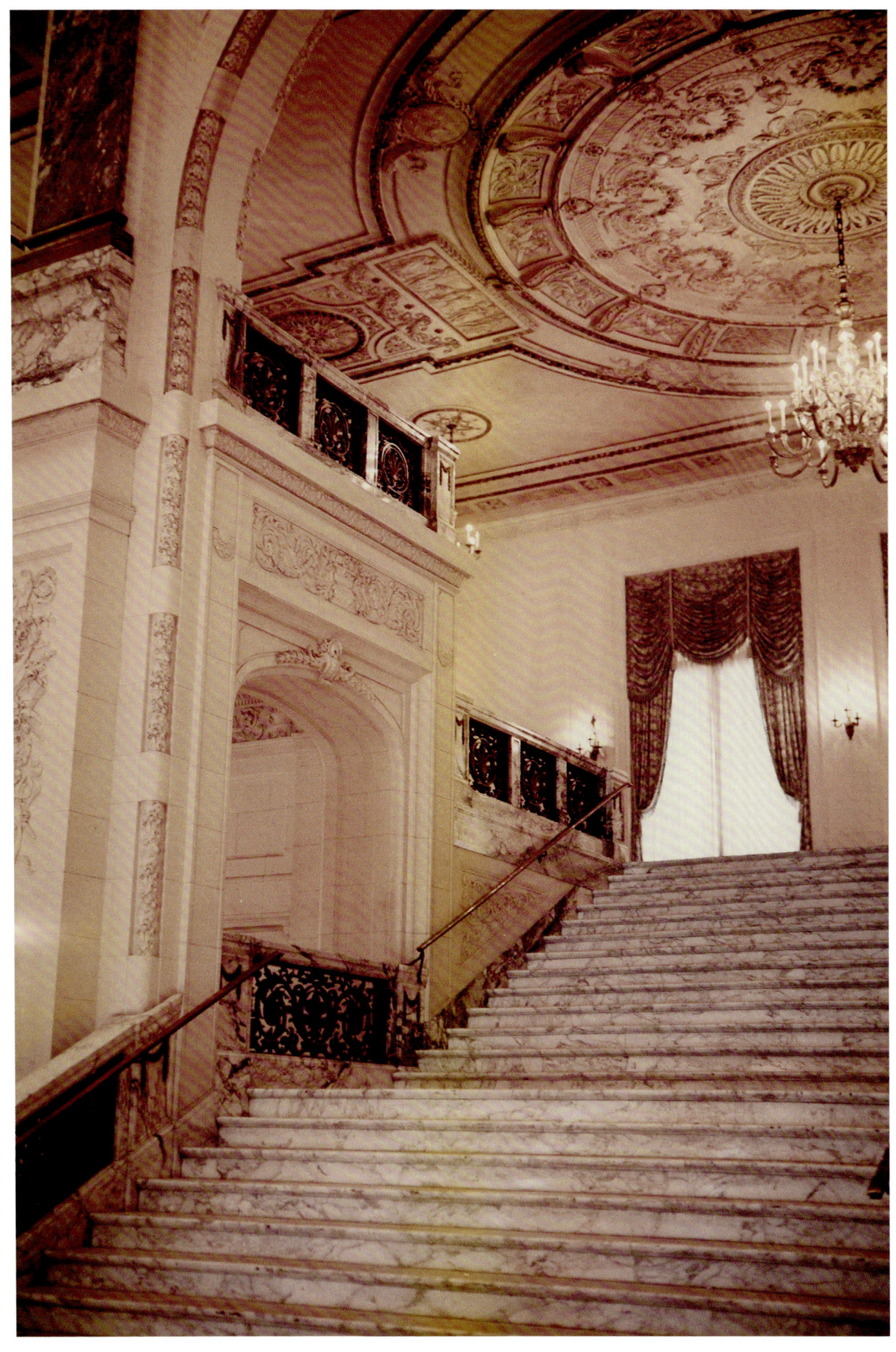

Untitled (Monmouth College, West Long Branch, New Jersey), 1982, from the assignment *Annie*. Resin-coated photograph. 1988.5.98.

William Eggleston Symposium

Friday, October 7, 2016

Sponsored by Friends of the Museum
with support from the University of Mississippi Lecture Series

Overby Center for Southern Journalism and Politics
The University of Mississippi

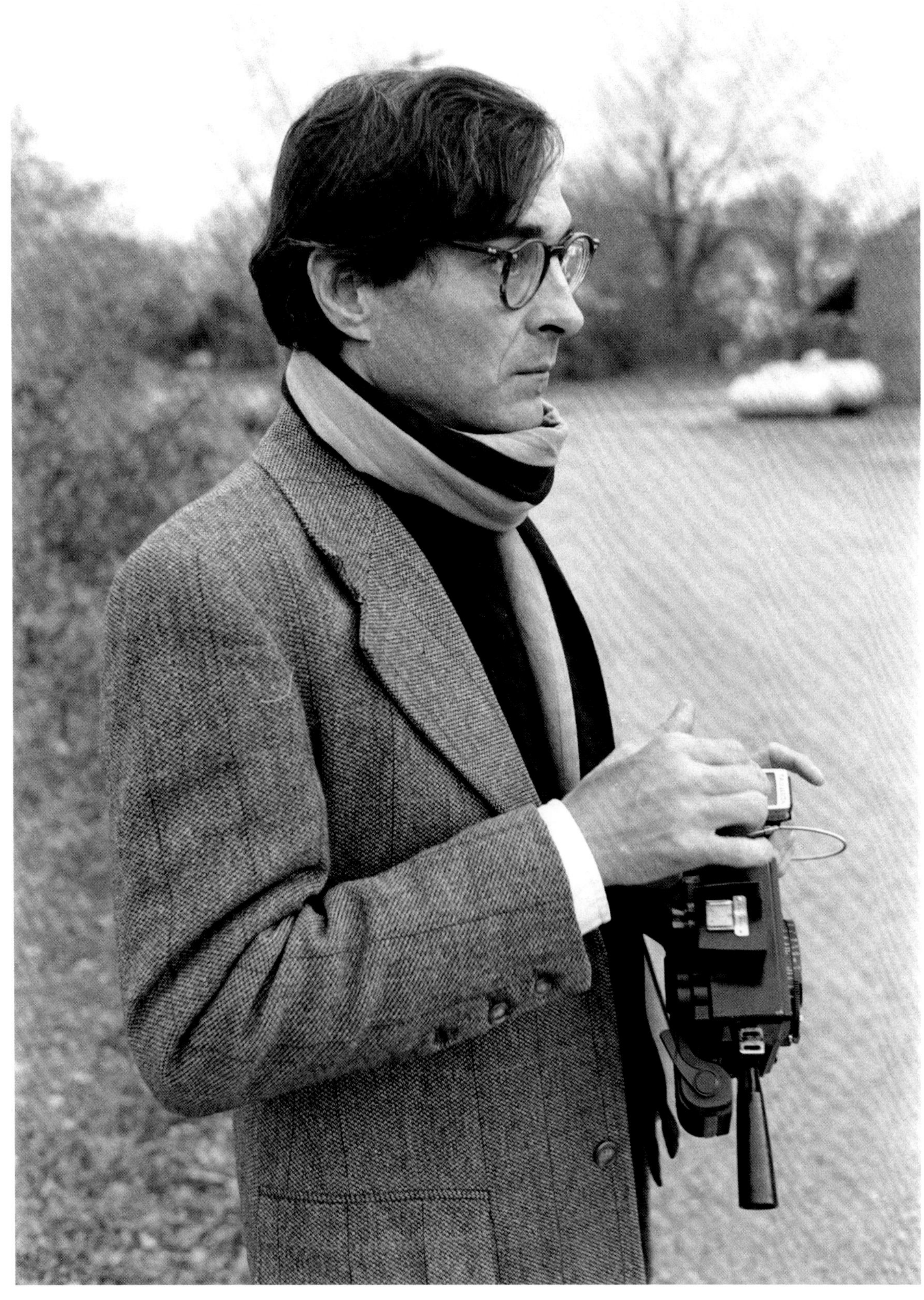

William Ferris, photograph of William Eggleston in Waterford, Mississippi, 1984. William R. Ferris Collection, Southern Folklife Collection, Wilson Library, The University of North Carolina–Chapel Hill.

William Eggleston Symposium

Morning Panel

Moderator: Lisa Howorth
Panelists: Megan Abbott, Maude Schuyler Clay, and William Ferris

Robert Saarnio: This symposium was financially underwritten by both Friends of the Museum and the University of Mississippi Lecture Series and would not have happened without that support. The exhibition itself entailed a thirty-month collaboration among Museum staff, including collections manager Marti Funke, and two essential partners, guest curator Megan Abbott and consulting advisor Maude Schuyler Clay. Suffice it to say that without Megan's brilliant curating, Maude's invaluable contributions, and Marti's coordinating efforts, this exhibition would not have been accomplished at the distinguished level that you see in our galleries.

We must also express profound gratitude to William Ferris, whose gifts of these Eggleston prints to the Museum's permanent collection made everything ultimately possible. Bill traveled from Chapel Hill to be with us today, serving as both panelist and moderator. We are indebted to this remarkable scholar, friend, and supporter. Please join me in extending the very warm round of applause to our great friend. Our panelist speakers today have traveled from the Delta, New Orleans, New York, Memphis, Chapel Hill, and across campus; and we are deeply grateful to each of them.

They will be introduced by their panel moderators, but we want to express unequivocally how proud and honored the entire Museum community is to be joined today by Bill Ferris, Megan Abbott, Maude Schuyler Clay, Lisa Howorth, Emily Neff, Richard McCabe, and Kris Belden-Adams. Thank you all so very much for the privilege of your participation and your expertise. It is now my distinct pleasure to introduce the moderator of our first panel this morning, author, art historian, and friend to everyone in this room, Lisa Howorth.

A native of Washington, DC, Lisa has lived in Oxford since 1972. She and her husband, Richard Howorth, founded Square Books in 1979 and later opened an annex store, Off Square Books, and Square Books Junior, a children's store. After earning an MS in library science and an MA in art history, Lisa was a reference librarian and an associate professor of art and Southern Studies at the University of Mississippi. She has edited four books, contributed to magazines and other publications, written the novel *Flying Shoes*, and is at work on a new novel. Please join me in thanking and welcoming Lisa Howorth.

Lisa Howorth: Thank you. Thanks to everybody involved. It's my pleasure to be part of this symposium, and I'm grateful to be invited. Let me go ahead and introduce the panel.

Miss Megan Abbott is the award-winning author of nine novels as well as a nonfiction book, *The Street Was Mine: White Masculinity in Hardboiled Fiction and Film Noir*. She's also the editor of *A Hell of a Woman*, an anthology of female crime fiction, and has written for the *New York Times*, *Salon*, and other publications. After receiving a PhD in literature from New York University, she taught at NYU, the State University of

New York, the New School, and the University of Mississippi, where she was Grisham Writer in Residence in 2013–2014. Much of her writing is inspired by William Eggleston's photography. We miss her, and we're glad to get her back here any way we can. I also want to add this, just in: she's a 2016 Edgar Award Nominee for Best Short Story with "Little Men." That's another feather in her cap, and we're so glad she's here.

Miss Maude Schuyler Clay was born in Greenwood, Mississippi, where her family has lived for five generations. That's saying something, isn't it? After attending the University of Mississippi and the Memphis Academy of Arts, she was an intern for her cousin, photographer William Eggleston. She then moved to New York City, where she worked at Light Gallery and was the photography editor and photographer for *Esquire*, *Fortune*, *Vanity Fair*, and other publications. After returning to the Mississippi Delta in the late 1980s, she continued her color portrait work and began a series of black-and-white photographs. The University Press of Mississippi published her monographs *Delta Land* and *Delta Dogs*, and Steidl published her book of color portraits *Mississippi History* with a foreword by Richard Ford. She's received five awards for her photography from the Mississippi Institute of Arts and Letters and was the 2015 recipient of the Governor's Award for Excellence in Visual Art. And, another tidbit of breaking news, her show at the Ogden Museum in New Orleans just opened to packed SRO crowds. We're very excited and proud of Maude for that.

Okay then, the big dog, William Ferris, is Joel R. Williams Eminent Professor of History at the University of North Carolina at Chapel Hill and adjunct professor in the Curriculum in Folklore. He is senior associate director at the Center for Study of the American South and a former chairman of the National Endowment for the Humanities. Prior to his role at NEH, Ferris served as director of the Center for the Study of Southern Culture at the University of Mississippi, where he was a faculty member for eighteen years. Wow. Amazing. Time flies when you're having a good time, right? We did. Ferris has written or edited ten books, created fifteen documentary films, and coedited the award-winning *Encyclopedia of Southern Culture*. His last three books provide an extraordinary trilogy of his documentation of life in the South through nearly six decades of photographs and interviews. I also want to add that Billy's entire family is one of artists, art supporters, educators, and writers. They're kind of a Mississippi treasure trove, and what the hell Bill's doing up there with all those Yankees, I do not know. It's a travesty, right? I hope someday to be asked to be on a panel about Bill Ferris, because I know some stuff. It would be a good panel. I guess that's all I have to say.

Megan Abbott: Before we start talking, Robert and Marti asked me to tell about my role in this rather miraculous exhibition. We first started talking about it in 2013; and I want to thank Robert, Marti, and the Museum for this incredible opportunity to play a small part in the exhibition that was a major undertaking for them. I thank Robert for engaging and shepherding me and Marti for all the stunning work she did in putting the exhibition together. For those of you who saw it last night or have seen it before, it feels like a whole new experience being in those rooms.

This morning we will talk about William Eggleston with those who know him and have stories and insight. I come as an outsider. His work has meant so much to me; and, like countless others, I was drawn to his photographs long before I even knew his name. I only know how the pictures made me feel, the kind of uncanny spell they put me under—first as a teenager and later as an aspiring writer yearning for transport. Looking for a cheat.

I think I thought, and I still think this: "Maybe if I look at that photo long enough, the back of the woman's head, her finely tended coiffure, a story will surface for me. I will know what I want to tell." Somehow for me, as for countless other writers, and filmmakers, and artists, it did work. It absolutely did. The photograph was there, and the spell was enchanted.

I'm fairly sure the first Eggleston I saw was the first color photo he ever made: the famous one of the grocery store clerk, his hair oddly lustrous, his mouth slightly open, pushing a hard, glittery tangle of shopping carts into the store. His palms are pressed just so. At the time, I didn't know about Eggleston's place in the history of photography, the breakthrough of color photography, the way he's been positioned often rather narrowly as a "Southern" photographer, a "regional" one, a photographer of the weird. All I knew was, when I looked at that photo, I saw a world I knew, part of the world I lived in: Kroger's and fluorescent lights and bright shiny wrappers, and the hard and soft faces of strangers and intimates. And part of the world that I experienced from the inside out: *fevered, heavy, mysterious, loaded, beautiful*. All the things I think we feel when we look at one of his photos.

Then it's no surprise that Eggleston is and always has been a catnip for writers, artists, storytellers of all kinds, from David Lynch, which is how I first discovered him, through Gus Van Sant to Sofia Coppola, and Harmony Korine. I suppose it's a cliché to say that when you look at Eggleston's photos, they seem to tell a story. I don't think that's true. They're not narrative images like we might see in, say, Robert Capa or Dorothea Lange. Eggleston's photos don't connect dots for us. They don't assert or announce. They don't *tell* at all. But maybe it's more precise to say that when you look at them, *you make the story*.

Stories, after all, have a beginning, a middle, and an end. We can see all three parts in a photo in an instant in some photos: a young boy of privilege, left alone, a toy grenade in his hand, to reference the famous Diane Arbus photo. It's all right there in the picture. With Eggleston, it's different. The photographs don't offer three acts, or even a first act. Instead, the photographs seem to come from the intense, hot *middle* of something. We are dropped in, immersed, sunk deep.

Eggleston has talked about trying to "creep up" on his subjects, and the photographs have that feeling. We encounter these jagged Eggleston worlds just before or just after something perilous or ecstatic has happened. Or both, but what? This brings me to the name of the show, which comes from an Albert Einstein quotation: "The most beautiful thing we can experience is the mysterious." Of course, the mystery lurks in every busy or barren corner of an Eggleston photograph. That mystery can feel like pathos: the man at the gas station gazing longingly at the liquor store sign glimmering darkly on the horizon. The mystery can feel like menace: the eerie eye-windows of a darkened church door. It can feel like a lot of things at once: the sweep of terrible history, as we might see in the white Winn-Dixie sign with its comic and tragic faces looming above.

Eggleston's photos encourage the pathetic fallacy—which I've never thought of as pathetic at all—an old term we learned in high school English about attributing human emotions to things or objects: a lonely window, a lusty pair of headlights. Eggleston's photos are so shot through, so infused with *mood*, with *feeling*, that they demand the pathetic fallacy. I have always felt, as critic Malcolm Jones writes, that Eggleston "addresses the meanest objects with unstuttering love." Consider the objects in this show: A lonely pink patio chair, squat and hopeful. A uniform starched on a clothesline, insistent and formal. A dishcloth with holes like eyes. The cluttered front seat of a car, white feathers dangling glamorously from the rearview mirror, promising a world more refined than the plastic McDonald's cup that's also there, or the brown paper bag that's shot through with light. The soulful gaze of a young man with a twin-scoop ice cream cone, seemingly change in hand. Even to describe these photos in sparest terms is to begin a story, but the story is ours. And it begins with feeling, trying to untangle the feeling we feel without knowing why we're feeling it: loneliness, the expectation, the wonder and longing.

This image of the young man with the ice cream cone drew me so closely the first time I saw it with Marti and Robert in the Museum. For me, it seemed to recall a lost frame from *The Last Picture Show*, the movie. Every time I look at it, I feel more story and more feeling. He's well groomed, dressed for a date who never arrived or arrived with someone else. It's my guess that he has change in his hand. It's my guess he looks deep in thought. I had this speculation that the twin scoop of the cone bespeaks something—a love lost or never won, a yearning, an aching disappointment. Does the change in his hand come from buying the cone, or is he about to play a sad, sad song on the jukebox we see in another photograph from the show, gleaming and machinelike and substantial? That change he carries as if it were Roman coins, heavy and substantial. Or maybe he's carrying them lightly, maybe he has not a trouble in the world and the stitch in the brow I think I see is really a mere matter of "Do I pick Sam the Sham or Jr. Walker & the All Stars?" Callow youth! Why am I assuming there's money in his hand? Maybe he's snapping his fingers. Maybe. Maybe, maybe.

See how quickly we get lost, subsumed into a narrative waist-high? I was talking with Phil Boyle last night (he's in the audience), and he said, "That's the most sinister photo in the exhibition." Then suddenly I looked at it and thought, "Maybe it is. Maybe this is like Dick and Harry. I don't know." At any rate, the story that springs from the photograph could never be the young man's story, nor Eggleston's or his magical camera's. The story is ours. The feeling is ours—spurred, sparked, inflamed by what we see here, the spell cast. "How democratic," as Eggleston himself might say.

I saw a 1990 interview where Eggleston says about Elvis Presley, "He fits the hole that there never was a hero for." The journalists point out that Eggleston could just as easily have been talking about himself. *He fits that hole that there never was a hero for*. There's something in these photographs we need without ever knowing why. "The most beautiful thing we can experience is the mysterious," says Einstein. "It is the source of all true art and science. He to whom this emotion is a stranger, who can no longer pause to wonder and stand wrapped in awe, is as good as dead—his eyes are closed."[1] These photos open our eyes. They drive the blood. They kind of ransack the heart. They bring us to the center of something. We feel them. We can't stop looking. We look again. We close our eyes and still see them. We're forever seeing them.

So maybe it'll happen for you today. A photo you've seen before perhaps or wondered at or thought you know. Or, more likely, one you're seeing for the first time. You'll look at it, you'll wonder, imagine something, remember something; and by the time you leave, it'll be a part of you, and it likely always was. Maybe, then, it's not we who might come to understand these photographs, but they who've always understood us, speaking to places deep inside. Years ago, Eggleston told an interviewer, "I would love to photograph dreams." Maybe he has.

Lisa Howorth: Okay. We're lucky to have Megan to do that lovely introduction to the whole topic. This panel feels weird, I realize, because Bill Dunlap isn't here! I don't think I've ever been to a panel in this room where it wasn't the Dunlap show. Something's wrong. Anyway, it'd be fun if he were here. Which I think I've been referring to as the Egg Bowl.

Since we've got two Williams or Bills, the Ferris one is Billy, and I may refer to Eggleston as Bill or Egg in case you get confused because that's what some people might do anyway, just to avoid confusion. Here's our charge: "This panel presents a unique opportunity to approach William Eggleston from the perspective of those who have known him personally over an extended time and from those whose work has been significantly influenced by his images." That's what we're going to try to stick to, and other things will be discussed during the afternoon session. I will ask each of our panelists a question, or just throw something out, and they'll have maybe ten minutes to answer, and I'll go around again so each panelist will have roughly two questions. We'll see what happens. Maybe at the end we'll have time for a Q&A or maybe some Eggleston anecdotes. I'm sure there are plenty of those out there.

First let me say about myself that my credentials for being on the panel are I'm old enough to have known Bill for about thirty years, which is saying quite a lot. He was coming to Oxford frequently when Richard and I and Bill Ferris were doing our various things. Billy was at the Center. Richard was getting the bookstore started. I was working on campus. Bill was coming down and staying at the Holiday Inn, room 117, smoking room. He'd have his guns, and his sound equipment, and his music, and his sketch pads; and he would just have a little vacation there.

Everybody was included, but he ended up running quite a lot with Barry Hannah—they had a lot in common—and Willie Morris. It was quite an interesting period to have the three of them here. Bill was working on *Democratic Forest* in the eighties mostly, and there are quite a few Oxford photos and

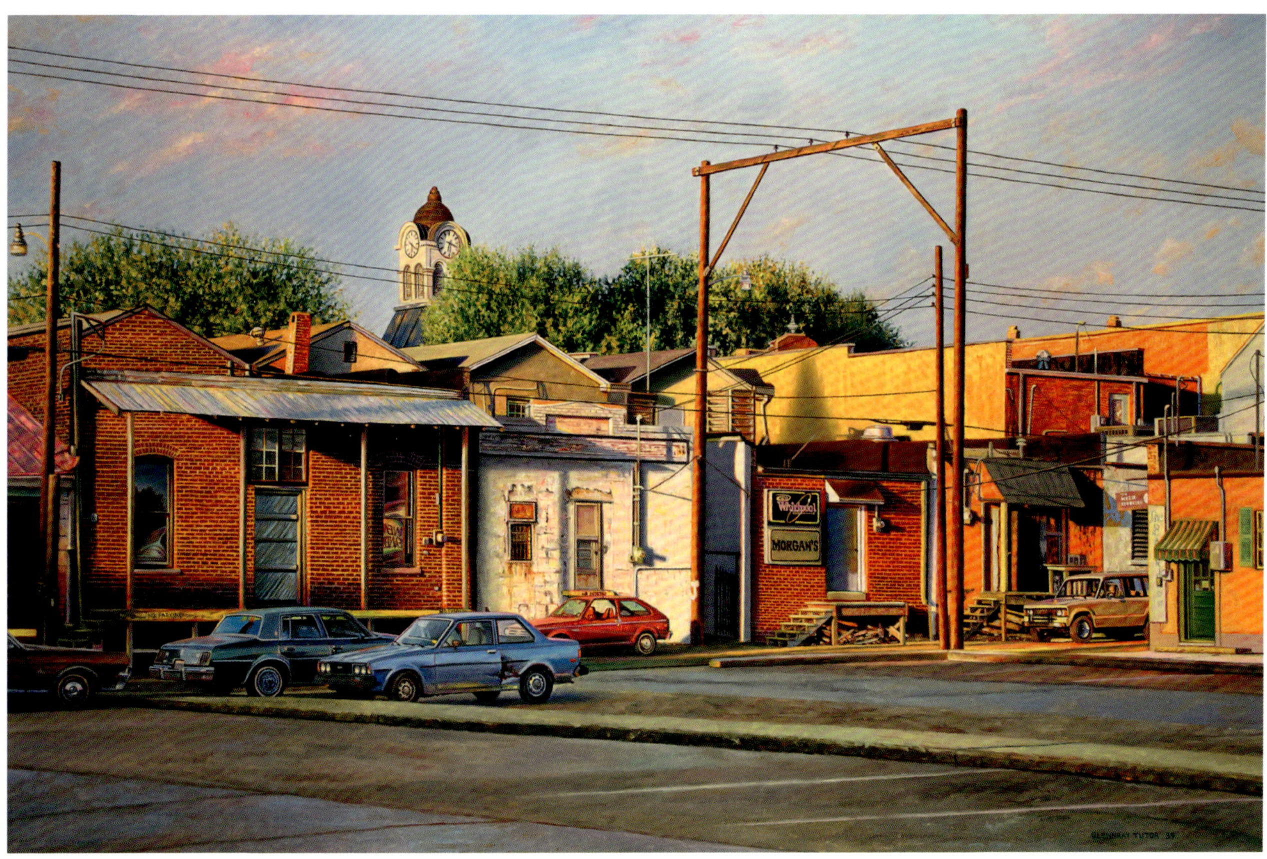

Behind the Square, oil on canvas, 26 × 40 inches. Painting completed: Summer 1990. Signed lower right: GLENNRAY TUTOR 39.

Lafayette County photos in that collection. He was skulking around, creeping up on people, or creeping up on things, and taking pictures. It was fascinating to watch him work. He was in a trance, as I recall, very much absorbed in what he did; but then at night he was running around and hanging out with these guys, and musicians, and everybody at the Hoka and wherever. Richard and I did a lot of wrangling of those guys in those days; and we became good friends with them—with Billy, in particular. I think Billy was also a wrangler to a certain extent. Anyway, it was an extraordinarily wonderful time in Oxford, and we were all so fascinated with Eggleston.

I brought a visual aid that illustrates the strong connection that Eggleston had to Oxford. This is the back side of City Grocery and what once was the original back parking lot of Off Square Books. I want to ask my husband, Richard, to tell a little story about that view and Eggleston.

Richard Howorth: I knew you were going to do this. Like you said, Eggleston came down here a lot. He and I were in the car one afternoon. I was driving, and we were riding around. When we pulled up to that intersection that's framed, we were in the car. What used to be Elliott Lumber is on the left, out of that perspective there; but right there at that stop sign, Eggleston said, "Stop! Stop! Stop! Just sit right here for a minute." I said "Okay," and he just sort of pointed out that way, and then he said, "That is my vision of Oxford." That stuck with me for a long time. This is a painting by Glennray Tutor. He does a fair amount of commission work, and I asked him if he would go to that particular spot and paint what Eggleston called his Oxford, and he did. You can see many things in there that Eggleston likes. I think it's one of the best paintings that Glennray ever did. Some future administration of the city came along and took down all those electrical wires and telephone wires and buried them underground, so we've lost a bit of the iconography here; but, at any rate, this is a painting. This is a vision.

Maude Clay: I thought you were going to say it's

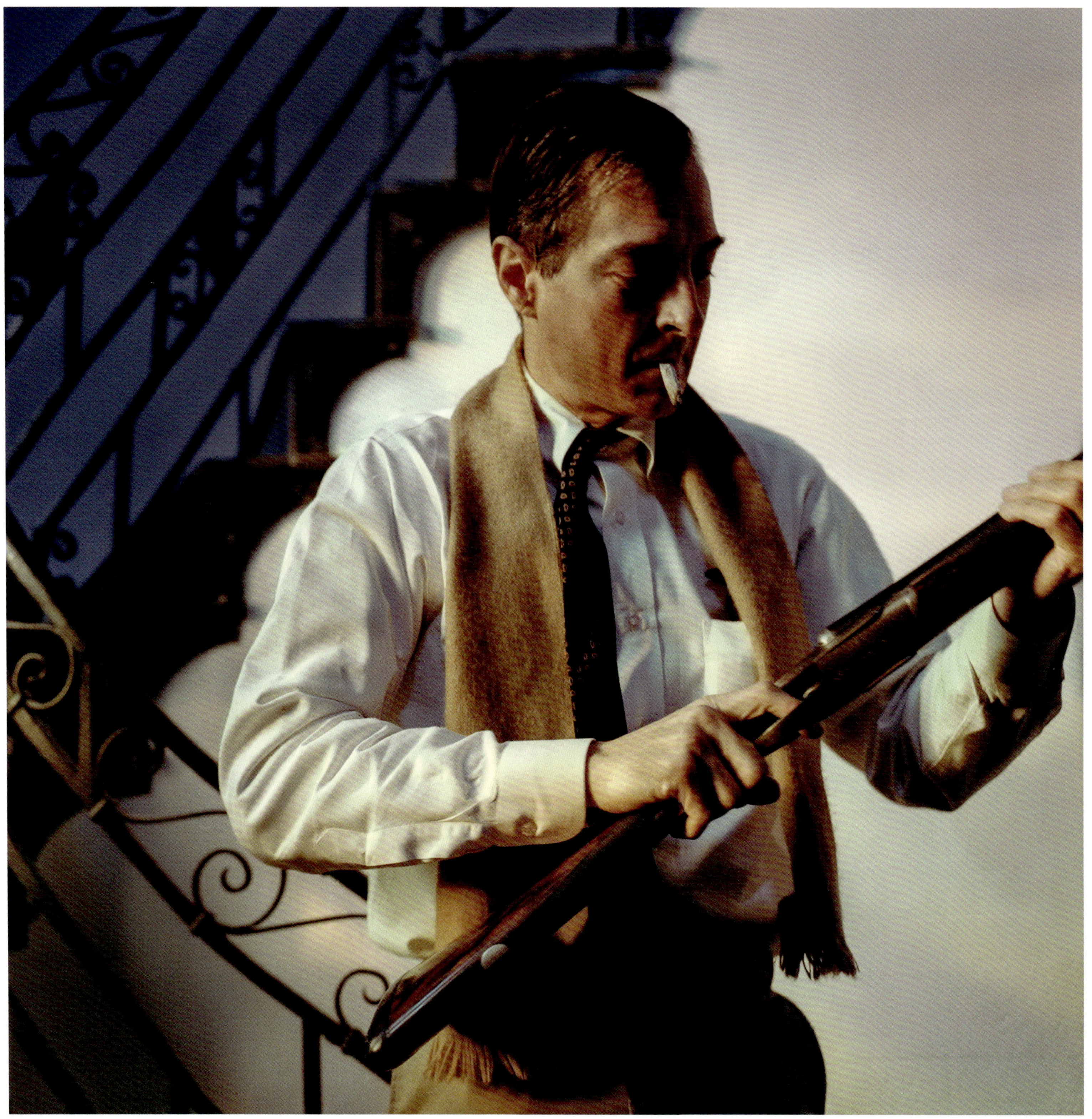

Maude Schuyler Clay. *Bill Eggleston with Gun*. Memphis, 1988.

a total coincidence that Glennray and Egg just happened to be in the same place without a commission.

Lisa Howorth: I think we traded Glennray seventy-five years' worth of books. That shows the kind of sensibility that Bill had. He wasn't interested in the charming street fronts of the buildings as much as he was interested in all the crazy stuff behind the buildings that also made the city really fun and made it much more intriguing to him, and the geometry of it. I thought that was an interesting little aside. Anyway, we were his friends; but he was so inscrutable and a little bit scary.

Here's a photograph that kind of shows you Eggleston's like a gangster, sort of an elegant gangster. He was messing with some guns, and you just don't know what's coming next with Bill. He was a little bit unknowable to us. Now I pick on Maude as a family member and a close friend.

Maude Clay: I'm thinking if those guns were ever loaded. He was just into the idea of the gun as a beautiful object, and he collects guns like he collects cameras or equipment for recording.

Lisa Howorth: You never knew.

Maude Clay: You never knew.

Lisa Howorth: The same with his cameras. You never knew. You never knew if he was really shooting sometimes. Let me point out some things, bring up some things that I would like for Maude to present to get better insight into Bill—who he was or is. Describe Bill and his family in relation to your family, things like when did y'all become aware of Bill's artistic nature and how does that manifest? Sumner with the environment there in 1955, of course, was where one of the most infamous crimes in American history occurred—the Emmett Till murder. Bill would have been roughly the same age as Emmett Till, a teenage boy. Do you have anything to say about that and your family's reaction to that? Did Bill ever take any pictures of the store in Money? Anything like that that you can recall that would be interesting to hear.

Maude Clay: Well, that sounds like big questions already. I hope I don't forget those.

Lisa Howorth: Make it kind of a timeline. Include the New York years, which I'm sure you were there for a good bit and just pack it on in.

Maude Clay: All right. I think the first question was about the Emmett Till story.

Lisa Howorth: Your family. Your connections.

Maude Clay: That all ties together because in the Delta, and the South in general, there are always two separate histories: one black history, and one white history. The Emmett Till case: I was only two years old in 1955, but Bill was fourteen years older than I, and there was a sign that was outside of the town of Sumner. It's now in the Civil Rights Museum in Memphis. I'm so glad somebody saved it. It said, "Sumner. A Great Place to Raise a Boy." Of course, the irony is that was that it *was* a great place to raise a white boy. A privileged person who grew up in Sumner, probably white himself, simply ignored a lot of bad things that happened. Even if you weren't actively participating in the bad things, you just went along with the status quo. Bill said on many occasions that he never set out to take photographs to make any kind of political statement or anything like that. From the get-go he was just interested in the way things looked.

Like I said, he was fourteen years older. When I was about maybe ten or twelve, he was already an adult. He was driving around in Ferraris and his black leather coat, and he had a pair of huge speakers in the back of his car with a reel-to-reel tape recorder. I think it was truly one of the first car stereo music systems. It was certainly the first one that I ever saw. He played Bach, and he built his own speakers. He was just kind of an anomaly. We had an interesting family, but they were rather prosaic. Bill was just in the right time at the right place, I think. I was easily swayed, because he just was always such an interesting guy, and he was sweet to a kid. He treated me like I wasn't just some little kid underfoot. He showed me books, and we listened to music, and then later I went to the Art Academy in Memphis. After I left this esteemed university, he let me be his "apprentice." I put that in quotation marks because all I did besides do a little darkroom work from time to time was just mostly create my own bad black-and-white photographs in his dark room. We just drove around Memphis in the right light. I kind of saw what he was interested in taking pictures of, so it was a real hands-on apprenticeship.

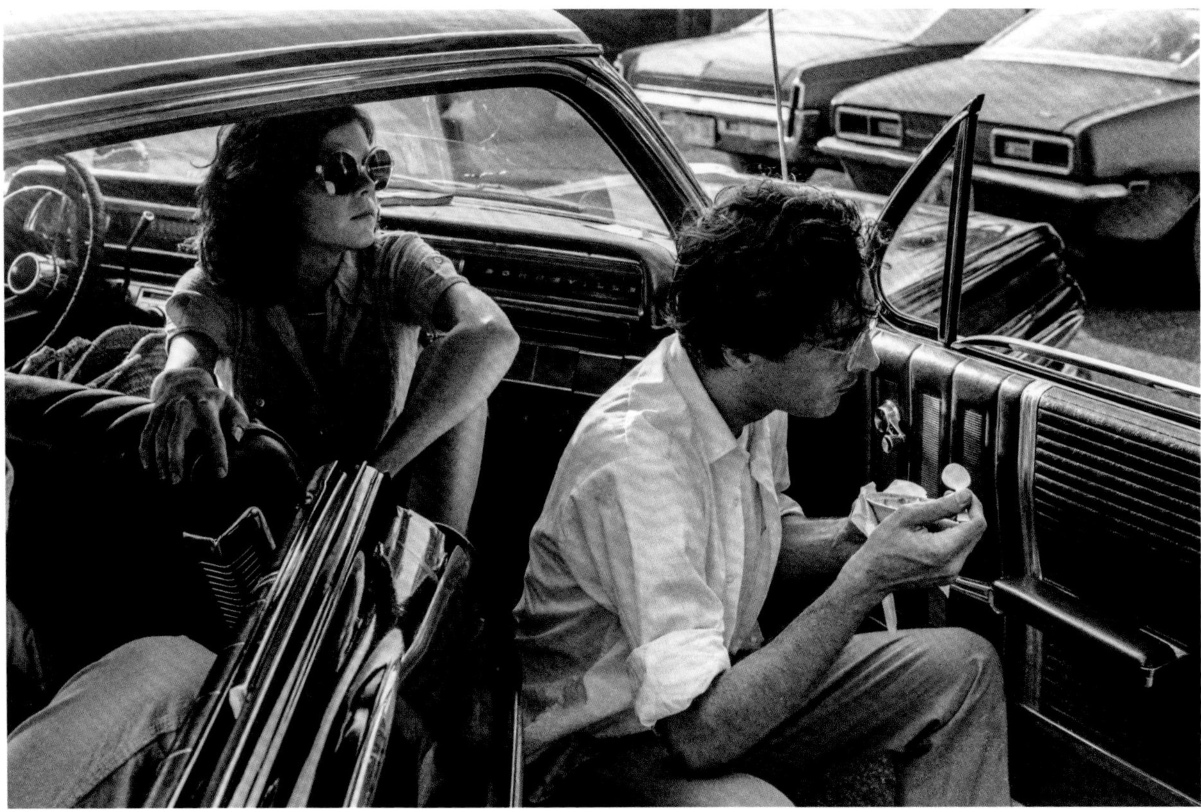

Tav Falco. Maude Schuyler [Clay] and William Eggleston in New York City, 1974.

Lisa Howorth: Tell us how his photographs maybe affected your way of seeing things, and don't forget New York.

Maude Clay: I started taking photographs, like I said, in Memphis and I had a Rolleiflex twin lens reflex 2 ¼ given to me. I think Bill was trying either to get rid of that camera or he was helping me out by giving it to me. I started looking at the world in a square; and I wanted to take color pictures because Bill was making color pictures, but I didn't want to take the same pictures he was taking. I think that anybody can safely say that, after 1976 or so, pretty much anybody that has taken a color picture has in some way been influenced by William Eggleston. That was why I started taking the portraits, because I wanted to differentiate my photography from his.

I moved up to New York, really on a wing and a prayer, and had no gainful employment, but I landed some great jobs. One was working for this place called Light Gallery. The only reason I got that job was Stephen Shore, who was a friend of Bill Eggleston's—and I met every photographer in the world who had come to Memphis, by the way, before I moved to New York—called up the people at Light Gallery and said, "I've got Eggleston's cousin here, and she needs a job. I think you guys need a class act out front." I got that receptionist job, and it was really like getting a PhD in the history of photography working at Light Gallery because at that time people like Harry Callahan, André Kertész, Ansel Adams, everybody came there. There weren't that many women photographers that I recall, but a lot of photographers congregated at this one gallery for contemporary photography in New York. That was the first lottery I won, maybe the second, in landing that job. Bill would come to see me pretty often. That show of his was in May of 1976 at the Museum of Modern Art, which is widely known as the first color photography show at the Museum of Modern Art. I think that's erroneous because Ernst Haas had a show of color photographs before that, maybe in the sixties, or fifties.

Lisa Howorth: Haas's was the first color show at the MoMA in 1962.

Maude Clay: That answered the question, Lisa.

Lisa Howorth: Okay. We want to hear some wild stories, the *Stranded in Canton* story.

Maude Clay: Oh, you can watch *Stranded in Canton* and get that whole story.

Lisa Howorth: You can *try* to watch it.

Maude Clay: Yeah. Well, I was sort of an aghast eighteen-year-old; I was just really riding shotgun. I think I was supposed to be the assistant on some level.

Lisa Howorth: Thanks, Maude. We'll dig deeper soon. It occurred to me also about the Emmett Till years, Bill might have been off at the Webb School at that point.

Maude Clay: He went off to school. He matriculated a few places. You know, that's really something you'd have to ask him. I don't know the full story of that.

Lisa Howorth: I may have asked him and forgot. I wasn't paying more attention back in the day, but his going to Webb School has always amused me. For those of you who don't know what Webb School is, it's in Bell Buckle, Tennessee. It's generally considered a place where bad boys from Mississippi were sent. Those bad boys would include Andy and Richard Howorth. I know he's sitting there. Bill, you got sent off somewhere.

Bill Ferris: Brooks School in North Andover, Massachusetts.

Lisa Howorth: Hard to handle! Okay, let's see. Okay, Billy. You were born in 1942, and Eggleston was In 1939, close in age or at least in cultural eras. How did you and Eggleston meet, and what has your relationship been since then? Not only early in life, but in your interest in photography that seemed to me to have taken very different paths. Do you agree with that, and can you recall a discussion you and Bill might have had about that? You and Bill were born in the era of the great documentarians. The WPA and the Farm Security Administration had tons of photographers who came through Mississippi and shot. Y'all are a little too young, but did you ever hear stories or talk to Bill about having crossed paths with any of these people, or were any of them heroes to you?

Bill Ferris: I am honored to be on the panel with Lisa, Maude, and Megan. I want to thank Robert and Marti for putting us all together. An aside, when I first came to Oxford, Ann Abadie was my partner; and we set about to do big things on this campus. There was no Faulkner manuscript collection at the University, so we encouraged Chancellor Porter Fortune to negotiate the sale of a Coptic Codex, a very valuable, totally unused document in the University Archives, for several hundred thousand dollars. The Williams Library used those funds to purchase the Rowan Oak Papers, a manuscript collection that was found under the stairwell in Faulkner's home. The Rowan Oak Papers were on loan at the University of Virginia's library; and the University of Mississippi bought the collection from Faulkner's daughter, Jill Faulkner Summers.

I later thought that it was an equally serious omission that the University had no collection of the photographs taken by William Eggleston, who also studied here. That brings us to our conversation about the William Eggleston photography exhibition, an exhibition that is of global significance because Bill Eggleston is *the* great color photographer who has transformed the field. He is from Sumner, Mississippi, and he studied at the University of Mississippi.

To answer your question about when I first met Bill, it was in the summer of 1975 when I worked with Judy Peiser at the Center for Southern Folklore in Memphis. Judy and I cofounded the center in 1972. When I taught at Yale from 1972 to 1979, I worked at the Center each summer. My old friend Perry Walker grew up in Holly Springs and lived in Memphis. He was a gifted photographer who did a book called *The Preacher and His Congregation* on Reverend Louis Cole, a black preacher who lived near Holly Springs. Perry Walker's wife, Mary Hohenberg, is also a photographer. One evening I was with Perry, Mary, and Mary's sister, Betsy Burr. They said, "You have to meet our friend William Eggleston."

We had been out for dinner. It was about eleven o'clock at night, and they said, "Let's go see Eggleston." We went to Bill's house, and all the lights were on. His children were running around the house. There were artists and musicians hanging out in the garden. Bill's mother was there. I had my parrot, Ogie, with me at the time. I left Ogie outside on the limb of a tree. A little later Bill came in, and he said, "Your parrot just bit my mother."

The whole evening was a surreal experience. At one point, Bill led me to his Steinway piano. The top was down, and several large piles of his incredible dye-transfer photographs were stacked on top of the piano. Viewing Bill's photographs for the first time was like an epiphany. It was as if I had never seen color photography before, certainly not color photographs like those. I looked at them for over an hour, and I was speechless. That was the beginning of our friendship.

The next year—1976—I invited Bill to speak to my students and to show his work at Yale. He brought an exhibition of his black-and-white photographs of Memphis nightlife and his video *Stranded in Canton*. When we spoke on the phone, Bill explained, "I'll need some special equipment to show the video." He gave me a list of equipment he needed, and I took it to the Yale media center. They looked at the list and said, "We have never heard of anything like this. We don't have it." I called Bill back, and he said, "Well, I'll just bring my own."

Bill flew up from Memphis with four video monitors and their support system; and he set them up in the master's living room of Calhoun College, where I lived as a resident fellow. The four large monitors faced each corner of the large room. The students were aghast and said, "We have never seen any equipment like this. Where did he find it?" I replied, "He brought it with him from Memphis." Bill gave a truly incredible program.

That was a highlight early in our friendship; and each time I was in Memphis, I got together with Bill. I never stayed with Bill because, as my brother, Grey, used to say, "You cannot fly with the owls at night and soar with the eagles in the day." Eggleston's day started about six in the afternoon. As far as I could determine, he stayed up all night. I could hang with him until around midnight, but I knew I had to function the next day. I loved him and everything he did. He is an artistic outlaw. He always breaks the established artistic laws and goes outside the box with his work.

When Ann Abadie recruited me to come to the University, Lisa and Richard Howorth had just moved back to Oxford after running the Savile Book Shop in the Georgetown district of Washington, DC. Lisa wrote me a postcard that said, "We look forward to meeting you."

Once I was settled in Oxford, I called Bill and said, "Come on down. I'm not in Memphis as much anymore." So he started coming to see me in Oxford. Usually, as Lisa said, it was on weekends, and he would get a room on the first floor of the Holiday Inn. Someone asked him, "Why do you always come and stay there?" Bill replied, "I like to wash my poodle in the bathtub." He always brought his poodle. Bill also brought an incredible sound system he would set up in the room at the Holiday Inn and play Buxtehude and Bach while he washed his poodle. Bill also played their compositions on his piano in Memphis.

We would go out on photo shoots around Oxford. Bill to me was like a ballerina with his camera. He moved in the most graceful way around the people and objects that he photographed. He engaged photography in important new ways. I visited yesterday with David Houston, who worked earlier at the Ogden Museum and at Crystal Bridges. I told David I was coming to the opening of the exhibition, and he already knew about it. He said, "Are you going to talk about Tom Young?" and I said, "No, but tell me more about Tom." He said Bill Eggleston worked with Tom Young when Tom taught in the art department at the University of Mississippi. Tom saw Bill working with black and white and said, "You need to work with color." Tom mentored Bill; and when I visit Bill, he often mentions Tom as a pivotal figure who inspired his work.

Eggleston is to photography what Faulkner is to literature, what B. B. King is to blues. He is an iconic figure, and he essentially builds on a long, rich tradition of photography in the American South. Bill is acutely aware of Walker Evans and of Eudora Welty. He is also inspired by the French photographer Henri Cartier-Bresson.

When Tom Young encouraged Bill to move from black-and-white to color photography, it was like the moment Sherwood Anderson told Faulkner, "Go back home to Oxford and focus on what you know there." Tom encouraged Bill to focus on the Delta, and also to move beyond the black-and-white traditional portraiture of children he was doing to more innovative color work. Theo Inman, who worked with the Mississippi Arts Commission in the seventies, once showed me portraits of her children Bill took. Other portrait photographers, like the Cofields, who photographed Faulkner in Oxford, and Bern and Franke Keating in Greenville, also did black-and-white portraits, and Bill knew their work well.

Eggleston moved from black-and-white sitting portraits to documentary color photography that differed dramatically from the work of Walker Evans and Eudora Welty. His color photography hits you in the stomach as well as in the head, and you internalize it. You cannot look at Eggleston's work without being moved by it. Sometimes as I watch scenes from the first year's series of *True Detective*, I think, "That looks like an Eggleston photograph." The camera will pause on a scene, and something about it is hauntingly familiar. Then I realize that the scene is inspired by Eggleston's photography.

In many ways, Bill's life and my own have moved on parallel tracks. His mother and my mother were students together at All Saints' Episcopal School in Vicksburg. I took photographs from the time I was twelve. I got a little Brownie camera for Christmas, and I immediately put a roll of film in it and photographed my grandmother's Christmas dinner with my family gathered around the table. Then that spring, I photographed a black baptism on the farm where we lived. That was 1954. Those images foreshadowed the intimate relationship I developed with what I view as my "extended family" of Mississippi people through photography. Balzac called it *La Comédie humaine*, the world within which we are all connected.

I always loved photography. As an undergraduate student at Davidson College in the early sixties, I stumbled on Frederick Ramsey Jr.'s *Been Here and Gone*, a book that features black-and-white

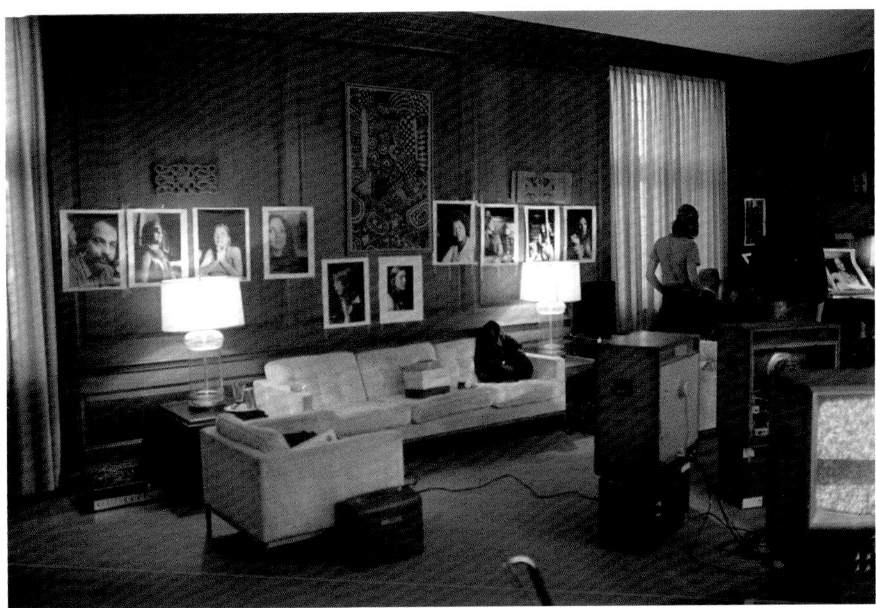

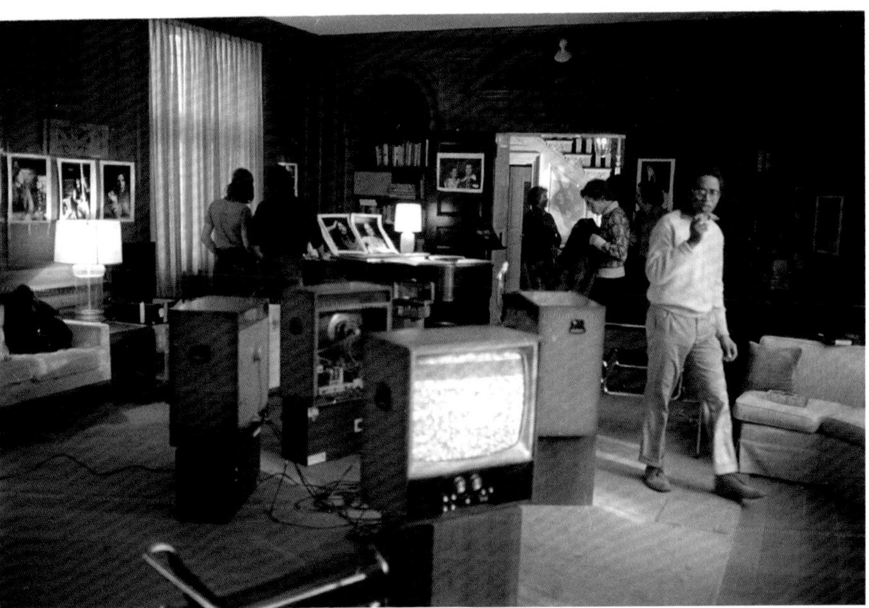

William Ferris, photographs of William Eggleston's images and audio and video equipment in the installation at Calhoun College (now Grace Murray Hopper College), Yale University, 1976. Detail of silver gelatin print contact sheet. William R. Ferris Collection, Southern Folklife Collection, Wilson Library, The University of North Carolina–Chapel Hill.

photographs Ramsey took in Mississippi and in my hometown of Vicksburg. Later, when I was a graduate student studying folklore at the University of Pennsylvania, Charlotte Capers introduced me to Eudora Welty's work. All those beautiful images were black and white, and their work inspired me to seriously pursue my photography.

From the beginning, I worked with both color and black-and-white film because I always loved color. But publishers would not use my color photographs, because of the expense of printing them. Even in my book about folk artists entitled *Local Color*, the publisher reproduced my color photographs in black and white. So I used my color slides to illustrate my lectures but almost never published them.

After I met Bill and saw his beautiful work, I began to think about the color photograph as a palette. Through his photographs, I realized that how you render color in an image is as important as the subject you capture on film. It's not the literal image of the face. Eggleston captured the rich, deep hues of yellows and reds. The natural beauty of the Mississippi landscape rendered in his drenched dye-transfer prints is unlike anything I have ever seen. Like a Rembrandt, they have the power of a classic painting. Inspired by Bill, I began to underexpose my film by a half-stop to achieve a deeper saturation of color on the film.

Bill Eggleston and Bill Christenberry influenced my work. Christenberry was a highly disciplined photographer, but Eggleston gave me license to do everything I wanted to do with my camera. He is a true genius, and he opened doors for me, for which I will always be grateful. That is how I view Bill.

Lisa Howorth: Thanks, Bill. That was a beautiful way of moving on. Going back to Miss Megan, you didn't know Bill, as you pointed out, unlike the rest of us, and you talk about your interest in his work going way back. I wondered if the sinister aspect of his work that you perceived is something that you've always felt or if it's something that occurred to you after you knew more about him, saw pictures maybe like that, and you thought, "This is scary. This is a dark artist."

Megan Abbott: Yes, I'm aware now that some of his photographs are sinister. Some of them, I guess, because people keep telling me that or I access them through David Lynch, who is a big Eggleston fan and collector and very influenced by him. I don't think that sinister quality is one I respond to. At least to me, what it was first in my teen years, I just couldn't wait to get out of the Michigan suburb I was in, which seemed to me so bland and lifeless and meaningless.

It was not inspiring me in any way as a writer, but then I would look at his photographs of grocery stores or parking lots, or *Leather Pink Patio Chair*. It was not unlike the world I was in, but suddenly it looked spectacular, strange, filled with feeling, and in some ways like the great melodramas I used to love watching. You know those great ones like *Gone with the Wind*. It just made everything that felt to me small, cramped, and simple look glamorous, complicated, foreign, and mysterious.

It made me realize the transformative power of art. I suppose it's not the object; it's the person looking at the object. It is the person sort of translating that through art—with personal history, associations. Like Arbus, you can get why people think they're sinister; but Eggleston, sometimes those responses—sinister, whatever—are more about you than about the photograph. The more you look, the more you see different things. The photographs seem to change when you look at them at different points in your life. I think that shows a sign of genius somehow. It's never the same photograph. I think because of the way we're trying to convey it, we're bringing ourselves to it each time, and it's giving us something new this time somehow.

Lisa Howorth: I agree with that, and I only became aware of this when I met him. I always thought, "Is this about the way I look at these photographs, or about him? About the man or about the photographs?" It's changed all these years.

Megan Abbott: Yes. I remember the first time I saw them in a group was at the Whitney's exhibition *William Eggleston: Democratic Camera, Photographs and Video, 1961–2008*. That was in 2008, the first time I saw them in a formal exhibition, the first time I saw them in real life other than in books. In showing some of his videos along with his photographs, the Whitney exhibition presented the wild Southern character he was. It was interesting to me because, of course, I was fascinated by that kind of artist's lifestyle—living his own way. That added another layer that changed the way I viewed the photographs. Seeing *The Beautiful Mysterious* exhibition has caused the way I look at some of his black-and-white photos to change again. I don't have the language of photography to speak of what it really means, but the black-and-white photographs in this exhibition are quite striking and extraordinary to me, filled with a kind of loneliness and beauty. I'm glad that he moved to color because of what the color ones brought, but those also deserve attention. Deep attention, I think.

Lisa Howorth: Have you ever tried to get one on the cover of one of your books?

Megan Abbott: Yes, I did. One of my books, *The Fever*, was very much inspired by Eggleston's famous photographs with the young girls with the long hair. The first shows one lying on the sofa with the other attending her. The second has one with blonde hair at a counter. These are glorious photographs of girlhood, of a kind of tricky girlhood that I loved and wanted to use, but they're expensive to put on the cover of a book.

Lisa Howorth: You never know, even still.

Megan Abbott: No.

Lisa Howorth: You might want to fix that.

Megan Abbott: I would like to make that happen.

Lisa Howorth: You may regret it.

Megan Abbott: I do like to hear the stories, though.

Lisa Howorth: Anything else you want to add? Anything you want to say?

Megan Abbott: I was unaware until much later of Eggleston's status as a Southern photographer. I know it's sort of complicated to get those kind of labels, but to me there's also something deeply universal. These photographs always felt deeply American to me, especially as someone in the Midwest. Those big swaths of parking lots, the Taco Bell. There are aspects of them that I feel need to be specific because there's so much he's offering in terms of his place in Southern history, but there's also so much that feels universal and big.

Lisa Howorth: Yes. One of my favorite shots I think was on the cover of *Artforum*. I forget when, Maude, but it was your dad and . . .

Maude Clay: Okay, that was my father, Adyn Schuyler, and a man that worked for the family for many years, Jasper Staples. The story behind that photograph is that we were at a family funeral. One of the many alcoholics of the family breathed his last, and somebody forgot to put on the emergency brake. Mr. Bob Flautt and his car rolled down the driveway and almost went into Cassidy Bayou. Everybody went down there to see about Mr. Bob Flautt's car. If you look closely in that picture, you see Mr. Bob Flautt as a little figure behind the wheel in the white car.

The interesting thing, I think, about that photograph is that Daddy and Jasper looked so similar in that stance. When that picture was in the Museum of Modern Art show in '76, one of the better reviews—not "The Emperor's New Clothes," which was my favorite because everybody was really upset about John Szarkowski's springing that work on the world unawares—described Daddy as a white Faulknerian figure in a black suit and Jasper as a black Faulknerian figure in a white suit. I just thought, "Well, that about says it all."

Lisa Howorth: When you first see it, you assume it's a picture about race. Of course, it is to a certain extent. Although I don't think Bill intended that so much, but it's also the contrasts and the colors and the open car doors. He's got each man standing next to the car, and the doors are opened, and it has a much more universal quality, like Megan was saying. I appreciate it as something else now.

Maude Clay: Well, for me, of course, it's always kind of a family picture. One thing I want to go back to, Lisa, is that I don't think Bill really sees that much difference in pictures of people and pictures of places and objects. He thinks of his photographs as one long continuous body of work. I know lately he was a little perturbed about showing at the National Portrait Gallery in London because it featured only his pictures of people. He said, "You know, I just don't want to separate the work out like that because it's all of a piece." Whatever that genius is that we've all been trying to describe is that he has seen the work as one long history of himself, of the place, of the world, of storytelling. Really to me it boils down to the storytelling, in that it's how he's telling the story or whether the person is perceiving a story as he sees the picture. I'm glad to be in that family. I can tell you some of it rubbed off.

Lisa Howorth: Some of it rubbed off on your lovely husband, too.

Maude Clay: Yes.

Lisa Howorth: Who's also a wonderful, well-known photographer, Langdon Clay. He's here.

Maude Schuyler Clay: It seems like there are a lot of professional voyeurs running around.

Megan Abbott: Jumping back to the object thing, that feels so true. I was speaking of the photograph with the front seat of the car where there's the McDonald's cup, the white feather hanging from the rearview mirror, and the paper bag. To me it feels as if a person is in the photograph, even though there's no person there. In some ways the objects seem as animated as people, and sometimes the people seem more like objects. I can see it. That makes so much sense. That's so interesting to me.

Lisa Howorth: Isn't one of the books portraits? Am I imagining that?

Maude Clay: There's the *5x7* book that's mostly portraits. The National Portrait Gallery's criterion is "It needs to be a portrait." I thought Bill would have been thrilled with that show and the book, but he said he just didn't like the way it was cut-and-dried to have only people in the photographs. If we had him here, we could grill him about it.

Lisa Howorth: Have we ever had him anywhere when we wanted to grill him? Maybe in Japan where he sang "Are You Lonesome Tonight?" to the crowd. I'd give a million dollars to have him here today. One of my favorite stories, Maude, since you brought this up, is regarding alcoholism. As far as Oxford and Mississippi writers and artists go, it's sort of an 800-pound gorilla in the room. You're talking about them as *people*. Probably most notably William Faulkner and Tennessee Williams, but I guess Miss Welty probably took a little nip every now and then.

Maude Clay: Oh, she could drink people under the table.

Lisa Howorth: I bet she could. But I don't want to pry. I want to pry a little bit! Let's put that out there because it's always such an issue. The reason I want to ask about Bill and drinking, I've heard it so many times talking with Barry about drinking, and how it affected their art, or how they thought it affected their art, talking about Faulkner and how they think maybe it affected his art, that kind of thing. Also, Michael Almereyda's documentary film *William Eggleston in the Real World* is very frank, and Bill makes no attempt to hide the fact that there's a hell of a lot of drinking going on all the time. I really want to know if there is a connection between that and his work? Does it enhance it? I know sometimes I'm trying to write something and I just need a little nip.

Maude Clay: I think this is not a problem that's particular to my family, or the South, or anything. Often with absinthe, and opium, and every drug that's ever been consumed, some people use it to get themselves into another state of mind. What was the question again?

Lisa Howorth: Talking about *Stranded in Canton*, the 1973 film. I guess it was the director who says that it brings out the sense of psychic disarray about Bill. It just makes you wonder.

Maude Clay: I do think he was merely recording. At that time, I don't believe he was doing that much drinking himself.

Lisa Howorth: I mean, do you think it is something that you realize? I remember Barry telling me that he worried that he wouldn't be able to write if he couldn't drink.

Maude Clay: I think essentially what I remember from growing up is that Bill's kind of shy. Liquor has that way of giving you courage, and of course eventually you're going to make a fool of yourself a lot of the time, but it gives you that dimension that you need I think sometimes to break into the world Barry Hannah has created. How the hell did he ever think up all that stuff? Some people can think it up without substances. I think for some people it enhances what they're doing, but that's another question you would need to ask Bill.

Lisa Howorth: I've asked him. We've talked about it. He's always very frank and open about it. That was a long time ago. Barry used to say that he would not be able to write at all if he were not drunk, which turned out not to be true; but his body of work is pretty much defined by the drinking period and then, when he stopped drinking, the nondrinking books. I can tell a huge difference, but you don't see any? I know Bill stopped drinking at certain points.

Maude Clay: Well, yes, I don't know if he ever has. I know he's still doing work. You know, he usually goes to exotic locales like Paris, or Japan, or Berlin, and it's remarkable about those photographs. As Megan was saying earlier, it's not just about making a record of the South or a record of Poland, or Jimmy Carter's election eve. Those are amazing pictures. I think he has this sort of vision that goes on no matter where he is. It's not so much about the place or the fact that he's a Southerner. I think maybe the light had something to do with his being a Southerner. I know that seems to be a real point for me because I love this light here so much. Anyway, I hope I've answered the question.

Lisa Howorth: Yes, I was just curious about it.

Maude Clay: This will be my last panel, I'm sure.

Lisa Howorth: Probably not. Okay, Billy. You've told us a whole lot of stuff already, but we haven't gone over everything, but you've just published your beautiful book. Most of those photographs date back to the seventies and some of them as early as the sixties. Eggleston began in '65 with black and white, and then in the 1970s he turned to color. Color was considered sort of the stuff of advertisements, and family photo albums, and snapshots. Since we've been talking about Walker Evans, it's time to bring up what he said about color photography: "There are four simple words for the matter, which must be whispered: Color photography is vulgar."

Obviously, there was a breakthrough at some point with Eggleston. To me, what he did with color photography was bring photography up to the achievement of painting, which had been going on since 1839 with the invention of photography. What do you think about the idea of its being vulgar, or tacky, or whatever when you started doing color? What do you remember talking to Bill about, what he thought about it?

Bill Ferris: I started using color film in the early sixties, and I loved color. I did not meet Bill until 1975.

We should think of Bill Eggleston not simply as a photographer, but as an artist who works in multiple fields. Just as Faulkner and Welty did fin de siècle drawings that are quite beautiful, Bill does watercolors and sketches. Bill's daughter, Andra, now designs textiles that are inspired by her father's watercolors.

The Bohemian South and the Gothic South are concepts that help us frame William Eggleston and his work. Since Edgar Allan Poe, Bohemian worlds have been an important presence in the American South. For a formative period in his life, William Faulkner lived in that "southern capital" of Mississippi—New Orleans—in the French Quarter and was immersed in its Bohemian world with a group that included Sherwood Anderson and William Spratling. A generation later, Eggleston was a central figure in the Bohemian world of the "northern capital" of Mississippi—Memphis.

The primary interest of the New Orleans group was literature. In Memphis, it was music. Bill was the epicenter of the Memphis Bohemian group, which included musicians, photographers, and painters. It was a counterpart of the Oxford Bohemian community who found their home in Ron Shapiro's Hoka, a coffeehouse, cinema, and concert hall where counterculture worlds thrived. Bill's life and his photography are firmly grounded within the Southern Bohemian tradition, which helps us connect his multiple talents as a visual artist, a pianist, and a photographer.

Since we first met in 1975, Bill has been an inspiration for my work. I view myself as a documentary photographer who aspires to creating art. If you craft the document well enough and long enough, you create art. You aspire to break through walls, which is what Bill does so well.

Bill's photography has an important association with violence. The violence is not always a literal depiction, as seen in his photograph of a man with a pistol in his hand. Equally important is what is not in the picture. What lurks behind the walls, the curtains, and in the dark hallways of his photography? He reminds us of a latent violence in the worlds he photographs, a violence that is a familiar part of the frontier experience.

We associate the frontier with the westernmost part of the United States. In the nineteenth century, the frontier was known as the "Old Southwest" and included Mississippi. While the frontier moved west, its association with violence and the use of colorful language is still alive and well in Mississippi and in the South today. The South should be viewed as a frontier society whose identity is deeply rooted in guns, violence, and colorful language. Bill distills those worlds through his photography.

Place defines people in powerful ways, and Bill is closely associated with the Mississippi Delta. When he travels to Berlin, Rome, or New York City, he makes exquisitely beautiful images, like a photograph he shot in a plane as light pours from the window through a glass of bourbon on a table. In a similar way, while Alan Lomax recorded music across the globe, his most famous recordings were in the Mississippi Delta and in the hills of Northeast Mississippi. Lomax found his soul in the fife and drum music of Gravel Springs, Mississippi. Similarly, Walker Evans was forever defined by the photographs he took in Hale County, Alabama. Bill Eggleston's artistic genius is fused inextricably with Sumner, Mississippi, and with Memphis. Those two worlds defined his work in powerful ways.

Bill rarely speaks about his work. In 1991 the University Museum featured an exhibition of Bill's photography, and Marie Antoon and a film crew from the media center tried to interview him. Each time Marie asked a question, Bill just sat and smiled. When I brought Bill to Yale, questions were asked about his work, and he just smiled. Just as when Eudora Welty was asked, "Why do you not take a public position on civil rights?" she replied, "Read my work." Eggleston's voice is best heard through his photographs.

Maude Clay: I have a funny anecdote about that. One time he was showing at the International Center of Photography in New York. Those were the photographs that were in the Museum of Modern Art show. A lot of the color work was in *William Eggleston's Guide*, and he showed two or three trays of his slides. At that time in New York, in the mid to late seventies, there were the Magnum photographers, and then there was this whole idea that photography was not really serious photography unless it was black and white or it was making a statement about some social concern.

Anyway, photography was blown out of the water by Bill Eggleston; but when the slideshow finished, there was an audience of these serious photography people. We got to the questions and the answers. One of the people said, "Why do you take photographs, Mr. Eggleston?" Then there was a very long pause, and he said, "*There just has to be some way to deal with all of this time.*" He allowed a few more questions, and he just sort of quietly left the stage. He's not one who loves to talk about photography or his work. As Bill Ferris said, you should just look at the images and make your own conclusions. We all have these stories we love to make up when we see some images, and he has provided some great ones.

Lisa Howorth: I think the shyness and the alcohol are things at work and are part of him and his public persona. Here's one more question for Megan. Can you come up with an author whose writing is as evocative as Eggleston, or can you come up with five or six people who you think are somehow on the same wavelength?

Megan Abbott: This is going to be anachronistic, but I always think of Eggleston when I read Faulkner, and I always think of Faulkner when I look at Eggleston. I think that the connection is articulated, is definitely there. When I read William Gay, I think of Eggleston. When I read Willy Wiseman, I think of Eggleston. I feel like he's sort of all over the place in terms of books that are unshy about extreme emotion.

I was thinking about what you were saying about painting, how it brought photographs closer to painting and how photography was closer to painting than it seems. That famous Eggleston one of the red ceiling that's redder than red could be, and he's talked about it as being redder than red actually can be in real life in some way. That seems to me what makes his photos expressionistic rather than impressionistic or realistic. That they're about how things feel. You think that writers who write with a heart, and libido, and other things first—those are the writers I associate with Eggleston. There's something very unafraid about that.

Lisa Howorth: I always thought that about Barry.

Megan Abbott: Yes, Barry is a wonderful example.

Lisa Howorth: That courage always fell out

throughout everything they did. They were going to do their part and report what they saw, and nothing else mattered or influenced them really. They were both really brave about their part in it. I think that's something I always think about with my reading Barry and viewing Eggleston.

Megan Abbott: Well, even someone like Shirley Jackson, who wrote Gothic novels, books that are very interior because they're about these characters' views of the world, that can become both terrifying and pulpy in an instant and then recede back; but you always have the feeling when you read Shirley Jackson's *The Haunting of Hill House*, or *We Have Always Lived in the Castle*, or I guess her famous short story "The Lottery" that everyone knows, but not everyone knows that from the outside these are quaint women walking down the lane. But you're reading a book on the inside, but the inside is redder than red, and every object is infused with meaning. Henry James's *Turn of the Screw* would be another example of that where everything is infused with sensation somehow.

Lisa Howorth: I hadn't thought of James. That's good—and the psychology.

Megan Abbott: Right, the psychology. Absolutely and unconscious. You could say that Eggleston's photos are the unconsciousness in a way.

Bill Ferris: When I first met Barry Hannah, I saw him as a kindred spirit. Barry and I moved to Oxford about the same time. When I read *Airships*, I thought, "I must introduce Barry to Bill Eggleston because they are the two bad boys of literature and photography and they need to know each other."

Lisa Howorth: It was a bad mistake!

Bill Ferris: They met. I later saw Barry, and I asked, "Are you and Bill still hanging out?" He said, "I couldn't hang with him. He was just too wild." One of the speakers at our conference on Elvis Presley was from Memphis and a friend of Eggleston, who was also visiting Oxford. They went out the night before the conference and went on a binge. The next morning the speaker got up to present his talk. He spoke about six words; then he stood there staring at the audience and collapsed. We had to carry him out. He just could not keep up with Eggleston.

I will mention one other Eggleston story. One of my old friends from Yale, Willie Ruff, with whom I taught, is a jazz musician, a bass player, who was part of the Mitchell-Ruff duo. When I brought Eggleston to Yale, Willie told me that he and Bill were old friends. Eggleston and Vernon Richards met Willie at a party in Harlem and became good friends.

I called Willie not long ago. He is now retired from teaching. I told him about this symposium, and he said, "God, I'd love to see Eggleston again." Willie had also visited Eggleston in Memphis. Bill and Willie's friendship suggests the power of the Bohemian worlds of Memphis and Harlem. Bill's world in Memphis was connected with Stax Records in Memphis, where white and black musicians played together in defiance of the Jim Crow racism that existed outside the studio walls. Inside that studio and at studios in Muscle Shoals, Alabama, musicians created a refreshingly new music that broke through racial barriers.

Through his photography, Eggleston embraced extraordinary people in New Orleans, Memphis, Harlem, and New York and made them part of his world. To view his photographs is to connect with those worlds.

Lisa Howorth: I'm so excited that Oxford has a part in the whole Eggleston thing. We're really lucky that he did spend time here, and he did some really incredible work here. He seems to love Oxford. Would you say he loved it here?

Maude Clay: I was also going to say to any budding Bohemians out there, it's not that easy to pull off, so watch it.

Lisa Howorth: Okay. We have ten minutes left. Anybody have any burning questions for our panelists?

Carlyle Wolfe (Oxford artist whose paintings and paper and metal silhouettes reflect the natural world)**:** Mr. Ferris, I'm having a hard time getting past your taking a parrot to dinner.

Bill Ferris: My parrot Ogie was a gift from a friend whom I knew at Yale in the seventies. His owner decided to give him to me because he was too loud. He was an important part of my life for fifteen years. He came with me when I moved to Oxford in 1979, and we lived together at 1700 Jefferson Avenue.

Having a parrot changes your life. The bird becomes an intimate part of who you are. I have a thick file of jokes and cartoons that friends sent me about parrots.

I learned that if you enter a restaurant and ask, "Can I eat with my parrot?" they always say, "No." But if I just walked in with Ogie on my shoulder, sat down, and ordered, they never asked me to leave.

So Ogie was with me when Perry Walker, Mary Hohenberg, Betsy Burr, and I went to dinner in Memphis after which we went to visit Bill. I never left Ogie in the car, because he would destroy it. When we arrived at Bill's home, I put Ogie on a limb. When Bill's mother tried to play with him, he bit her. You have to own a parrot to appreciate their personality.

Lisa Howorth: Anybody else?

Ron Shapiro (owner of Hoka Theatre and Moonlite Café from 1975 to 1996 and other cultural establishments in Oxford)**:** It was always my understanding that Eggleston was inspired by newspapers, especially the Sunday newspapers, when they first began to print in wild fluorescent colors. Those colors had never been seen before. I heard that. Is there any truth in that? Would he do something that would help him make colors like that?

Bill Ferris: I think Ron made an important point, which is that Bill is not only an artist. He is also a genius at technology, and he pushes printing technology to its limit to reproduce color. In the seventies, he found a lab that understood the new technique of dye transfer, and he realized that it could produce the most vivid color ever seen in photographs. When he was frustrated by limitations of his cameras, Bill designed new lenses for both his still and video cameras. He pushed his cameras to their limits, and he was equally demanding with his color printing. Once he was focused on color, he pushed it beyond what the existing technology allowed.

Glenn Cofield (financial advisor in Memphis, grandson and great-grandson of Oxford photographers)**:** Isn't there a story about the Walgreens print machines?

Maude Clay: Before he transferred to the dye-transfer people in Chicago, he was having all his work printed at the drugstore. They would make 8-inch by 10-inch copies of each 35-millimeter negative, and he would have hundreds of those things made. He'd go pick them up at the drugstore.

Glenn Cofield: Not just his work, but it seems all the other stuff.

Maude Clay: Yes. In fact, there's a picture in *2¼* that Twin Palms Publishers issued, and it's a picture really of a quintessential little old lady with a fur around her neck and with a grandson. That's always been attributed to Bill, but he claims he never took it. He says it was mixed up in the drugstore. He might have just decided that it was a wonderful story, and he really did take that one.

Lisa Howorth: He reminds me of another Popeye, not the Faulkner Popeye, but the real Popeye: "I yam what I yam." Anybody else, ladies and gentlemen?

Lynn Wilkins (Oxford grantwriter and arts patron)**:** Bill, I wonder if you would talk for a minute about that process for you as a collector, and friend, and building up that body of work, and how you did it.

Bill Ferris: Each time I visited Bill, there were piles of photographs on his piano, and I would go through them and pull out ones that I thought were especially beautiful. I would say, "Bill, I really love these five. Can I buy these from you?" He would reply, "Yeah. Give me so much for them." I bought them because they reflected what Bill was working on at the time. Some of these black-and-white photographs, like the one of a teenage boy with the pointed finger, are especially powerful.

Although Bill is best known for his color work, his black-and-white photographs are equally striking. These photographs remind me of our long friendship. I often visited Bill in his home on Walnut Grove, and usually his photographs were always stacked on that Steinway piano.

On one visit, there was a Gatling machine gun just inside his front door with a cloth cover over it. I said, "What's that, Bill?" He took the cover off. It was a work of art, a beautiful brass machine gun standing on three metal legs. Bill showed me the cartridges for the gun that were stored in a metal box below it. If fired, the gun would have cut his front door in half. Bill also kept rare shotguns near his piano. He is a fine pianist and he loves to play Buxtehude and Bach. He sometimes played Bach for me. He plays Bach fugues with great skill. It all seemed to be of a piece.

Marcie wanted to use Bill's color photograph of a dinner on the table for her book *The Edible South*. I called Bill, Rosa, and Winston, and they were all enthusiastic about the idea. Bill's wife, Rosa, said, "Bill took that photograph when he visited his grandmother. She fed him what she had in the kitchen, and he snapped a picture of it."

The photographs in this exhibition are images that I saw on Bill's piano, admired, and picked up. It was random, but perhaps not so random. They were whatever he had shot and printed when we visited. I selected only a few out of probably 1,000 or more that I looked at during my visits with Bill.

I loved them all, but there were certain ones that struck me as especially beautiful. Those are the ones I pulled out, and thankfully they ended up here in Oxford, where they should be. Bill's time as a student at the University of Mississippi was a transitional moment, just as it was for Faulkner. Important artists have studied here and been inspired to write, paint, and photograph in ways that we should recognize and honor.

The University will always nurture young artists. This exhibition is an important way to share Bill's genius with future generations of artists and writers. Square Books is part of that tradition. It's like a university in the community that brings in a steadily growing number of writers who present readings and sign their books. The bookstore is a national treasure. No other community in the nation has a bookstore like Square Books. Let's hear it for Lisa and Richard Howorth and for their great team at Square Books.

Lisa Howorth: Okay. I guess we've got to recognize one last question from Ann Abadie.

Ann Abadie: Tell about the experience of exhibiting Eggleston at the museum the first time, *William Eggleston: Artist's Choice*, consisting of sixteen or so photographs he selected from his private collection and exhibited in the fall of 1991. He came to Oxford for the opening of the exhibition.

Bill Ferris: It was like a homecoming because, as Lisa's mentioned, Bill loves Oxford. He began to come regularly on weekends to wander around and to photograph in the early eighties, and he agreed to come for the 1991 exhibition of his photographs. Marie Antoon brought a film crew to interview Bill. He was seated there with the cameras rolling, but no pearls of wisdom were spoken because that is not who he is. But the exhibition was a very significant moment for all of us, and Bill loved it.

Maude Clay: I think Susan Hannah helped organize the exhibition.

Bill Ferris: Yes, Susan worked for the museum then.

Maude Clay: She was special, too. They were good buddies. I just want to say that I think this current version of the exhibition—*The Beautiful Mysterious*—is just over-the-top great. The aubergine walls are magnificent. That was a stroke of genius, whoever did that. I think that the professionalism—just the way everything is: the selections, the way it's lit, the mixing of black and white with the color—is a fantastic thing that's happened here, and it should really be seen around the world. This exhibition is tantamount to, as Bill Ferris was saying, Bill Eggleston's roots in this place. Thank you to everybody who did this exhibition. It's over-the-top great.

Lisa Howorth: That's a wonderful way to end. We're a little over time. Thank you all for coming, and don't forget to come back at two o'clock.

Note

1. Albert Einstein, *Living Philosophies* (New York: Simon and Schuster, 1931), 2.

William Eggleston Symposium

Afternoon Panel

Moderator: William Ferris
Panelists: Kris Belden-Adams, Richard McCabe, Emily Ballew Neff

Robert Saarnio: Welcome back. Thank you to our morning panelists and moderator. That session was extraordinary, incredible. The afternoon will be equally compelling. Thank you all again for being here today. We are immensely grateful to have as moderator of our afternoon panel distinguished author, photographer, filmmaker, and scholar William Ferris. This university has an extraordinary collection of William Eggleston prints, thanks to Bill's gift of fifty-five prints, with thirty-six of them featured in the Museum's current exhibition.

To introduce him as moderator and speaker this afternoon, I will read from last week's press release in which the Mississippi Arts Commission announced him as the recipient of the 2017 Governor's Lifetime Achievement Award in the Arts. "William Ferris grew up on a farm south of Vicksburg and developed an early love of storytelling, books, art, and music. He served as the director of the nationally recognized Center for the Study of Southern Culture at the University of Mississippi from 1979 to 1997, when he became chair of the National Endowment for the Humanities. Since 2003 he has served as Joel R. Williamson Eminent Professor of History and senior associate director of the Center for the Study of the American South at the University of North Carolina at Chapel Hill. He continues to be one of the country's preeminent scholars on the American South." Please join me in extending a very heartfelt welcome.

William Ferris: Thank you, Robert. It is an incredible honor to be here. Robert and Marti have outdone themselves with this symposium, and I feel especially privileged to be able to talk about Bill Eggleston with people whom I have known for so long and who have been such a special part of the artistic and intellectual family within which I have worked for decades.

I want to explain the procedure for this session. First, I will introduce the panelists; then we will have four presentations, after which we will take questions.

Kris Belden-Adams received her PhD in modern and contemporary art history with a specialization in photography from the City University of New York Graduate Center and has an MA in art history, theory, and criticism from the School of the Art Institute of Chicago. She has numerous scholarly publications and is editor of the book *Photography and Failure*. Prior to joining the University of Mississippi Art Department in the fall of 2013, she taught at the Minneapolis College of Art and Design in Minnesota.

Richard McCabe is the curator of photography at the Ogden Museum of Southern Art in New Orleans. He received an MFA in studio art from Florida State University and was a fellow at the American Photography Institute, the national graduate seminar at New York University. While living in New York City from 1998 to 2005, he worked for numerous art galleries and museums, including the International Center for Photography. His photographs and other art have been exhibited in galleries and museums throughout the United States.

Emily Ballew Neff was named the fifteenth executive director of the Brooks Museum of Art in April

2015 after spending twenty years at the Museum of Fine Arts in Houston as its first curator of American painting and sculpture. She has organized more than twenty exhibitions and coordinated fourteen traveling exhibitions from other institutions. She holds a BA from Yale University, an MA from Rice University, and a PhD from the University of Texas at Austin. Neff is a recent fellow of the Center for Curatorial Leadership in New York City and was president of the Association of Art Curators from 2013 to 2015.

Now I will make the first of our presentations this afternoon.

William Ferris: William Eggleston's color photography is a gateway to the American South through worlds that are both beautiful and frightening. The exhibition *The Beautiful Mysterious: The Extraordinary Gaze of William Eggleston* is an opportunity to better understand Eggleston's Mississippi roots and his experience as an undergraduate at the University of Mississippi from 1958 to 1960. During that period, the University's Art Department produced important painters like William Dunlap, M. B. Mayfield, and George Wardlaw. William Faulkner's presence was influential then, as George Wardlaw recalls: "He was a model for me as another artist working in a different medium. . . . I went to the same restaurant that Faulkner did every Sunday evening because I wanted to sit next to him. I felt that some of his genius might rub off on me. I never spoke to the man, but he was one of my superheroes."[1]

Eggleston grew up in Sumner, Mississippi, at a time of great artistic productivity; and the state's writers, artists, and musicians clearly influenced his photography. William Faulkner, Elvis Presley, and B. B. King were an important presence during his formative years in Sumner, Oxford, and Memphis. Eggleston's photography in the book *Faulkner's Mississippi* and in his portfolio *William Eggleston's Graceland* shows how he focused his eye on both Faulkner and Presley.[2]

As a young artist, Eggleston was inspired by French photographer Henri Cartier-Bresson. In 1947 Cartier-Bresson visited Oxford and took a classic photograph of William Faulkner standing in his garden at Rowan Oak with his two Jack Russell terriers beside him. Eggleston also admired Martin Dain's photographs in his book *Faulkner's County*.[3] Like Dain, Eggleston was drawn to places associated with Faulkner. "I know Martin Dain's book on Faulkner's country. Some of these photographs are taken near Oxford, Mississippi. This might be a guide to Faulkner's stuff, too. He is writing about what it is like in that region."[4]

Eggleston felt the presence of Faulkner's fiction and compared his photography to literature. He reflected, "I think that a series of photographs is like a novel. If a person went slowly through that body of work, it would be roughly like reading a novel. Now and then you would remember, information would add up, at the end you would remember a lot of things. The order is not significant. The order is random. I do not really care about the value of one picture over another."[5]

Like Eudora Welty, whom he admired and photographed, Eggleston rarely speaks about his artistic work and its relation to race. Welty recalled how "I got lots of phone calls in the bad sixties when we were having all the troubles here. People . . . saying 'What do you mean sitting down there and not writing stories about your racial injustice?'. . . I have always written stories . . . about human injustice. . . . I was looking at it in the human—not the political—vision, and I was sticking to that. . . . I still feel that way. All great works have been moral documents. It is nothing new."[6]

Interestingly, many artists often shift between literature, art, and photography as they seek the right fit for their talents. Welty seriously considered a career in photography when she wrote for the Works Progress Administration. She took photographs "for my own gratification on the side. I was not the photographer of the WPA. I was a journalist, and I was doing a newspaper job, interviewing. . . . They were pictures because I would see something I thought was explanatory of the life I saw. I think those experiences are bound to have shaped my stories, indirectly . . . provided the raw material. It was the reality that I used as a background."[7]

Like Welty, Faulkner was attracted to photography and used an old Zeiss camera that he had purchased in Europe. Oxford photographer Colonel J. R. Cofield developed Faulkner's negatives for him and recalled that they "usually turned out to be a hodgepodge of double exposures, overtimed or undertimed. . . . He finally gave it up in disgust, even though cameras always did fascinate him."[8] Colonel Cofield and his son, Jack Cofield, ran a photography studio in Oxford and made portraits of Faulkner throughout his life. Colonel Cofield photographed Faulkner as a young man, and Jack did portraits in his final years.[9]

As students, Faulkner and Welty both drew fin de siècle line drawings that are important counterparts to their prose. One of Faulkner's classmates remembers that as a child in school "he would do nothing but write and draw—drawings for his stories."[10] Like Faulkner and Welty, Eggleston is also an artist whose sketches and watercolors suggest the similar breadth of his aesthetic.

While an undergraduate at the University of Mississippi, Eggleston earned money making black-and-white portraits of children for friends like Theo Inman. Eggleston knew the work of Greenville, Mississippi, photographers Bern and Franke Keating. The Keatings were award-winning photographers who photographed prominent white families throughout the state. Thus, both in the Delta and in Oxford, Eggleston knew photographers who worked for Mississippi clients, one of whom was a Nobel laureate.

Eggleston began with traditional portraits and soon moved towards documentary photography that captured people in motion, rather than in static, staged poses. That work was strongly influenced by Walker Evans and William Christenberry. Eggleston was inspired by Evans's black-and-white photographs of sharecroppers in Hale County, Alabama, in *Let Us Now Praise Famous Men*. He acknowledged that "Walker Evans, of course, is an influence. You cannot forget images like his. It is impossible not to be influenced."[11]

Bill Christenberry's ancestral roots are in Hale County, Alabama, where he and Walker Evans both photographed extensively. When Christenberry taught at Memphis State University from 1959 to 1961, he met Eggleston and encouraged him to expand his palette from black-and-white to color photography. Eggleston acknowledges that "Bill Christenberry's work has had a big influence on my work. Christenberry works in color. He is one of the few that does."[12]

In Sumner, Eggleston's ancestral home, photography was integrated into family life. His cousin Maude Schuyler Clay and her husband, Langdon Clay, are both gifted photographers who now live in the Eggleston family home. The Clays support a vibrant arts scene in the town through the Cassidy Bayou Gallery.

When Eggleston was sixteen years old, an act of violence and the trial that followed in his hometown galvanized the world. On August 28, 1955, Roy Bryant and J. W. Milam murdered Emmett Till in Money, Mississippi, and their subsequent trial was held in Sumner. Till was fourteen years old when he visited his family in Money that summer and was said to have wolf-whistled at Bryant's wife in her country store. Bryant and Milam kidnapped Till from his great-uncle's home, then beat him, gouged out his eye, shot him through the head, and dumped his naked body tied to a cotton-gin fan into the Tallahatchie River. Till's barely recognizable body was found by a fisherman several days later.

Emmett Till's mother, Mamie Till, decided to display his disfigured body in an open casket at his funeral in Chicago, "so all the world can see what they did to my boy." The *Chicago Defender* estimated that over 250,000 persons viewed the body of her son. The photograph of Till's disfigured face lying in his open casket was reproduced throughout the world. Representative Charles Diggs said, "I think the picture in *Jet* magazine showing Emmett Till's mutilation was probably the greatest media product in the last forty or fifty years." In his book *The Blood of Emmett Till*, Timothy Tyson argues that "perhaps no photograph in history can lay claim to a comparable impact in black America."[13] That photograph, like Harriet Beecher Stowe's novel *Uncle Tom's Cabin*, changed American history. Today, the events surrounding the photograph are commemorated by historic markers in Sumner.

In 1972—seventeen years later—Eggleston took a color photograph of Mississippi Fred McDowell lying in state in his coffin. The peaceful, calm expression of

McDowell, dressed in a black suit and string tie that contrast sharply with the white lining of his coffin, offers a dramatic counterpoint to the black-and-white photograph of Till's mutilated face in his coffin. These two portraits of black men lying in their coffins reflect the slowly changing South in which Eggleston worked as a photographer.

Ernest Withers, an important black photographer, grew up in Memphis after his parents moved there from Marshall County, Mississippi. Like Eggleston, Withers was drawn to photography at an early age. During his career as a professional photographer, Withers amassed an archive estimated to contain over five million images. Withers photographed musicians at Stax Records for twenty years. He also took a legendary picture of Elvis Presley and B. B. King at the Memphis Goodwill Review in 1957 and titled it *The Two Kings*. Withers's extensive photography of the civil rights movement includes images of Martin Luther King in the Lorraine Motel shortly before his assassination. Eggleston is aware of Withers and of his career as a professional photographer in Memphis.

A traumatic event during the civil rights movement occurred toward the end of Eggleston's time at the University of Mississippi, when James Meredith enrolled as the school's first black student in 1962. The subsequent riots and the death of two men—one a French journalist—during the evening of September 30, 1962, shaped Eggleston's experience as a white Mississippian finding his way as a photographer.

While Eggleston's roots in Mississippi and the state's complex mix of artistic genius and racial violence are an important background to understanding his art, Memphis has an equally important influence on his photography. Described as "Mississippi's northern capital," Memphis was home to Eggleston and other Mississippians, including Shelby Foote, B. B. King, Elvis Presley, and Rufus Thomas, all of whom lived in the city. Known as the "home of the blues and rock and roll," the river town was also home to those who sought artistic freedom to write, sing, and photograph.

Talented artists from Arkansas, Mississippi, and Tennessee gathered in Memphis as part of a

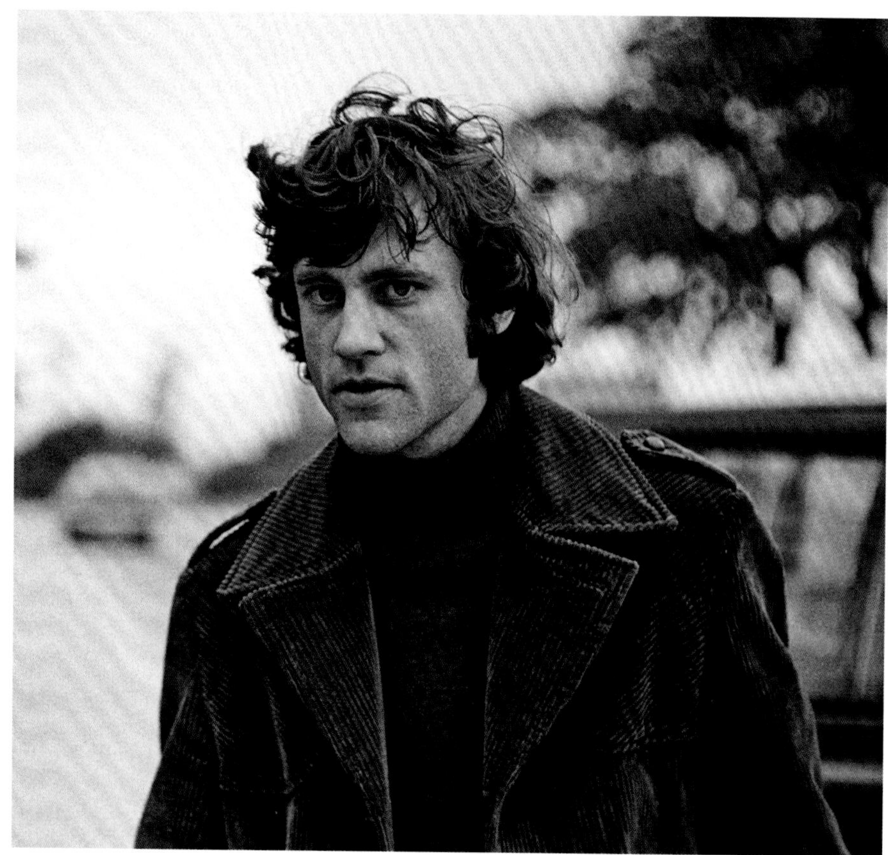

Bruce Jackson, photograph of William Ferris, 1972.

Bohemian world in which Eggleston was a central figure. Faulkner was part of a similar Bohemian group in New Orleans, where he lived and worked with William Spratling, who taught at Tulane's architecture school. As the acknowledged leaders of the French Quarter Circle, Faulkner and Spratling were joined by Sherwood Anderson and fifty-two others who formed a loosely organized artistic community.[14] New Orleans and Memphis were important Bohemian communities in the American South, a tradition that dates from Edgar Allan Poe to the present.[15]

Eggleston was a central figure in the Memphis Bohemian community that emerged in the sixties and seventies in Memphis. His love of music and his photographs inspired Memphis musicians Alex Chilton, Jimmy Crosthwait, Jim Dickinson, Tav Falco, Phineas Newborn, Robert Palmer, and Sid Selvidge, several of whom featured Eggleston's photographs on the covers of their LP recordings. These musicians were also inspired by blues artists like Furry Lewis, Mississippi Fred McDowell, Bukka White, and Reverend Robert Wilkins, and they helped organize the annual Memphis Blues Festival that was held at the Memphis Shell in the 1960s. Writers Robert Gordon and Steve LaVere, photographers Maude Schuyler Clay and Perry Walker, and philanthropist Julien Hohenberg were also part of the group.

Unlike the New Orleans Bohemians, who were inspired by literature, the Memphis group focused on music. Eggleston photographed and filmed musicians and nightlife extensively in edgy places like the Antenna Club.[16] Lawyer Saul Belz did pro bono work for struggling artists and musicians in the group, and Randall Lyon and Pat Rainer promoted and photographed their work. Lyon grew up in Arkansas with Robert Palmer and once told me, as we looked at the Mississippi River from his apartment in downtown Memphis, "If we were in Paris, we would be living on the Left Bank. But since we are in Memphis, we must think of ourselves as on the Left Bank of the Mississippi."

I consider William Eggleston a spiritual brother. His artistic sensitivity and his intense focus on creating beauty through his photography are an inspiration for my own work. We did photo shoots together in Waterford and in Oxford at Faulkner's home, Rowan Oak. With the grace of a ballet dancer, Eggleston positioned himself for each shot. He relentlessly tracked the everyday life that surrounded him. During the day, he photographed the lunch his grandmother served him, barren Mississippi Delta fields, a solitary dog wandering along the road, and the intense colors of sunrise and sunset. At night, he was drawn to dark rooms with their incandescent and neon lights.

William Eggleston imprints our memory with the familiar, and he burns color photography into our souls. Just as Richard Wright, Eudora Welty, and William Faulkner touched us with their prose, just as B. B. King, Elvis Presley, and Jimmie Rodgers moved us with their music, Eggleston embeds his "Egg Yellow" in our visual memory. He introduces us to both familiar and hauntingly strange worlds. Eggleston constructs a narrative tale through his photography, and as we move from image to image, we understand their meaning. Like Faulkner's stream-of-consciousness literary style, Eggleston's photographs merge with our consciousness. They link us to a place that once seen can never be forgotten.

To see an Eggleston photograph is to be forever touched by his eye. He brings us face-to-face with moments that are both intensely beautiful and deeply troubling. His unflinching eye peers through his camera's dark, private lens, his finger presses, and the shutter's familiar click locks down another image. The visual genius we witness through Eggleston's photographs is his gift to the viewer. As Faulkner might say, that is how Eggleston etches "his name on the face of oblivion."

I will close with a recording of Bill speaking about his photographs: "Being like a novel, there are pages. If a person has the patience to look at all, there are 320. So, if the person went slowly through that body, it would be roughly like going through a book. Then you'd remember, the information would add up at the end, you'd remember a lot of things. I don't really care about the value of one picture over another. One might be a little prettier than a certain other one, but that might not be the best thing."

Our next speaker is Kris Belden-Adams. Please join me in welcoming her.

Kris Belden-Adams: Thank you all for coming. Thanks to Robert and Marti for organizing this conversation and to the Friends of the Museum for making everything happen today. It's a pleasure to be here. It's also a joy to see so many students in the audience when I know that on a Friday afternoon they might rather be somewhere else. Incidentally, William Eggleston probably would approve of that.

As a historian of photography, I will look at Eggleston's work in terms of what I see as the various key figures who influenced the dialogues and themes of his work.

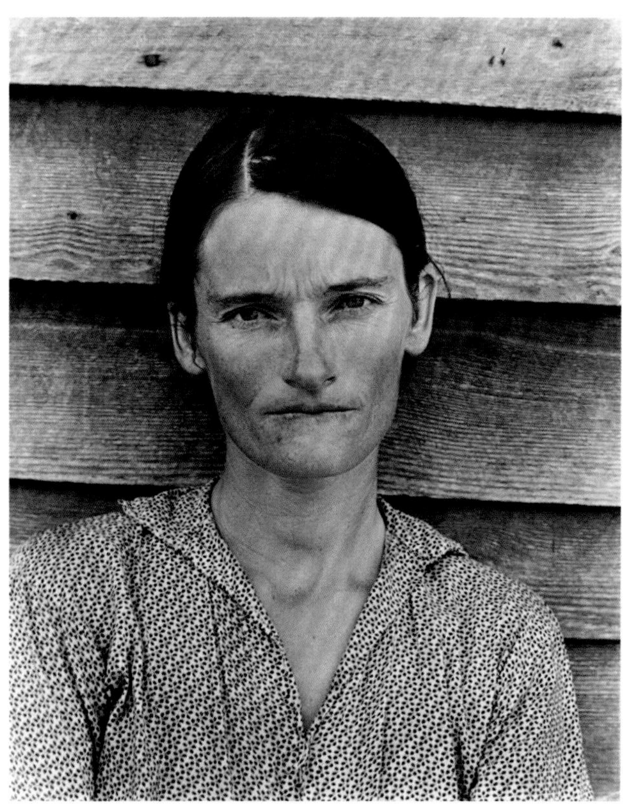

Walker Evans. *Allie Mae Burroughs, Wife of Cotton Sharecropper*. Hale County, Alabama, 1936. Photograph. Library of Congress.

Walker Evans, who grew up in Toledo, Chicago, and New York City, worked in the South for the Resettlement Administration and Farm Security Administration. His work begins a conversation about what the South looks like through the lens of an outsider. The most famous of Evans's Alabama photographs is one taken in 1936 of Allie Mae Burroughs, who was then twenty-seven years old and enduring the depths of the Great Depression. She is the wife of a sharecropper whose four children have gone hungry, night after night. The horizontal movement of the texture of the wall of her makeshift home in the background has the air of temporariness about it—and echoes the horizontality of her mouth. She does not smile. Here we see an earnestness, a sense of temporariness, and, formally speaking, a beautiful juxtaposition of flatness and texture behind this very human portrait. As viewers, we each enter the picture and create a narrative for it. Many works by Evans employ juxtaposition of volume and areas of insistent flatness, such as *Roadside Stand, Birmingham, Alabama* (1936). Eggleston's urban atmospheres often do the same.

Another photographer from the Resettlement Administration/Farm Security Administration who provided a view of the twentieth-century South was Dorothea Lange, who photographed extensively in the Clarksdale, Mississippi, area. She is most famous, though, for being the photographer of *Migrant Mother*, taken in Nipomo, California, in 1936. As the story goes, Lange was driving home after a month of photographing for the Resettlement Administration

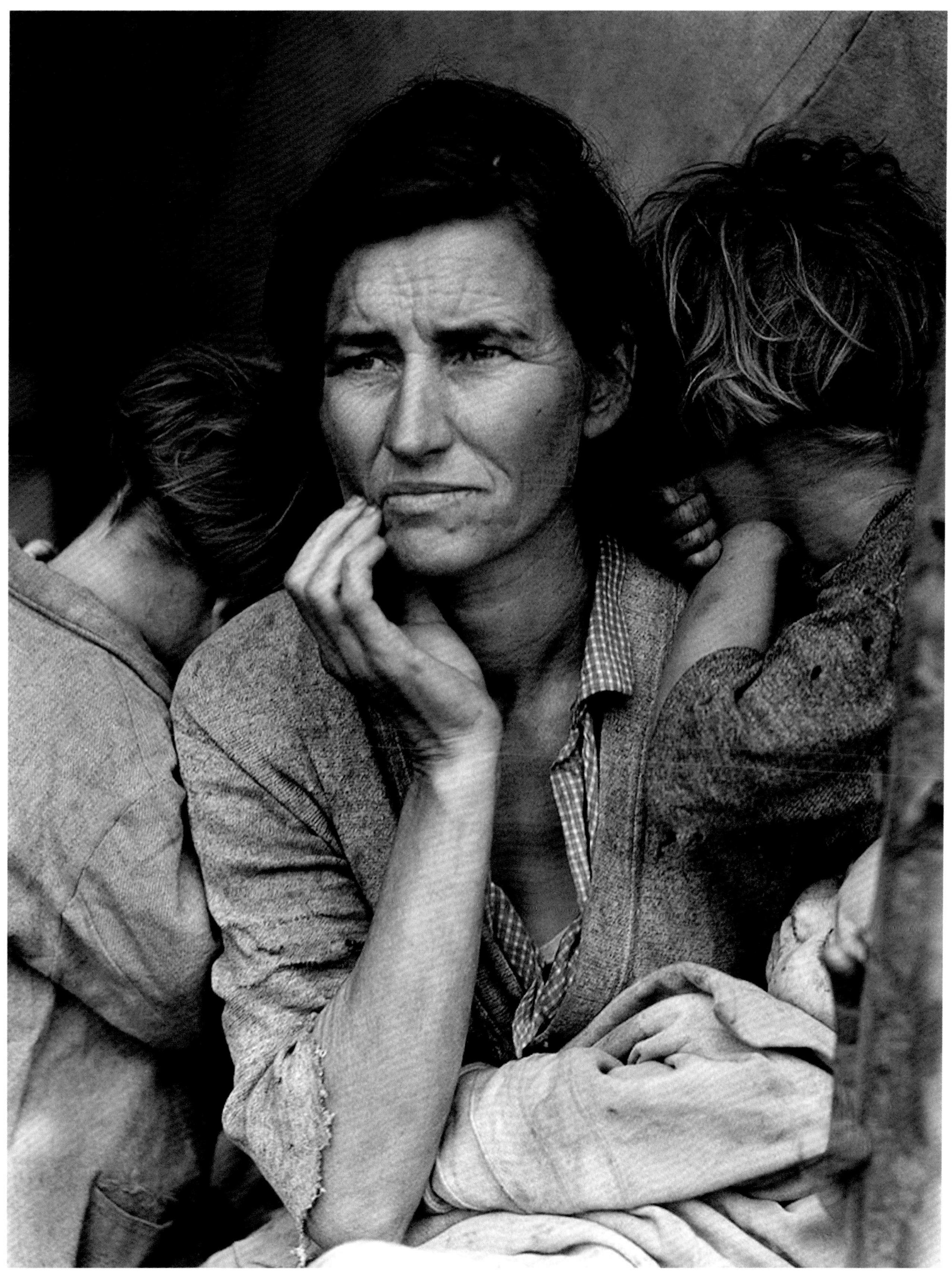

Dorothea Lange. *Migrant Mother / Destitute Pea Pickers in California. Mother of Seven Children. Age Thirty-Two*. Nipomo, California, 1936. Photograph. Library of Congress.

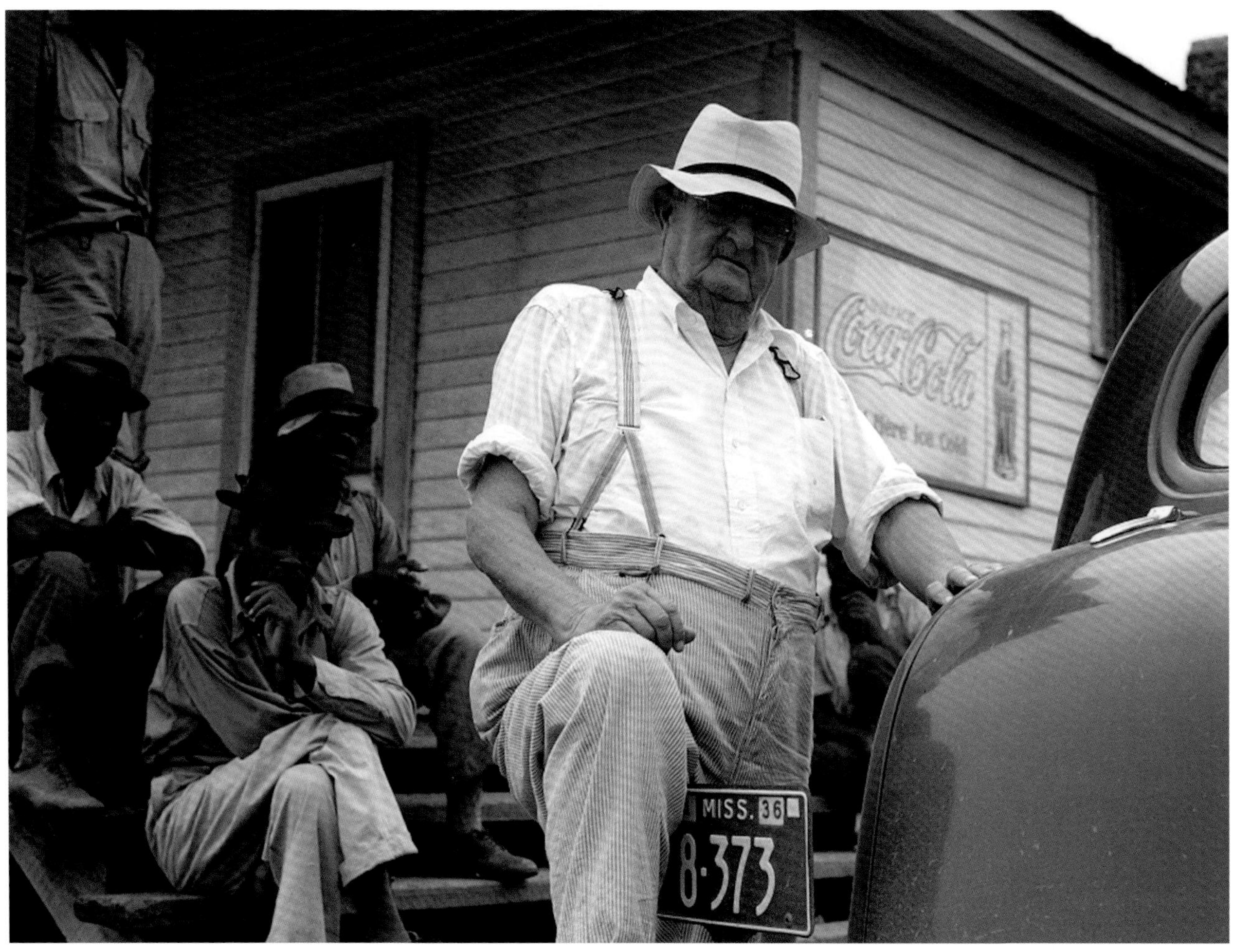

Dorothea Lange. *Plantation Overseer*. Mississippi Delta Near Clarksdale, Mississippi, 1936. Dorothea Lange. Photograph. Library of Congress.

when she saw a woman with her children huddled around her. Many of us have seen this image. Well, it almost didn't happen. As Lange was driving her car away, it took her twenty minutes to decide to turn around, go back, and shoot these frames. From them we see the iconic image of Florence Owens Thompson and her kids, who were living off frozen peas they picked from the field and birds they had killed for food. Notice that I'm building a narrative here, and Lange encourages this. In a very long caption, she also tells us that they had sold the tires off their car for food. Here we have these children left alone with only their mother, no father figure; and they're left essentially at this pea pickers' camp to starve. However, it turns out that there was a car, and there was a father figure. He would come back with the car after he'd got it repaired, pick them up, and they would move on to the next town. By the time federal relief arrived, they were long gone.

These kinds of iconic pictures were published nationwide, free of charge. Lange also spent a substantial amount of time right in the middle of summer in Clarksdale. In the image known as *Plantation Overseer* from June of 1936, we see a white man, leaning on a car, with five black men around him at a plantation store in Sunflower County. With the help of surviving Clarksdale residents, I have since identified the white man as Boon Mosby Partee. Some of his surviving family members and people whose parents worked for him said he was "the meanest man that ever lived." He stares earnestly at Paul Taylor on the far left-hand side of another version of this image. Paul Taylor is Dorothea Lange's husband, and Paul Taylor smokes a cigarette and talks to the plantation owner as we see these black men gathered idly in the background.

Lange was determined to bring up issues of race in her work—particularly in Clarksdale. But hardly any of that work was published across the United States, because boss Roy Stryker felt that the country wasn't quite ready for that discussion in the 1930s. A generously cropped version of *Plantation Overseer* appeared in national Formalist poet Archibald MacLeish's *Land of the Free*, a 1938 publication of his poem with eighty-eight photographs by Lange, Walker Evans, and others. Many of Dorothea Lange's images also appear in F. Jack Hurley's *Portrait of a Decade: Roy Stryker and the Development of Documentary Photography in the Thirties*, published in 1972, when it became more fashionable to discuss race.

New York City's influence on many of the people in Eggleston's circle has been noted by several speakers today. Weegee, or Arthur Fellig (1899–1968), was a tabloid photographer known for his gritty street photography of crime and murder scenes made in the 1930s and 1940s. He had a darkroom equipped with a police scanner in his van and was nicknamed Weegee because he had a knack for knowing, like a Ouija board, exactly where the next grisly crime was going to happen. He also had a knack for being right there to capture the discovery of a severed head found in the cake box, or a fire engulfing a building that was adorned by a sign reading "simply add boiling water." He quickly rushed his freelance photographs straight to publishers. The International Center for Photography sponsored a popular retrospective exhibition of Weegee's work in 1998, and for the past two decades his work has frequently been represented in television, film, and other forms of popular entertainment. The craze continued with another ICP Weegee exhibition in 2012 and the publication of *The Weegee Guide to New York* in 2015. Weegee's work has a dark humor, a wonderful dark humor, I think. You certainly can find that sort of humor and macabre in Eggleston's work.

And speaking of humor, Swiss-born Robert Frank went on one of those great Kerouacian journeys across the United States in 1955 to create a typographic view of "Americans." In his book *The Americans*, we see lots of bored housewives, suburban dystopian society, checked-out waitresses at the diner. We see television providing a human presence in an atmosphere in which there is no actual human presence. Many of Eggleston's photographs have this implication of human presence without an actuality of human presence. Frank also prominently featured the American flag in different images throughout *The Americans* to question blind patriotism and pride. Formally, the photographing of a symbolic textile appears throughout this Eggleston exhibition.

Frank's *The Americans* was published first in Paris in 1958 and a year later in the United States—with an introduction by Jack Kerouac. It was received as a biting critique of American society. It also was around 1955 that the first fast food (also the subject of one of Eggleston's photographs in this exhibition) was being invented, that American consumer culture moved from town to the suburb. That's a world that Eggleston has critiqued as well.

The Museum of Modern Art is an important player in determining the "who's who" of contemporary photography and in determining the shape of the medium's history. In fact, Beaumont Newhall's *A History of Photography from 1839 to the Present*, first published by MoMA in 1937, is still used as a textbook, or at least versions of it still are in our classrooms today. In 1967, John Szarkowski curated an exhibition called *New Document*s that featured the work of three photographers—Diane Arbus, Lee Friedlander, and Garry Winogrand—who created a new take on the documentary from what we saw in the Resettlement Administration/Farm Security Administration's stress on sympathy and economic reform. The new photographers, Szarkowski wrote, "redirected the technique and aesthetic of documentary photography to more personal aims. Their aim has not been to reform life but to know it." All three had "a shared fascination with the commonplace."

In one Friedlander photograph we see a woman in a fur coat walking away, down the street, with the shadow of a stranger falling upon the back of her head (*New York City*, 1966). We get to complete the narrative, and it's chilling. In another Friedlander photograph, we can see a man lying stretched out on the street under a store window displaying a gigantic, inflated, twisted bottle of booze (*New York*, c. 1963). People just walk on by. Winogrand shows glamorous women in Los Angeles walking by, casting beautiful shadows on the ground as a presumably homeless man is slumped over in a wheelchair (*Los Angeles, California*, 1969).

In addition, Winogrand captures an image of a man driving in a convertible with a bandaged nose (*Los Angeles*, 1964). The car—which also appears in many Pop Art paintings—represents the 1950s–1960s boom of American "car culture." Being set in Los Angeles gives the image the suggestion of glamour and the possibility that the man nurses not an injury from a fight or accident, but is recovering instead from a nose job. Again, the viewer gets to complete that story. Diane Arbus presents viewers with square-format photographs that included one of her most well-known images, *Child with Toy Hand Grenade in Central Park, N.Y.C. 1962*. In it, a perturbed and impatient young boy holds a hand grenade. At the time, the United States was engaged in the Vietnam War; and the loss of young lives was not far from mind.

Some of Arbus's photographs also addressed suburban dystopia. In the 1968 photograph *A Family on Their Lawn One Sunday in Westchester*, Arbus shows a couple sunbathing in their yard in Westchester, New York, as their child prepares to play in a wading pool behind them. The man rubs his eyes. His gesture suggests that he may be unsatisfied, or deeply worried. Yet this is the very picture of the 1950s and 1960s American Dream. Is it all it's cracked up to be? All these images convey an urban dystopia and an edgy, cynical view of American and human nature.

It's also important to discuss color because it is perhaps the first thing people think of when they see Eggleston's work. During World War II, all color film was used for aerial photography by the US military and was not commonly available for vernacular use. After the end of the war, it became quite popular and grew to be associated with nonprofessional, non-fine-art photography, like family snapshots. For a photographer to be taken seriously as an artist, he or she needed to shoot in black and white. That's what the Museum of Modern Art showed. To use color was to be vulgar, to borrow from the "low" common culture and to bring it into the gallery. We often forget how subversive that was for Eggleston. And he didn't just *use* color. He *flaunted* it.

As I think about Eggleston's work, I also think about picturing the South and how that historically has been done by other photographers from both inside the South and from outside of it, like Evans and Lange. Eggleston challenges existing traditions and norms in the fine-art world in general, while also connecting to these more edgy, dark dialogues about subject matter, Americana, and human nature. He dabbles with the formal flatness of Evans; the issues of narrative that Lange suggests; the critiques of Frank; notions of subject sympathy that are suggested by Arbus; and the nonheroic, dystopian subjects that often emerge in the work of Winogrand and Friedlander. Eggleston integrates color—a piece of a vernacular practice—into fine art.

But he also uniquely prompts us to consider him apart from tradition and the New York–based conversations about fine-art photography. For example, he makes us wonder how someone from the South, who has grown up here, might convey its identity. He explores how suburbanization and globalization have changed the South, especially Memphis. It's all quite a fun and rich conversation.

William Ferris: Emily, would you like to begin?

Emily Ballew Neff: I'm glad to. Thank you to Robert and Marti and to Maude and Bill. As an art museum director, I find it stunning to walk into such a beautiful room of Bill Eggleston photographs and learn that it is through your generosity that you have made this happen for the University of Mississippi. It's a very big deal, and I am honored to be a part of this symposium. I also thank Friends of the Museum and Carlyle Wolfe and others who put on a wonderful lunch today.

William (or Bill) Eggleston's photographs were familiar to me long before I knew the name attached to them. It started at the Museum of Fine Arts, Houston, the museum I grew up in and my work home for several decades. My office when I was an assistant curator was next door and slightly catty-corner to the office of Anne Tucker, the Wortham Curator of Photography. Anne recently retired after a great career building the distinguished collection of photographs at the Museum of Fine Arts, Houston. Her track record is legendary; but, important to this story, she had worked at the Museum of Modern Art's photography department under John Szarkowski, who organized Eggleston's breakout solo exhibition there in 1976.

Anne's office was delightfully cluttered: a large jar of candy greeted anyone walking in the door, and wind-up toys were scattered all over her desk. Maps and images adorned the wall, and books were stacked in large piles everywhere. Among the jumbled, mixed-up things, one image never failed to catch my eye: a photographic reproduction of an outdoor scene in which a big, white sedan appears at left, and two rhyming figures can be seen at roughly center. One figure is a well-dressed middle-aged white man with his hands in his pockets and, behind him, an African American man in a servant's uniform. It is a fall or winter day—leaves, hints of orange especially vivid, blanket the ground, which also reveals what might be a bit of trash. A driver appears in shadow in the front seat of the car, and a bayou with outbuildings in the distance completes the view. The figures appear at ease, casual, as if they had been talking. And yet the moment seems tense, and the image feels weighty and potent. The reproduction was of Eggleston's *Sumner, Mississippi, Cassidy Bayou* (c. 1970).

As I came in and out of my office, probably twenty times a day over a seven-year period, I always saw that image out of the corner of my eye. I was drawn to it, even mesmerized. I may be more familiar with that image than any other in a lifetime of studying art. How could something so seemingly incidental to my daily life take such powerful hold of my imagination?

For nearly two years now, I've served as the executive director of the Memphis Brooks Museum of Art. One of the institution's attractions, for me, was its significant holdings of works by Eggleston, whose work Anne introduced to me long ago, and whose *Sumner, Mississippi, Cassidy Bayou* had become a kind of talisman for me.

The Brooks began collecting Eggleston's photographs in 1977, a few months after the artist's exhibition at the Museum of Modern Art closed. The Brooks acquired a dozen photos at that time and borrowed thirty more to produce the second museum show of Eggleston's career. The iconic tricycle was one of those photographs we purchased. Our holdings grew significantly in 1985 with the addition of 110 prints from *The Louisiana Project*. Ten photos commissioned by First Tennessee Bank in 1984 came to us in 1986. Two series, both dye transfers, came in 2001 as a gift of AutoZone: *Troubled Waters* in 1980 and *Southern Suite* in 1981. We also have photographs from the *Los Alamos* portfolio and 130 images from Eggleston's *Egypt*, which the Brooks commissioned in 1986. The Brooks now includes 279 original Egglestons in its collection and, as a major repository of his work, has ambitions to expand and more fully understand its holdings.

Early on in my tenure at the Brooks, I met the photographer's son Winston Eggleston, and later the artist himself, who is a close neighbor of the museum. My experience meeting Winston and talking to him about *Sumner, Mississippi, Cassidy Bayou* has come to be emblematic of our new life in the Mid-South, where everyone can be so friendly, casual, spontaneous, and full of hilarious stories, yet simultaneously aware that they inhabit a place that runs deep with culture and a complicated history. As I began describing this one photo to Winston, he immediately grinned and said something to the effect of, "Oh yeah! That's a funny one! That's a family picture. There's Maude's dad [referring to Maude Schuyler Clay]; he's my dad's uncle; and there's Jasper, who worked for the family. They were at a funeral. No one put the car in neutral; and seconds after my dad took the picture, the car slid backward towards the water, and everyone went running after it." He then burst out laughing. In one brief second, this monumental, to me, photograph proved to be also an amusing personal footnote. But that is the very nature of an Eggleston photograph: familiar and elusive, incidental and timeless, witty and dead serious.

I had the pleasure of meeting the photographer a couple of weeks ago and spending one-on-one time with him. We talked about Anne and about the late Walter Hopps, a leading curator of twentieth-century art and founding director of the Menil Collection in Houston, who is said to have played a role with Eggleston, developing or encouraging him in the incredibly expensive dye-transfer color process. We mostly talked about our fathers' involvement in World War II. Both were naval officers in the Pacific theater during the war. This meeting was important, because one of the reasons I was attracted to the Brooks was its holdings of Eggleston works and the opportunity to play a role in stewarding the Eggleston legacy. When I say Eggleston legacy, I'm aware that he has not passed away. Bill is very much alive; and yet if you have 279 of these originals, then you hope to have many more. You're both excited by the opportunity but also weighted by it. I hope with the great work that all of you are doing here at the University of Mississippi that we can be working together on a path forward. I think the opportunities and the potential are incredibly great.

One of the first things I did when moving to the Brooks was knock down walls so we could make more room for installing some of these great photographs. We now have about thirty-five on view in the space that we completely reconfigured. I can't stand the idea that anybody would come to Memphis, visit the Brooks, and not become aware of the Bill Eggleston connection. If I look out the front door of the Memphis Brooks, I can practically wave at Bill across the other side of Overton Park.

A topic of interest to me is the Memphis reception to Bill's show in 1977 in the wake of the '76 show at MoMA. Even to this day some people feel very strongly one way or another about his work, both positive and negative. I want to know what Memphis said. The level of conversation was incredibly serious, with Guy Northrop doing the review of the Brooks exhibition on Eggleston for the *Commercial Appeal* on February 20, 1977, just a few months after the one at the MoMA closed. In Northrop's "Learning How to Look at Eggleston's Photos," the real subject was the debate among the Brooks board, not about the importance or quality of the work. It was accepted, it was understood, that we are dealing with a great photographer. The debate was about the longevity of the color medium, how long before they fade. That is an important question because some photographs that have come into our collection previously hung on AutoZone's walls, in people's homes, at First Tennessee Bank. A few did fade to some degree over time, though not much. The closing line from that review in '77 is that we are "wrong if we look for permanence in these transitory moments of light and color."

Another article appeared in the *Titled Untitled: A Mid-South Quarterly Review of the Visual Arts* on February 14, 1977, edited by Gary Witt, and including a transcription of a conversation among F. Jack Hurley, associate professor of history at Memphis State University (now University of Memphis); Richard Reep, photography instructor at Memphis Academy of Art (now Memphis College of Art); Steven Cushing, senior photography major at MAA (MCA); and Gary Witt. It's a sort of random, free-wheeling conversation; but I love what Gary Witt says: "With a famed innocence, Eggleston is registering his intuitive love, or maybe hate, of his surroundings. He seems delighted with what he sees as true out there." But it was interesting to me coming to Memphis to recognize that from the get-go there was an elevated conversation and understanding of his work.

I want to close by going back to the *Cassidy Bayou* picture, which has been important to me since I first saw it. It's been one of those images that I cannot get out of my mind. Maude says she always thinks of that as a family picture, Winston too thinks of it as a family picture, and it's brilliant that something like that could be so utterly open-ended. There is no one way, one right way, wrong way to understand it. For me it will continue to be a kind of talisman or lodestar as I would walk up and down that hallway passing Anne's office; and it was a way for me to measure, in a funny way, my own progress, my own thoughts about the South, my own thoughts about photography, my own thoughts about art in general, and it continues to function for me in that way to this day.

William Ferris: Thank you, Emily. Now it's time for Richard's presentation.

Richard McCabe: First, I want to thank the

University of Mississippi Museum for inviting me and to say that the exhibition is gorgeous. I thank Bill Ferris for donating that work, which encapsulates William Eggleston's most important era of work from the early sixties to mid-eighties. I think that's when he was at his peak, just making really great work, and he was in time with the times. It's also important because it's a transitory time when he was going from black and white to color, and it's all that and adopting the dye transfer. The exhibition is a beautiful overview of an important period of his work.

It's hard to look at a William Eggleston photograph today and not wonder why his work was so misunderstood and controversial when he first burst upon the scene with the Museum of Modern Art's 1976 exhibition *Photographs by William Eggleston*. Famously, the *New York Times* art critic Hilton Kramer described Eggleston's MoMA exhibition as "perfectly banal . . . perfectly boring," with "dismal figures inhabiting a commonplace world of little visual interest." What was it that Kramer and other art critics did not understand or see in Eggleston's photographs—that now forty years later are considered modern icons of art and Eggleston one of the greatest photographers of the twentieth century?

First, there's the Southern thing—the cultural divide between the South and North, the slower Southern way of life and Southern culture that New Yorkers and especially New York art critics didn't understand. Also, Kramer and others could not comprehend the context of Eggleston's work—not just the cultural context, but also the art historical context—because there really was no context in which to view Eggleston's work. Eggleston's photography was simply ahead of its time—avant-garde. Yet his art was distilled from multiple influences within twentieth-century art. Pivotal moments in his life shaped the trajectory of his art and informed his visual language. There were content and context to his work; yet it was sublime, underplayed, and mysteriously veiled.

The legend goes that, at some point in the early 1960s, Eggleston was confused about the direction of his photography. He said to his friend Tom Young, the abstract expressionist painter, something to the effect, "I don't know what to photograph—I don't like what's around me . . . everything around here is so ugly." Young replied, "Then why not photograph what you don't like, what's around you—the ugly?" Eggleston took the advice and began photographing the ugly, the obvious, the local—his immediate surroundings of Memphis and the Mississippi Delta.

The ugly, the obvious, and the local were the new suburbanization, or suburban sprawl, that was spreading like kudzu over America and the South. The New South began to look like everywhere else in America. Fueled by the rise of the automobile and white flight from traditional urban centers, shopping centers sprang up, interconnected by highways to new neighborhoods filled with ranch-style houses at the edge of town. These were the trappings or the product of a postwar booming economy. Eggleston's first color photograph is said to be of a young man pushing a shopping cart in a Memphis grocery store parking lot. It was this blandness of mindless consumer culture that Eggleston made strangely beautiful through his photography. Eggleston captured the loneliness and isolation brought about by the changes in physicality of American society and culture—the topography of the New South—and in the process produced one of the definitive visual documents of the American South in the 1960s through the '80s.

Henri Cartier-Bresson's book *The Decisive Moment,* published in 1952, had a profound influence on Eggleston. He freely admits that he was co-opting Cartier-Bresson's style with his early black-and-white photographs. He speaks of making perfect Cartier-Bresson fakes by combining elements of documentary or straight photography with a refined fine-art sensibility. Both Cartier-Bresson and Eggleston photographed with small, hand-held, 35mm Leica cameras. This portable device facilitated a quick and fluid form of reactionary picture-taking, thus creating the shoot-from-the-hip or snapshot aesthetic. Both employ similar compositional strategies of stacking visual signifiers within the foreground, midground, and background of the picture plane. Both expand the photograph to the edges of the picture space, filling the frame and sometimes dissecting and cutting off key figures on the edge of the scene. All elements of design are employed, and rules are broken in their photographs to create order out of chaos.

Yet Cartier-Bresson, born in 1908, was from a different generation than Eggleston, born in 1939. Eggleston was a man of his time, the 1960s. In the 1960s, street photography was at its zenith, and Pop Art dominated painting and sculpture. Eggleston fused elements of both street photography and Pop Art into his oeuvre. Like Lee Friedlander, Garry Winogrand, and Stephen Shore, Eggleston shot from the hip, blending the new apolitical snapshot aesthetic with the older and more traditional stylings of Cartier-Bresson.

Appropriation of consumer and popular culture iconography was a staple of Pop Art. Andy Warhol's soup cans and Brillo boxes, as well as Roy Lichtenstein's washing machines and comic book heroes, are examples of the everyday elevated and empowered within the context of high art. Eggleston incorporated similar consumer and popular cultural motifs into his visual vocabulary—ceiling fans, tricycles, ovens, freezers, gas stations, parking lots, refrigerators, cars, shopping centers, and fast food. Many of these vernacular subjects had been previously ignored in photography. With the dye-transfer printing process, Eggleston employed another design component associated with Pop Art—color. Previously used exclusively in applied or advertising photography, the dye-transfer process allowed Eggleston to isolate, manipulate, and saturate individual colors in his photographs—thus turbocharging the color of his prints. The dye-transfer process gave Eggleston's work its distinctive look and separated the appearance of his photographs from other art photographers of the time.

Another aspect of Eggleston's work that set him apart from other photography in the 1960s and '70s was not only the much-talked-about "subject matter" or "lack thereof" in the everyday, but also how he photographed the everyday, the so-called mundane and banal. Eggleston photographed his world as if he were from another planet. He photographed as if all his mundane surroundings were endlessly fascinating, fresh and new—which they were. He saw beyond the ordinary to the extraordinary. Through compositional elements and camera angles, subject matter, color, and lighting, Eggleston's photos took on a feel of otherworldliness. Nan Goldin, Alec Soth, Mark Steinmetz, Martin Parr, Paul Graham, Juergen Teller, and about every contemporary art photographer have been influenced and emboldened by his work.

As with all great art, poetry, literature, and song lyrics, the combination of the specific and the open exists side by side in Eggleston's photographs. His is art that asks more questions than it answers—an ambiguity that lets the viewer into the picture to fill in the blanks. Warhol once said, "If you want to know all about Andy Warhol, just look at the surface of my paintings." And like Warhol, it is the surface of Eggleston's photographs that sheds light onto its maker and, in the process, revolutionized twentieth-century photography. But underneath the surface exterior of an Eggleston photograph, something strange and unspoken is happening that leaves so much to the imagination. Masked within the facade of normalcy resides tension—a strange energy and an unsettled beauty that fascinates and tantalizes when gazed upon. Eggleston's art is paradoxical; it is simple and complex, anti-intellectual and, at the same time, so smart.

Going back to Eggleston's reception in 1976 at MoMA when Kramer at the *New York Times* and others called his exhibition the worst one of the year, I think the critics didn't understand him for two reasons: he was ahead of his time, and he portrayed Southern art, life, family, and place that perplexed them. In addition, he was working in isolation in the fifties and early sixties. There was not the photography industrial complex that there is now. The South didn't have photo galleries; few museums in the nation showed photography, and no one had Collector's Base, PhotoNOLA, Art Houston, and all these other places that show photography. Eggleston was working in complete isolation. The only place that he would even be exposed to photography was New York City, if he went to MoMA and saw a Cartier-Bresson show.

Luckily enough, one of his roommates at the University of Mississippi had a copy of Cartier-Bresson's *The Decisive Moment*. Before then, all the photography he had seen was from *Look* magazine, *National Geographic*, *Time*, *Life*. It was all basically photojournalistic stuff. This is the first time that he says that he saw art photography. It was in a documentary style, but it was done in such a fine art aesthetic it was painterly. It was more like a Degas painting, or Toulouse-Lautrec. This wasn't Edward Weston or Ansel Adams, who were the art stars of that time of photography. They were doing black and white with cameras. He was a guy with a Leica camera basically doing street photography. Seeing Cartier-Bresson's *The Decisive Moment* was one of the moments I think was critical for him.

What did he do after that? He went to Paris. He wanted to shoot like Cartier-Bresson, so he went to Paris, didn't take a single picture. He was there for two weeks, didn't take a single picture; he was out of his element. Then he came back to Memphis, came down here to Ole Miss, where Tom Young was teaching painting in 1960 and 1961 as artist in residence. Tom Young was a fighter pilot in World War II. He got out of the war on the GI Bill, went to school, moved to New York in the fifties, and was one of the founding members of the 10th Street Galleries with Willem de Kooning, Franz Kline, Roy Lichtenstein, and Philip Guston. Eggleston was in total isolation here in Mississippi, where he couldn't get a photography book, and he met Tom Young, an abstract expressionist painter. That was like a library, like a visual library that he had access to now, here at Ole Miss.

Taking Tom Young's advice, Eggleston went out and photographed what was ugly at the time—suburban sprawl. That was the beginning of the suburbanization of the South, when the region was starting to look like everywhere else in America. This was a different South than Walker Evans saw. That South still existed, but it was changing. This was the changing South. This was during the civil rights movement, during segregation, when integration was starting to happen, and white flight from the cities began. Suburbs were starting to build outside of Memphis, and he started photographing there, in grocery stores, in parking lots, and in gas stations. He invented this visual language, and he was photographing things that nobody had photographed; that's the beauty about Eggleston. He was so sublime in his approach, you might have seen some Edward Hopper paintings, or something like that, and the loneliness that the twentieth century brings upon us.

But he was influenced mainly by Abstract Expressionism and Tom Young. That's something that people don't really talk about. Tom Young was an Abstract Expressionist; and Eggleston loves to paint and draw, and the book with his artwork is coming out sometime soon. Somebody's sitting on that, and there are a bunch of shows there. I think he approaches photography in a painterly way. He sees things that we don't see when he looks at art. And his black-and-white work, which I see as little sketches, is nice before he realizes color stuff. To me the preliminary sketches for his color work look like they're little rushed, five-minute sketches, and then he moves on.

When he gets to color, I see him as very abstract. I see him as lines and shapes and forms and colors, and that possibly goes back to Cartier-Bresson. He talks about being influenced by Walker Evans, and how can one not be influenced by Walker Evans? I think Walker Evans is one of the greatest photographers of the twentieth century, if not the greatest. Walker Evans was very formal, very compositional. Walker Evans was Mondrian. Everything was straight on, squares, rectangle, triangle. Cartier-Bresson approached things from an angle and kind of wedged them in from the side. In *Holly Springs Road at Waterford, Mississippi* [1982], Eggleston photographed a store from the side, cut it off at the top. Nobody else would photograph it that way, but that's very much a Cartier-Bresson influence there.

I see Eggleston's photographs as abstractions and painting. He's a very painterly photographer, and the abstract painter Tom Young was an influential figure in Eggleston's development. I have heard that he had told Eggleston about going to color. I've heard the story about Eggleston going in Christenberry's studio and seeing Christenberry's colored photographs tacked on his studio wall. Like Walter Hopps said, "If Walker Evans hadn't told William Christenberry to go back down South and photograph, Eggleston wouldn't have met Christenberry, and Eggleston would probably still be shooting in black and white."

That's pretty incredible. Walker Evans telling Christenberry to go South, and he meets Eggleston. It's unbelievable, really. I will say this one last thing. This is an Eggleston quote, "You can't follow up photography with words; it doesn't make sense."

William Ferris: Thank you, Richard. Now we open this up and take questions and comments.

Gaetano Catelli: I would like to hear Kris talk about her new book.

Kris Belden-Adams: The book *Photography and Failure*? It began as a panel that I chaired at the College Art Association conference in New York a couple years ago. I initially looked at photography as literal and technical failure and marveled at how so many of photography's pioneers died penniless, with nothing. We celebrate Alexander Gardner, Mathew Brady, and other all-stars of the history of photography; but they died penniless. Even Joseph Nicéphore Niépce, who created the earliest known photograph, spent everything he had on inventing photography; and his family remained in debt when he died.

My look at "failure" then expanded. I started looking at stories of practitioners' struggles against the medium to achieve something that the medium just won't do—such as providing an absolute "truth." I started thinking about our failure to theorize and recognize the medium as a fine-art medium. And I finally decided that this project might best be a multiauthored volume and invited others to weigh in on the topic. The book also addresses individuals who felt they failed, but whom history acknowledges as successes. History is relative and therefore anything but settled fact. Philosophically, writing history is an endeavor doomed to "failure," too.

Sometimes our histories also fail to acknowledge dialogues started by practitioners who were working off the beaten path. In a way, Eggleston fits into that category. While many photographers were working in New York City, here's this guy in Memphis, working in relative isolation from the MoMA-centered dialogue that becomes the history of photography. The book has been a fun project.

Lisa Howorth: This question is for Richard. It's sad, ironic anyway, that Cartier-Bresson was here shooting in Oxford when Bill was a youngster in Sumner, eight years old. Did their paths ever cross?

Richard McCabe: I don't know about that.

Lisa Howorth: Cartier-Bresson photographed Faulkner at Rowan Oak in 1947 during a trip across the United States with poet John Malcolm Brinnin commissioned by *Harper's Bazaar*, ten years after Walker Evans and author James Agee made a similar trip for *Fortune* magazine.

Richard McCabe: Those photographs Cartier-Bresson took of Faulkner are amazing. I suppose that was before he was in New Orleans. We have two of these photographs in the collection, and they're not very good. That's why when Eggleston goes to Kyoto and other places, he's out of his element; it's not the same. You guys said he was grounded here, and he is. That's the work that he will always be remembered by. That's the strongest work; it's that sense of place. You can tell there is that love there; in other places, he's an outsider looking in.

Lisa Howorth: Was Eggleston aware that David Smith, the great American sculptor, taught here?

Richard McCabe: I haven't heard that.

Lisa Howorth: It's a little-known but fascinating fact. Smith taught here for one semester in 1955, before Eggleston came to Oxford.

Ed Croom (botanist, photographer): The MoMA exhibition was the defining moment for Eggleston. How did that come about?

Richard McCabe: William Christenberry took Eggleston to meet Walter Hopps at the Corcoran Gallery of Art around 1970. Hopps and Eggleston worked together on the *Los Alamos Project*, which later resulted in several books and an exhibition that featured eighty-eight dye-transfer prints taken between 1965 and 1974 in Memphis and during numerous cross-country road trips they made together in the southern United States. Hopps introduced Eggleston to John Szarkowski in 1974 while planning to exhibit Eggleston's work at the Smithsonian's National Museum of American Art as that institution's first exhibition of photography as fine art. Szarkowski wanted MoMA to be the first to exhibit Eggleston, and Hopps deferred to him.

Emily Neff: Walter was the great matchmaker.

Richard McCabe: Yes. He was ahead of his time in visualizing art in museum settings, which were more like mausoleums than museums at that time. Living artists weren't shown in museums, just dead artists. Hopps was one of the first people to really promote living artists. He brought the Marcel Duchamp retrospective to America, promoted some of the other greats, and then Christenberry, Eggleston, and so on.

Lisa Howorth: Bill brought Walter Hopps over to our house one day, just making his Oxford rounds, and I had a painting that was done by my great aunt, some sort of lady painting. Walter Hopps walked in and zeroed in on that little still life, and he actually dated it to the year. He said, "I know when this was painted; it was about 1935." I was very impressed.

Emily Neff: Mrs. de Menil brought Duchamp and then Walter to Houston. It's interesting how it's all connected.

Ron Shapiro: What is the status on color photography as far as retaining the colors as time goes on? There are new processes, aren't there?

Emily Neff: It's called the most expensive refrigerator in the world. Seriously, it's sort of a Sub-Zero on steroids.

Maude Clay: And no hanging on the wall where there's any light. That color photograph I took of Bill in 1988 is on the wall at Square Books. You can see that it's no secret that's almost faded into a black-and-white print. The material is supposed to be much more stable today, especially with the digital prints. I just don't think anybody really knows.

Emily Neff: But meanwhile, what you'll find in many art museums where you have your normal "storage for gelatin silver, or other media," there is always a separate area that is for the C-prints. Like my late director before I left Houston said, "It's the most expensive Sub-Zero in the world." It's a huge investment, but it's important.

Langdon Clay: By contrast there are black and whites from the 1850s that are still gorgeous.

Maude Clay: That's been a battle, all right. The black-and-white/color thing.

Richard McCabe: The dye transfer is much more archival than the C-prints.

Emily Neff: I want to follow up on something that you said, Richard, because I think all of us would agree that Eggleston's enduring work is his immediate surroundings, whether it be Sumner or Memphis; but one of the things that I've been trying to do as an outsider coming in is understand the critical reception of Eggleston in Memphis, where he's very much alive and a very powerful presence. Memphis is a really cultured city in terms of that kind of Southern tradition of appreciating literature, music, and art; and I'm interested in how he was immediately highly regarded by all Memphians as an artist but, with so many of his commissions, he was also the go-to photographer. Memphis says, "Yes, we're doing this Egypt show; we should send *our* photographer to Egypt." I agree that the Egypt work will never measure up to the enduring work that he did in this area.

Nonetheless, there's a story there. I'm not sure what it is, because I don't have my head around that work, but all the different commissions that he did for First Tennessee Bank and AutoZone comprise a corporate art collection. Why did they choose Bill Eggleston? You don't necessarily square that with the Bohemian South that you're talking about, and I don't have my head around it, don't have a magic answer, am not sure there is one; but my antenna is up in terms of trying to make sense of that, and what is it that they see besides that he's "one of ours." He's "our photographer." There's more to it than that.

Amanda Malloy: I notice with a lot of Eggleston images, and in particular many images in this exhibition, there is a lot of trash, and there are a lot of abandoned rural and agricultural spaces. Is that a criticism of FSA photography, or perhaps the contemporary South, or is he just continuing that narrative?

William Ferris: Bill's best friend arguably was Bill Christenberry, who traveled back to Alabama each year to photograph buildings and places as they deteriorated and in many cases disappeared, to look at the effect of time on people and landscape. When Bill Eggleston spoke to my students at Yale, somebody asked, "What is your next project?" He replied, "I have to keep going back South. I have a lot more work to do." I think there is a deep love between Bill and the American South. It is a love/hate relationship like that felt by Faulkner's Quentin Compson when he says, "I dont hate the south, I dont hate it. I dont." Well, Bill is trying to document the South in the most honest way; his photographs are not the posed relationships. It may be a parking lot with trash and a pool of water. If he sees the right light there, he photographs it. He keeps track of the South, and it is a changing relationship. He grew up on a plantation world in Sumner; he lives in Memphis with its incursion of suburbia on the rural landscape around the city. His celebrated photograph of the tricycle captures the intersection of rural and suburban worlds. He might say, "That is my world, and I do not have to love it. I photograph it."

Eggleston is an artist, and an artist who crosses boundaries. He is a photographer, but he is also a painter and a gifted musician who plays Bach and Buxtehude on the piano.

Eudora Welty, early in her life, thought she would be a photographer. She exhibited her photographs in New York; and then Cleanth Brooks and Robert Penn Warren, at their newly created *Southern Review* at LSU, discovered Welty and published five of her short stories. Those early photographs influenced her writing. Phoenix Jackson in "A Worn Path" was inspired by a solo figure of a black woman whom Welty saw walking in the distance. Ernest Gaines also photographed his childhood worlds in the quarters in Louisiana that influenced his novel *The Autobiography of Miss Jane Pittman*. Faulkner and Welty also did fin de siècle drawings, which were indirectly linked to their writing.

There is a porous relationship between the visual arts and the literary tradition. Eggleston's artistry spans the worlds of photography, painting, and music. He is a gifted concert pianist. He could also have designed cameras and audio speakers. Bill has enormous knowledge about each of those worlds, and thankfully for us, his focus has remained on color photography; but there is a lot more that is on the outer edges.

Kris Belden-Adams: It's hard to follow that.

Emily Neff: Yes, it is hard. You're hard to follow, Bill. Everything is a complete thought and a complete sentence.

Shaun H. Kelly: I was wondering if perhaps we could talk a little bit about how Eggleston and Christenberry, and other Southern photographers, have formed our recollection of Southern history and about how that relates to Eggleston's saying that everything he sees is boring. Agnès Sire, in her essay "The Invention of a Language" for the 2014 exhibition *William Eggleston: From Black and White to Color*, describes Eggleston's subject as "the creeping decay of the American South." That is not a foreign feeling to contemporary Southern artists, who see the South's creeping decay as very slow and always changing. Perhaps photographers like Eggleston inform what we recollect through artistic work and what we see in a contemporary world. Which is more accurate, recollection or the contemporary South?

Richard McCabe: Are you asking how photography affects the memory?

Shaun H. Kelly: Sure. To see the contemporary South as boring now is not the same thing that Eggleston recognized thirty to forty years ago. Our recollection is perhaps a little bit romanticized when we call upon Southern artists to assist us.

Richard McCabe: You were in Athens about six months ago when they did the Do Good Fund exhibition of twenty portraits by photographers from the Southern states. They had Mike Smith, a great photographer from East Tennessee; Mark Steinmetz, one of the best contemporary photographers now; and Baldwin Lee, who is amazing. They all talked about how they didn't want their photography to be romantic. That's exactly what they didn't want; and I was thinking, "Well, Southern photography, I guess, can get a little nostalgic and romantic. I love that stuff, so I'm not going to knock it. Sally Mann's very romantic. I love that about her work."

I don't think Eggleston when he took a picture thought of it as romantic; it was contemporary art when he was making it, and he thought of it as contemporary. I don't think he thought what this would look like in thirty years. Maybe it's nostalgic or romantic now because you look back at it and you see all these cool cars, all those great hairdos, and everything. It makes you think of that, but I don't think it was ever intentionally that. Another thing Sally Mann talks about a lot is the way that she says photography corrects memory, which I don't really agree with. I always use photography and photo albums to remember things.

Kris Belden-Adams: I might add that every time we look at a photo album, it jogs different memories and associations in viewers. Eggleston's work also has a great open-ended narrativity that also is changeable. You may look at an Eggleston image one day and see something different in it. I think that photography's relationship to memory is very complicated. On one hand, it gives you what Roland Barthes called "that-which-was," a sliver of a time and space that you can never relive but can revisit in the photograph. But then, for the viewer, it embodies not just that encapsulated moment, but an infinite possibility of multiple "times" and memories.

Bill Ferris: I think you must take Eggleston's statements with a grain of salt. I do not think for a moment he ever sees his work as boring. He has spent too much time and care making photographs.

Thank you all for being here.

Notes

1. "George Wardlaw," in William Ferris, *The Storied South: Voices of Writers and Artists* (Chapel Hill: University of North Carolina Press, 2013), 243.

2. Willie Morris (text) and William Eggleston (photographs), *Faulkner's Mississippi* (Birmingham: Oxmoor House, 1990); William Eggleston, *William Eggleston's Graceland* (Washington, DC: Middendorf Gallery, 1984), 11 dye transfer prints, edition of 31.

3. Martin Dain, *Faulkner's County: Yoknapatawpha* (New York: Random House, 1964); Martin Dain, *Faulkner's World: The Photographs of Martin J. Dain* (Jackson: University Press of Mississippi, 1997); William Eggleston, *William Eggleston's Guide* (New York: Museum of Modern Art, 1976).

4. "William Eggleston," in *Storied South*, 193.

5. "William Eggleston," in *Storied South,* 190.

6. "Eudora Welty," in *Storied South,* 39–40.

7. "Eudora Welty," in *Storied South*, 32–33.

8. J. R. Cofield, "Many Faces, Many Moods," in *William Faulkner of Oxford*, ed. James W. Webb and A. Wigfall Green (Baton Rouge: Louisiana State University Press, 1965), 110.

9. Jack Cofield, *William Faulkner: The Cofield Collection* (Oxford, MS: Yoknapatawpha Press, 1978).

10. Joseph Blotner, *Faulkner: A Biography*, 2 vols. (New York: Random House, 1974), 1: 154–55; see also Candace Waid, *The Signifying Eye: Seeing Falkner's Art* (Athens: University of Georgia Press, 2013), Lothar Hönnighausen, *William Faulkner: The Art of Stylization in His Early Graphic and Literary Work* (London: Cambridge University Press, 2009), and Patti Carr Black, "Introduction" in *Eudora* (Jackson: University Press of Mississippi, 1984).

11. "William Eggleston," in *Storied South*, 194.

12. "William Eggleston," in *Storied South*, 194.

13. Timothy Tyson, *The Blood of Emmett Till* (New York: Simon & Schuster, 2017), 75.

14. John Shelton Reed, *Dixie Bohemia: A French Quarter Circle in the 1920s* (Baton Rouge: Louisiana State University Press, 2012), 1–6.

15. Shawn Bingham and Lindsey Freeman, *The Bohemian South* (Chapel Hill: University of North Carolina Press, 2017).

16. "William Eggleston," in *Storied South*, 196.

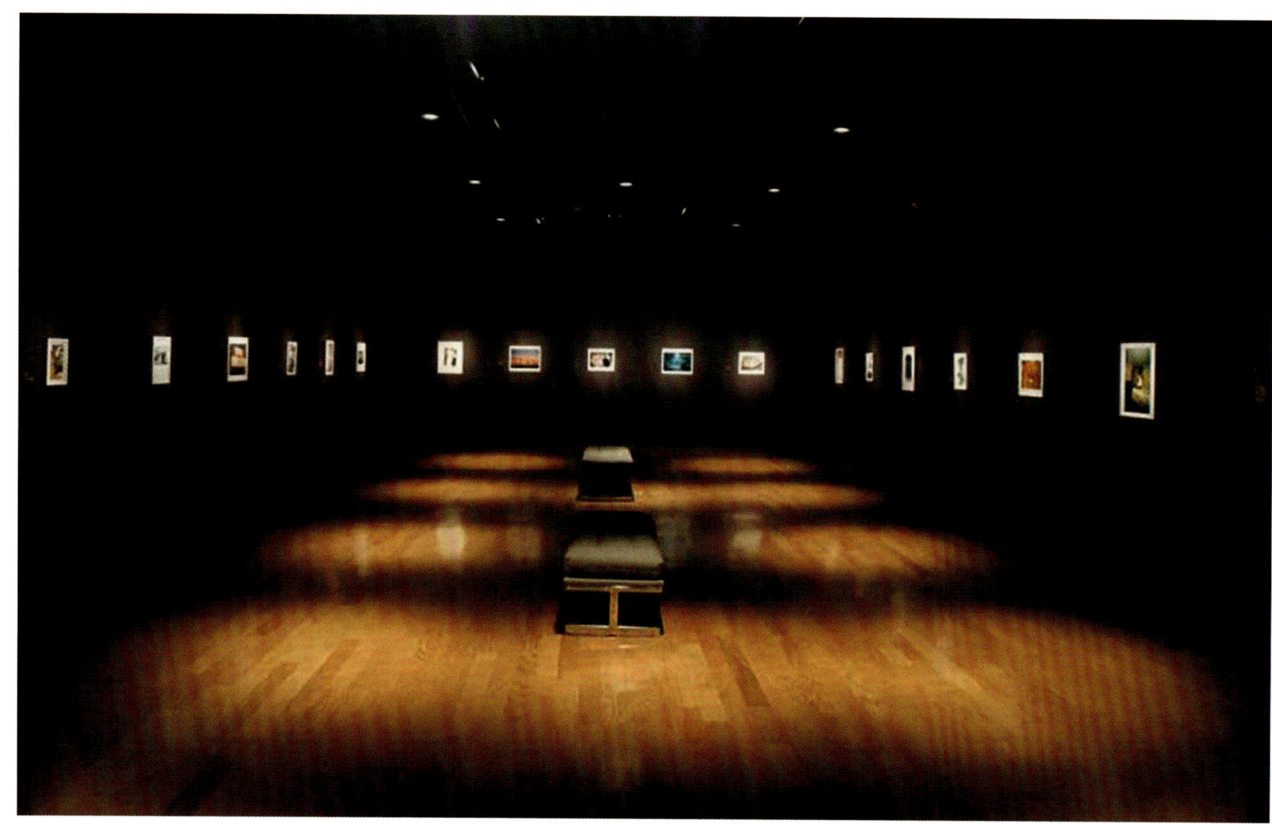

Amanda Malloy. *Main Gallery Space*. Permission and courtesy of the William Eggleston Artistic Trust.

The Beautiful Mysterious: The Extraordinary Gaze of William Eggleston

AMANDA MALLOY

William Eggleston's use of deeply saturated color and seemingly mundane subject matter may have caused some controversy at the photographer's premiere exhibition at the Museum of Modern Art in 1976, but today Eggleston is widely considered one of our greatest living photographers. Thirty-six prints of Eggleston's extraordinary work are on view at the University of Mississippi Museum from September 13, 2016, through February 18, 2017.

Upon entering the exhibition space, museumgoers are transported to another world. The deep eggplant gallery walls complement the rich ambers, rusty reds, and the pops of turquoise in the artist's photographs. Megan Abbott, Edgar Award–winning novelist and curator of *The Beautiful Mysterious*, notes this otherworldly ambience of Eggleston's images: "When you look long enough at his photographs, like the gorgeous, lonely blue parking lot chosen as one of the exhibit's central images, you get lost in it. You're in another place."

That "place" can inspire a sense of "romantic loneliness," as Abbott describes it. People are rarely seen in these thirty-six images. The human form, when present, is often detached; eye contact or recognition of the camera is almost never present. A young man looks despondently out of the frame of one photograph as he eats alone at the counter of a fast-food restaurant. A grocery store clerk loads paper bags into the backseat of an automobile; his eyes are cut off by the car's roof, leaving his full face teasingly out of view.

Abbott's introduction of the exhibition details Eggleston's ability to make our own world mysterious through his use of color and composition. Abbott suggests that more exceptional than Eggleston's innovative use of color is his work's ability to be felt and experienced: "he drops us in the middle, or near a shuddering climax, or in the chilly moments after."

Museumgoers will encounter the imprinted remnants of traumatic climax through Eggleston's landscape photographs, where rural architecture sits long forgotten, skeletal in the aftermath of fire or decay. As often noted of Eggleston's photography, it is not human interaction that conveys much of his work's sentiment, but it is the material objects with which humans interact and their inevitable mark on the landscape that tell the stories of Eggleston's world.

Eggleston's architectural depictions are particularly stunning. The artist's camera details the vertical and horizontal intersecting wood slabs of worn Southern buildings and the faded, hand-painted signs and religious iconography that adorn them. The exhibition also includes images commissioned by Ray Stark, producer of the film *Annie* (1982), who asked several photographers to film as they pleased on the set located at Monmouth University in New Jersey. Eggleston's shots focus on lavish interior architectural adornment, resulting in a beautifully haunting series of photographs.

Seven black-and-white images are dispersed throughout the collection, all from the early to mid sixties, before Eggleston fully realized the possibilities of color photography. While these prints do not carry quite the same emotional weight as those in color, they do highlight Eggleston's early ability to capture line and depth. Through a monochrome palette, the artist portrays an empty gas station or a diner at night with inventive composition and framing, skills that have likened him to photographers like Walker Evans and Henri Cartier-Bresson.

Enriching the exhibition is the commentary of Eggleston's first cousin and protégée, Maude Schuyler Clay, an accomplished artist and author of three acclaimed books of photography. By offering particular insight to the locations and people, Clay presents a personal and familial understanding of Eggleston's photographs.

Longtime lovers of Eggleston and those new to his work will find in *The Beautiful Mysterious* a rewarding balance of the artist's singular and identifying photographs with images they've likely never seen before. Narration by Abbott and Clay offers astute interpretation and biographical context, further enhancing the collective experience and deepening our appreciation of this native son now known to the world.

Color Is Everywhere

W. RALPH EUBANKS

"I want you to know that your parrot has just bitten my mother," William Eggleston first said to William Ferris. During a trip up to Memphis from Oxford in the 1970s, Ferris had received a spur-of-the-moment invitation to a party at Eggleston's home. Given that Eggleston, the pioneer color photographer, held a reputation as a loveable eccentric central to the city's emerging Bohemian community, and that Ferris, the celebrated folklorist, took his yellow-headed parrot, Ogie, with him everywhere, it would follow that a man like Ferris would be welcome at an Eggleston gathering. To play it safe, Ferris left Ogie on a perch outside, at what he thought was a fair distance from the boisterous revelers in the house. Ogie had proven him wrong.

In spite of this awkward introduction, the two shared a few drinks, and Eggleston allowed Ferris to look through the prints he kept stacked on top of his Steinway grand piano. Ferris purchased several on the spot. "When I first saw Eggleston's photographs, it was as if I had never seen a photograph before," he recently recollected, "I was speechless"—and that night a collection and friendship were born.

Ferris shared this story at a symposium on *The Beautiful Mysterious*, an exhibition from more than fifty Eggleston prints Ferris donated to the University of Mississippi Museum during his long tenure as the director of the Center for the Study of Southern Culture. Throughout the 1980s the two men would often travel throughout Mississippi to photograph together. (Whenever he came to Oxford, Eggleston would stay in the same room at the old Holiday Inn, surrounded by cameras and the elaborate stereo system he traveled with.) Steeped in the folkways of the American South, Ferris understood Eggleston's work in the context of the photographer's roots in the Delta, with its complex culture of both artistic genius and racial violence. Eggleston's 1972 portrait of bluesman Mississippi Fred McDowell lying peacefully in his coffin serves as a counterpoint to the image of Emmett Till caught by Memphis photographer Ernest Withers fifteen years before.

The exhibition is a sort of Faulknerian stream-of-consciousness narrative, moving seamlessly from subject to subject. Tattered orange and red dishtowels on a clothesline, each piece of cloth shot through with holes; a line of railway freight cars shrouded in the evening light of the Mississippi Delta; thin shadows cast on brown cinderblocks below a periwinkle-blue sky. The Bohemian and Gothic Souths collide in Eggleston's photographs—his bright colors and distinct perspectives imbue rusting signs and aging buildings with a spiritual, emotional darkness that speaks to a decaying world of an older South fading into suburbia and industrial development. The pictures can be disturbing in their marriage of stark ordinariness and psychic disarray. What James Agee called "the cruel radiance of what is."

Ferris compared Eggleston with another photographer friend, Agee's collaborator Walker Evans. "With the grace of a ballet dancer, Eggleston positioned himself for each shot," he said, whereas "Walker would seek for hours to find the right light and shadows to capture his photographs." Like Walker, Ferris shot mostly in black and white; sometimes he pointed his camera at Eggleston, perhaps with the folklorist's impulse to document the creative process. What Ferris remembers most vividly about his many trips with Eggleston is how Eggleston chose his subjects democratically—and only if they provoked an immediate emotional reaction. Perhaps that is why Eggleston says he never takes more than one image of an object. As the exhibition's curator, novelist Megan Abbott, notes, Eggleston doesn't see much difference between people and objects. It is all one long body of work.

Thirty years have come and gone since their house party meeting, but the two remain close and continue to spend time together. On their most recent visit, Ferris asked Eggleston why he decided to photograph in color. The answer was simple. "Color is everywhere," Eggleston said, "even in the black hole of space."

Family Ties

MAUDE SCHUYLER CLAY

I grew up in the Mississippi Delta within an interesting but fairly prosaic family. As soon as I became cognizant, one of the main things I realized was this: the stories they told about themselves and others were more than enough to sustain an imagination. One cousin in particular, Bill Eggleston—his mother and my mother were sisters—fascinated me. Fourteen years my senior, he rode around in exotic cars, smoked filterless French cigarettes, and wore clothes that an Englishman would wear. (I saw a lot of Hollywood movies at the Tutrovansum Theatre in nearby Tutwiler.) I also noticed that he carried around a beautiful little Leica camera and took pictures of the most mundane things, such as signs and old buildings and rusted bicycles. He designed and built his own tall-as-a-person stereo speakers, and mostly listened to Bach. He spoke to me about things musical, scientific, and literary, not seeming to register that I was merely a child.

When I grew up, attended, then left the University of Mississippi, I moved to Memphis to go to the Memphis Academy of Arts. Bill, who lived—then and now—in Memphis, offered me an "apprenticeship." He was a great mentor, and I learned as much from him as I did from any teacher at the Academy. We rode around in the late-afternoon light in Memphis and its environs, where I observed what he thought worth photographing (pretty much everything!). It was an education in how to look at the world and take away a little piece of it, and for that I'll always be grateful.

I later moved to New York City, where Bill had the first color show at the Museum of Modern Art (*Photographs by William Eggleston*, 1976). Not everyone—especially critics and viewers caught off-guard by this interloper from the Deep South taking color pictures of prosaic people and places and calling them art—quite understood the work then. (My favorite negative "review" was titled "William Eggleston: The Emperor's New Clothes.") Not very much later, they did understand and laud this breakthrough work. When I once asked him about all the negative press, he rather naively and sweetly said, "I really felt sorry for them because they just didn't get it."

Eggleston's work has been much written about elsewhere, so there is little I could add in the way of critical analysis. What my short contribution here would be, most likely, is one of eyewitness: an early eyewitness to the family history (or is it lore?); to the Mississippi Delta; and, later, to the Memphis that intrigued Bill, prompting him to form his unique vision. In the very beginning, our family's version of "remembrance of things past," Bill's and my maternal great-grandfather, Nathan James McMullen, came to the largely unpopulated—except by Native Americans and all types of wild animals—Mississippi Delta from Carroll County,

Tennessee, and before that, from the Carolinas (this a typical Scots-Irish migration) in or around the 1830s. He came to Tallahatchie County by boat, as the roads then were few and the Mississippi River flooded the Delta on a yearly basis until levees were constructed after the Great Flood of 1927. The cotton farm he settled, on a landing on the Tallahatchie River, a tributary of the great Mississippi River, was called Graball. Our grandmother, Minnie Maude McMullen, the last of seven children born there in 1884, grew up and married Joseph Albert May. They built a house about 1910 in Sumner, a settlement some ten miles north of Graball, and had two daughters, Catherine Ann May (1912) and Minnie Maude McMullen May (1918).

Jumping forward a generation, my mother, Minnie Maude, Bill's aunt, was an early proponent of Bill's artwork: his Kandinsky-like drawings, his Mondrian-like wood block sculptures, his Joseph Cornell–like collages. Bill had a general interest in art before he "discovered" photography. At our modern summer house at Mayfair in Sunflower County, my mother had an eclectic collection of art, such as paintings by Theora Hamblett and Carroll Cloar; prints by Picasso, Miró, Matisse, and Van Gogh; Russel Wright furniture; and light fixtures, pottery, and garden sculpture by local potters Lee and Pup McCarty. To this collection she proudly added Bill's artwork. We grew up knowing that Bill was a "genius" and gifted artistically. But not only was he prolific in the visual arts, he played and composed music on our grandmother's Steinway grand and was an electronics whiz. He built his own early car music delivery system, a Tandberg reel-to-reel tape deck connected to speakers in the backseat of one of his cars.

While this is just a sketch by an early observer of the man who took the photographs you see here, I think the idea comes across that he always saw things differently and, from the start, had a unique point of view and vision. It has been an honor to be intimately connected to Bill Eggleston for most of my life. I like to hope some of his magic rubbed off on me, and just what the nature of that magic might be is in every one of these photographs.

William Eggleston: Some Thoughts and Reflections

WILLIAM DUNLAP

I walked into William Eggleston's 1976 photography exhibition on the Mid-South at the Museum of Modern Art, cold. Just back from Europe and steeped in Old Masters lore, I was hitting New York's cultural high spots only to be confronted in MoMA's hallowed galleries with pictures, vivid in color of places and people not only familiar to me, but some known quite well.

There was Bob Bailey, a tiny cup in his hands and a Theora Hamblett over his right shoulder. And Vernon Richards, in the backseat of a white car, bare feet and Johnson grass in the foreground. There were the obvious and unquestionable images of the landscape and cemeteries of Tallahatchie County, the towns of Sumner and Morton, Mississippi, and a number of pictures made in one of the nation's most ornery and unique cities, Memphis, Tennessee.

In his essay in the exhibition catalog, *William Eggleston's Guide*, John Szarkowski, the museum's longtime head of the Department of Photography, waxed eloquent about Bill's work, his breakthrough with color, and the sheer perfection of looking at these pictures selected from some 375 photographs made in 1971.

Szarkowski, himself a fine photographer, seemed to almost brag about never having been to the Mid-South, suggesting that Bill Eggleston's photographs would do quite well, thank you very much. He also questioned whether someone who was, in fact, familiar with the place could fully comprehend the impact and importance of the work before them.

"A new work of art," he said, "that describes something we had known well is likely to seem as unfamiliar and arbitrary as our own passport photos."

That was hardly the case with me. Not only were Bill Eggleston's dye-transfer photographs ravishing and enjoying a kind of ultimate celebration, I felt a special access because of that familiarity. The formal issues and characterizations, such as Bill's revelation that all compositions were based on the Confederate flag, were not to be taken seriously. (So much of Bill's subsequent behavior has been with tongue planted firmly in his, if not someone else's, cheek.) These pictures, like the best fiction, were specific yet universal, local and at the same time worldly.

Bill's slightly over-the-top personality, his Southern manners, quirky wardrobe, elegance, and refinement have added to the mystique and aura around his photography. Eggleston stories abound. He has been known to walk into a room, go directly to the piano, and play the evening away, giving no recognition to his host or their guests. There are the all-around eccentricities, passing out, slurred speech, and on and on, but they have nothing to do with his art. They just keep tongues wagging, and, needless to say, East Coast Art Intelligentsia eats this up.

Harry Callahan, among others, made color photographs long before Eggleston, but not quite like these. Familiarity and informality are keys to understanding his iconography, as is the often-alluded-to "snapshot" quality of his work. This illusion of familiarity brings one into the picture plane, as if to say, "I could have made that photograph." But, of course, you didn't.

Bill has stayed the course, remained constant, and continues to show us something we didn't know we knew. And then there is the long and beneficial relationship with William Christenberry, but that's a story for another time.

Now this generous bequest comes to the University of Mississippi Museum, and rightly so. Who better to understand, enjoy, and revel in these works of art and autobiography than people of Bill's own kind? As if to predict the future, John Szarkowski in his 1976 essay on Bill Eggleston's photographs concludes, "These seem to me perfect: irreducible surrogates for the experience they pretend to record, visual analogues for the quality of one life, collectively a paradigm of a private view, a view one would have thought ineffable, described here with clarity, fullness, and elegance."

To my mind, John Szarkowski got it just about right.

Born Six Years and 367 Miles Apart

ANNE WILKES TUCKER

Reading John Szarkowski's introduction to *William Eggleston's Guide* forty years after it was published, I am struck by Szarkowski's struggle to distance Eggleston's pictures from their referents. His first sentence declares, "I have not yet visited Memphis, or northern Mississippi, and thus have no basis for judging how closely the photographs in this book might seem to resemble that part of the world and the life that is lived there."[1] Later, he further shifts Eggleston's focus from being specifically about Memphis or northern Mississippi to the photographer's "place" that he describes as "consistently local and private, even insular, in its nominal concerns . . . appearing not at all as it might in a social document, but as it might in a diary, where the important meanings would be not public and general but private and esoteric." Szarkowski's essay never mentions the South again but finally summarizes that Eggleston's pictures are "patterns of random facts in the service of one imagination, not to the real world."

Eight years later, Ingrid Sischy was more discerning about the personal and public balance of Eggleston's vision. She recognized his pictorial vocabulary as "edited bits from his local world."[2] Then her article notes that he gives "form and its consequence—meaning—to visible data that in life we take for granted and forget to observe." She acknowledges, "Eggleston is from and lives in the South, which is, to borrow a term from nuclear physics, the strong force that binds and centers his compositions." Then, she, like Szarkowski, returns to color as being "key with Eggleston's vision of his subject. . . . It is the big wave on which all the information rides."

In 1999 the screenwriter and novelist Bruce Wagner mentions color only in a list of other qualities and ignores the role of "form."[3] For him, Eggleston's images are mysteries that "will not go away when daylight comes." Wagner makes lists of the "sad, joyful, and indifferent" things captured by Eggleston's expeditionary eye: "radiators and false flowers, colloquial signs and ghost cafes, gasoline and soda logos and startled foliage . . . beneath blue skies."

In his response to such specific subjects, Wagner's readings of Eggleston's works are closer to my own, both when I first saw them at the Museum of Modern Art in 1976 and now. Szarkowski calls Eggleston's vision "private and esoteric." A woman next to me in the MoMA exhibition exclaimed that his pictures were "so exotic!" I call them home. Eggleston and I share certain biographical data. We were born six years and 367 miles apart. I grew up in Louisiana, and, like Eggleston, members of my father's family have lived for multiple generations where they now reside. The Wilkinson/Tucker families settled on both sides of the Mississippi River. Those on the west side grew sugar, and Eggleston's family planted cotton. Because an uncle on my mother's side of the family sold weight scales to cotton gins, my treasured childhood include memories of riding with Uncle Bill through the cotton fields of the Mississippi Delta. Eggleston's pictures evoke those memories. I can't be objective, whatever that means. His photographs evoke the hot, humid quality of Southern summers as well as depict languid puffy clouds, rust-colored dirt, faded and rusted signs, two-lane blacktop roads, and dried wild grasses with burrs that would stick to your socks and scratch your legs. I can smell the sappy pine forests and hear the cicadas. I recognize that, as Eudora Welty wrote, "in the Delta, most of the world seemed sky."[4]

Szarkowski was right that Eggleston was photographing places. All his early titles identify the place, or the place and season, but not individual people or what they were doing—when and where, but not who and what, and never why. *Sumner, Mississippi, Cassidy Bayou in Background* is a personal favorite and one of Eggleston's most reproduced images.[5] That was its title in the MoMA catalog, but in recent years more narrative information about the picture has been revealed. It was taken after a family funeral. The two men are Eggleston's "Uncle Adyn Schuyler Sr. and his assistant Jasper Staples." I don't want them identified and wonder why Eggleston has. I also think the words "his assistant" are too contemporary and politically correct, however true in reflecting Mr. Staples's services to Mr. Schuyler. Identifying them as specific people implies that this is primarily a portrait and diffuses the importance of other aspects of a complex picture that is classically Eggleston's precise recognition of an ordinary Southern moment.

The strength of this extraordinary picture is its balance between color and content. As photographer William Williams wrote, "The photograph literally is a composition of color in which black and white are the subjects."[6] One sees a white car, a black man in a white jacket and black slacks, and a white man in a white shirt and black suit. His red-and-black power tie is a noticeable and symbolic accent that distinguishes the bearer. I queried both Williams and the photographer Dawoud Bey asking, "How radically would it have changed my response to the picture had the black man been standing in front of the white man, but still with both in identical positions?" Williams's response made it clear that such a flip would have destroyed the critical rhythm of black and white forms. The uncle's central position, a black slash between two white entities, anchors the picture, formally and socially. Bey addressed the social component, writing, "That black man was never going to be standing in front of the white man whom he stands behind, invisible from his field of vision. No telling the exact degree to which Eggleston staged this situation, but it rings true to the social circumstances of the time, and I can't imagine the black man standing in front of Eggleston's uncle . . . even had the request been made. I'm sure he'd have found a way to politely, but persistently, decline. What's interesting is not only the position they each occupy in the social narrative and the actual place where the picture was made, but how—with the uncle in the foreground of the picture plane—the position that they occupy within the two-dimensional space of the photograph: one man pushes into our space while the other recedes. Their common gesture, for me, only reinforces the sad poetry and dynamic of the situation."[7]

What I saw forty years ago was a complicated bond suggested by their positions. The mirroring of their stances implies familiarity, but of a particular kind between white employers and African American employees of long service. There is both companionable comfort and enduring distance. Many of Eggleston's pictures are fresh, engaging, and at times disturbing without conjuring an identity with his vision. Other images preserve scenes that are gone and situations that needed to be gone. Above all, he also stopped to see—really see—that life is so daily.

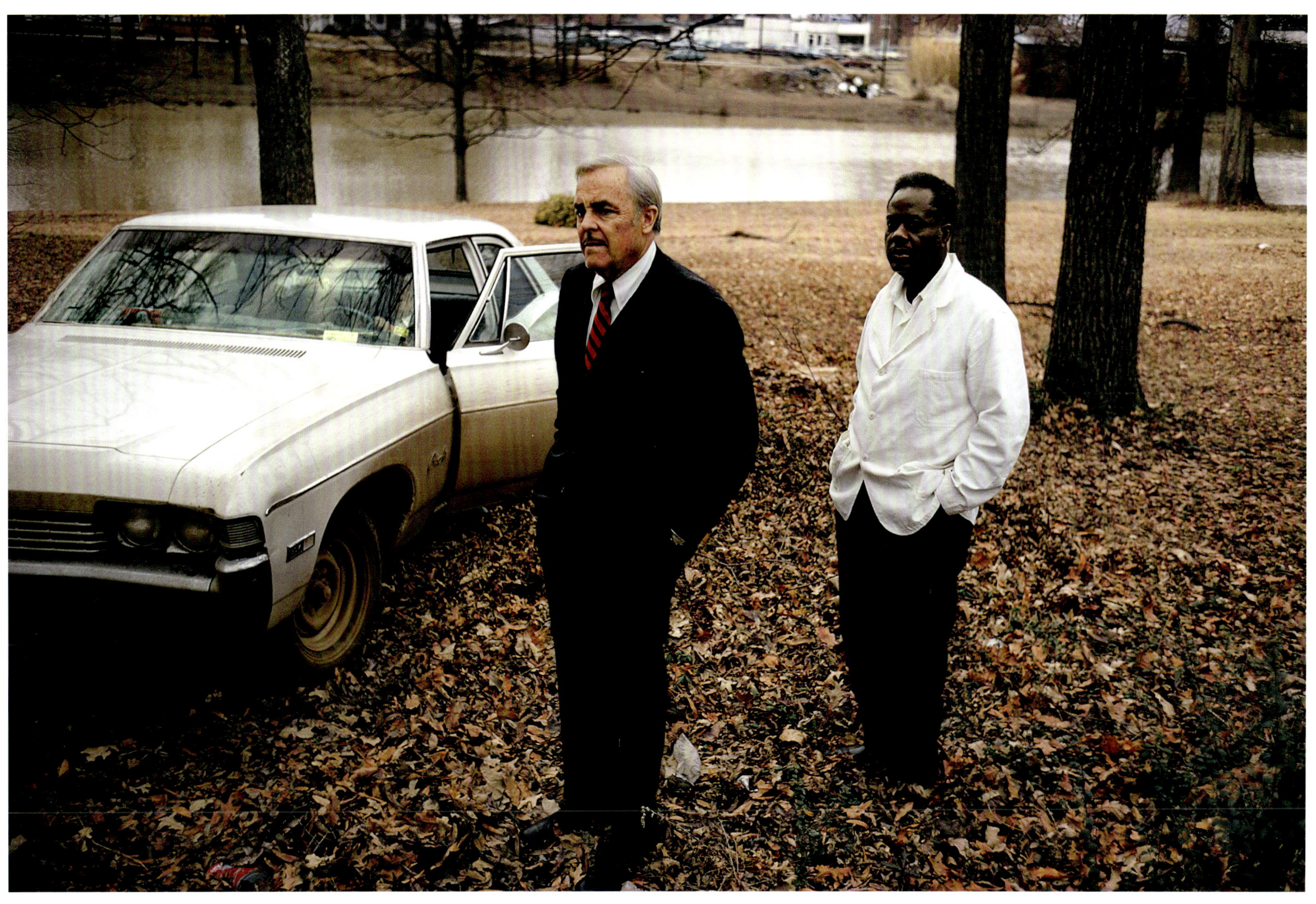

William Eggleston. *Untitled*, 1969–1970. © Eggleston Artistic Trust. Courtesy Eggleston Artistic Trust and David Zwirner.

Notes

1. John Szarkowski, "Introduction," in *William Eggleston's Guide* (New York: Museum of Modern Art, 1976), 5.

2. Ingrid Sischy, "William Eggleston's Color Photographs: Masters of Record," *Artforum* 21: 6 (February 1983).

3. Bruce Wagner, "William Eggleston, Mystagogue," in *William Eggleston: 2 ¼* (Santa Fe: Twin Palms, 1999), unpaginated.

4. Eudora Welty, *Delta Wedding* (New York: Harcourt, Brace, Jovanovich, 1979), 4.

5. I'm not sure the photographer was accurate about its being summer, because the carpet of dead leaves at their feet evokes fall, not summer. Whether he cared whether it was accurate is the subject of another essay.

6. William Williams, email to author, August 17, 2016.

7. Dawoud Bey, email to author, August 19, 2016.

Eggleston Unexplained

LISA HOWORTH

On a frigid night in January 2005 I went to MoMA hoping to see the premiere of Michael Almereyda's documentary *William Eggleston in the Real World*. To my disappointment and amazement, both showings were sold out, and the line was a block long, as if it were a big Broadway opening. I stood in the falling snow like the Little Match Girl, holding a sign that read "I NEED A TICKET."

Of course, I knew that Eggleston was internationally acclaimed, but I suppose I didn't really get it until that night. As far as I was concerned, William Eggleston was just our unusual friend Bill who in the eighties and early nineties often came down to Oxford from Memphis. Here he'd hole up in Room 117 of the old Holiday Inn with vodka and smokes and tinker with guns, sound equipment, and a very loud keyboard. He'd sketch and play music and roam Oxford and Lafayette County with his Leica and hang out with Willie Morris or Barry Hannah and whoever else was out until all hours. (A number of those Oxford shots are in his well-known collection *The Democratic Forest*.)

Some kind soul gave me a ticket. The crowd of Sophisticated New York Art People buzzed excitedly until the film began to roll, when a churchlike silence fell. The footage was rough, inscrutable, and painfully frank. Almereyda spoke after, admitting that he was somewhat at a loss to explain how such a *rara avis* of a man had arisen from Cassidy Bayou. Or much else about him. It was thrilling to realize how fascinated people were by Bill's life and art.

We think we want Eggleston Explained, but do we really? I prefer the mystery—we have so few these days. We want to find some familiar territory. We want to compare Eggleston's art to that of other geniuses: he understands light like Caravaggio or atmosphere like Vermeer or color like Klee, his subject matter is like the great Mississippi writers, he breaks rules like Picasso. But to me his work is incomparable. Until 1976 we'd not seen anything like it. That his printing technique was inspired by commercial technology only deepens, not cheapens, his photographs. Eggleston's art is where photography finally meets the achievement of painting, a journey begun in 1839. He changed the course of modern art.

I think that Oxonians feel entitled to brag on our part in this, and certainly to celebrate William Eggleston, Global Art Hero from Down the Road. Thank you, University Museum, and thank you, Jesus.

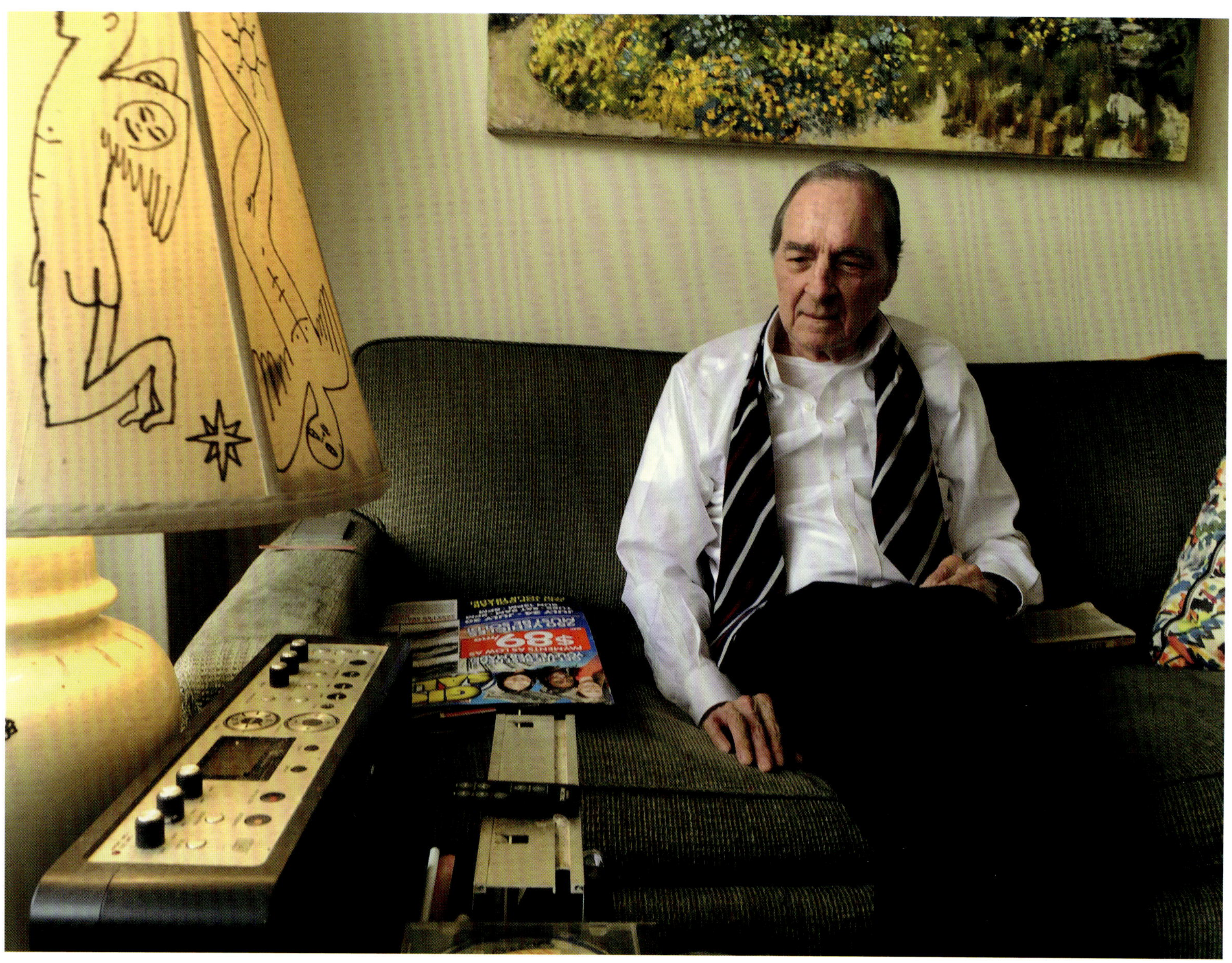

Michael Almereyda, *William Eggleston in Memphis, Tennessee, July 29, 2018*

"Mercy Mercy Pudding Pie": Notes on Some New Old Eggleston Pictures

MICHAEL ALMEREYDA

Venturing through the University of Mississippi Museum to view the bequest of Eggleston photographs installed on the museum walls, I was more than a little enchanted. The sense of enchantment may be attributed to a charge of metaphysical playfulness wafting in from an adjacent room, where a group of Theora Hamblett paintings are on permanent display. (Hamblett, as most Mississippians know, painted visionary tableaus of faceless figures assembled under vast trees the color of ice cream.) In another room, close at hand, stood a group of stern and magnificent portrait busts from ancient Rome, illustrated urns from ancient Greece, and an array of obsolete scientific instruments from the nineteenth century—archaic telescopes and optical devices as well as instructional paintings from that era depicting optical properties of color and light. Somehow, the Eggleston photographs seemed right at home.

The photographs range across the early decades of Eggleston's career, and they struck me as alternately innocent and sly, wonderful and odd, their oddness underscored by the sense that many of them had somehow slipped loose from the herd of better-known pictures. Years earlier I'd spent a great deal of time rummaging through a museum without walls in the Memphis headquarters of the Eggleston Artistic Trust, selecting digitized scans off Winston Eggleston's laptop, the repository of his father's entire photographic output up to that time. (The previously unknown images were gathered in a book, *William Eggleston: For Now,* published by Twin Palms in 2010.) I thought I'd seen just about all the Egglestons under the sun, and it was a poignant surprise to encounter fresh pictures in Oxford, Mississippi. The seven black-and-white photographs, especially—four of them made when Eggleston was in his early twenties—seem as random and precious as photos you might rescue from a shoebox, stashed in an old desk beside unreadable receipts and a pine cone. Most of the black-and-white images seem exploratory and offhand, though at least two—the jukebox glistening on the diner counter, the lone man under the blazing fluorescent gas station awning—have the laconic authority, the vibrant matter-of-factness, of iconic Eggleston pictures.

It's good to be reminded that Eggleston worked in black and white for a dozen years before committing to color, and his black-and-white pictures are often remarkable and satisfying. They tend to be spare and dry, elliptical and elusive, centered on people sitting around doing next to nothing. Eggleston's indebtedness to Cartier-Bresson—he's on record referring to the Frenchman as "my hero"—may allow us to savor the impression that he's always been seizing *the decisive moment*, but it's safe to say he resists the common misunderstanding of what the decisive moment must be. Eggleston pretty decisively *avoids* moments—scenes, people, architecture—that might be considered important, urgent, or dramatic. What we get in his pictures, more reliably, is a sense of alert alien intelligence hovering within a spirit of bemusement, plus an appreciation of natural and unnatural light, though it's seldom foregrounded as a pictorial effect. The implicit conviction, flowing through image after image, is that the decisive moment can live within an arena defined by the humble parameters of the photographer's home turf.

In the mini-trove of black-and-white pictures now in Oxford, another standout shows a young woman at an outdoor table at night, bringing a cup with a straw to her open mouth, her other hand reaching into a bag of fries. She's staring directly into the camera, but the picture's full upper half features the gaseous glare of a parking-lot light fixture, and surrounding darkness. This can be considered a portrait only in the loosest sense, allowing for an element of detachment and plain mischief. Similarly, there's a photo taken from the backseat of a car, showing a young man with muscular arms leaning in to deliver groceries. He's wearing a short-sleeved shirt and a bowtie, and the doorframe crops his face above his nose. A particular moment, and a particular world, has been caught on the fly, but there's a curious aloofness, a chill.

More to the point, and plainly enough, Eggleston was training his attention on unspectacular local reality, going after seemingly commonplace, fugitive moments involving people in fast-food joints, parking lots, and cars. Early on, he had a capacity to make arresting pictures out of stuff that routinely escapes notice. Greil Marcus has pointed out that action and motion are unusual in Eggleston's photographs, as if movement would detract from the main event, a haunted and haunting stillness that gathers power in and through color. That is to say: what may seem cold, austere, and even astringent in Eggleston's black-and-white work gets heated up in color. In color, Eggleston's aloofness shades into tenderness.

One of the most exciting surprises, for this viewer, among the previously unseen images collected here, is another inside-the-car picture, whose contents would be unlikely and unlovely in black and white: an untended steering wheel, a paper bag between seats, two frayed white feathers (dangling from the rearview mirror), a laminated folder, a dim, plastic-lidded McDonald's cup with a protruding straw. This jumble of things becomes dramatic and stirring because Eggleston's camera captures the riot of sunlight splashing in from the open door, light catching on the pale yellow cloth covering the seat cushions, brightening the feathers and the upper length of the brown bag. And so a glimpse into somebody's not-so-pretty car interior becomes a sumptuous still life, a celebration of textured light.

I visited Eggleston in Memphis before driving out to see the exhibition in Oxford. A painting of Bach—an actual mail-ordered canvas, copied from the famous 1748 white-wigged portrait—is tacked up on one wall of Bill's living room, where not a single photograph is in evidence. Bill had stationed himself on a long couch adorned with brightly colored pillows and two packs of American Spirit cigarettes. I assume he was aware of how effectively, how cheerfully, the stripes of his unknotted tie chimed with the colored chevrons of the pillows.

We spent some time talking while a DVD of *Baby Doll* played without sound on a flat-screen monitor across the room. *Baby Doll* is a distinctly striking and uncomfortable movie made by Elia Kazan in 1956, based on a Tennessee Williams play—a provocation that still provokes. In the film, a luminous Carroll Baker plays the virgin bride of loutish Karl Malden. Much of the action, as I recall from that afternoon in Bill's apartment, involves Baker and Eli Wallach (Malden's rival) lunging toward and away from each other on the premises of a decaying Mississippi mansion that, Bill explained, stood a few miles down the road from the plantation where he himself spent the better part of his boyhood. Even without sound, sexual frustration roils off of *Baby Doll* like waves of heat.

I have no idea how carefully or often Bill has looked at this movie. (It had been playing in the background when I visited the previous day.) Half-watching with him, I was reminded of the well-established, hectic, and hysterical qualities of the Southern Gothic, and how these qualities can be explicit and glorious in Faulkner and Tennessee Williams, Flannery O'Connor and Barry Hannah, but they can feel forced and grotesque when crossing the border into visual art. Eggleston tends to deny or deflect them in his work. Nonetheless, on occasion, they register as undercurrents, intimations of anxiety or dread, and they can announce themselves within distinct details: a red crucifix on a rural church facade, bullet holes in a road sign, the blade of an ax. Even as our apprehension of an Eggleston image can veer from flat "documentary" fact to dreamlike beauty, the pictures lead us to recognize that facts are seldom altogether innocent; the dream is not always serene.

I found myself telling Bill about Boris Kaufman, one of the most gifted cinematographers in the history of cinema, the man behind the camera for *Baby Doll*, *On the Waterfront*, and, years earlier, the extraordinary films of Jean Vigo. Bill seemed politely interested. Do I need to mention that we were drinking bourbon? After a while, he got up from the couch and made his way to the piano in the back room. Before joining him there, I sat watching *Baby Doll* for a few minutes as if it were a silent movie scored by William Eggleston, who supplied a lush improvised accompaniment, leaping off a musical cliff provided by Bach.

Eggleston has testified often enough to his love of Bach, and we should not undervalue the depth of that bond. All the same, in closing, I feel gratitude to Bill for bringing my attention to another musician, LaVern Baker, and her 1955 hit single "Tweedlee Dee," written by Winifred Scott. If this were a slide lecture, I'd play the last verse through to the end.

The lyrics go like this:

Tweedlee tweedlee tweedlee dum
You're as sweet as bubble gum
Mercy mercy pudding pie
You've got something that money can't buy
Tweedlee tweedlee tweedlee dum
Ow, tweedlee tweedlee dum
Ow, tweedlee tweedlee dum
Ow, tweedlee tweedlee dum
Ow, tweedlee tweedlee dum
Ow

Contributors

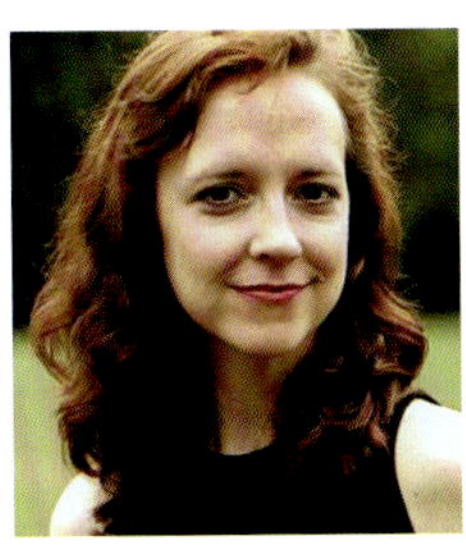

Megan Abbott is the award-winning author of nine novels—*Die a Little*, *The Song Is You*, *Queenpin*, *Bury Me Deep*, *The End of Everything*, *Dare Me*, *The Fever*, *You Will Know Me*, and, her latest, *Give Me Your Hand*—as well as a nonfiction book, *The Street Was Mine: White Masculinity in Hardboiled Fiction and Film Noir*. She is also the editor of *A Hell of a Woman*, an anthology of female crime fiction, and has written for the *New York Times*, *Salon*, the *Guardian*, the *Wall Street Journal*, and other publications. Her work has won or been nominated for the CWA Steel Dagger, the International Thriller Writers Award, the Los Angeles Times Book Prize, and five Edgar Awards. Her novel *Queenpin* was awarded an Edgar. After receiving a PhD in English and American literature from New York University, she taught at the State University of New York, the New School University, and the University of Mississippi, where she was the John and Renée Grisham Writer in Residence in 2013–2014. She lives in Queens, New York. Much of her writing is inspired by William Eggleston's photography.

Michael Almereyda's films include *Hamlet* (2000), *Experimenter* (2015), and *Marjorie Prime* (2017). *William Eggleston in the Real World*, his documentary portrait of the photographer, premiered at New York's Museum of Modern Art in 2005. Almereyda supplied text for the 2007 Eggleston book, *5 x 7*, and he edited and wrote an afterword for *William Eggleston: For Now* (2010), a selection of previously unpublished photographs. Almereyda's essays on film and photography have appeared in the *New York Times*, *Film Comment*, *Artforum*, *Aperture*, the *Believer*, *Triple Canopy*, and booklets for the Criterion Collection.

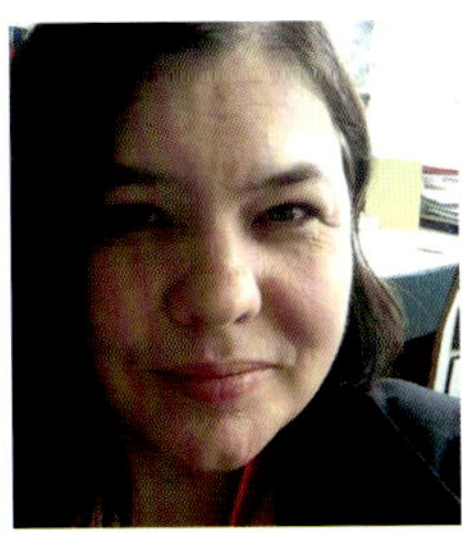

Kris Belden-Adams received her PhD in modern and contemporary art history with a specialization in photography from the City University of New York Graduate Center. She also has an MA in art history, theory, and criticism with a concentration in contemporary art from the School of the Art Institute of Chicago. Her scholarly work on the history of art, photography, and visual culture has been published by the Metropolitan Museum of Art, *Photographies*, *Southern Studies*, *Afterimage*, and *Cabinet*. She is editor of *Photography and Failure: One Medium's Entanglements with Flops, Underdogs, and Disappointments* and contributed chapters to that volume, as well as to *Before-and-After Photography: Histories and Contexts*. Prior to joining the University of Mississippi Art Department in the fall of 2013, Belden-Adams taught at the Minneapolis College of Art and Design in Minnesota. PHOTO BY KRIS BELDEN-ADAMS

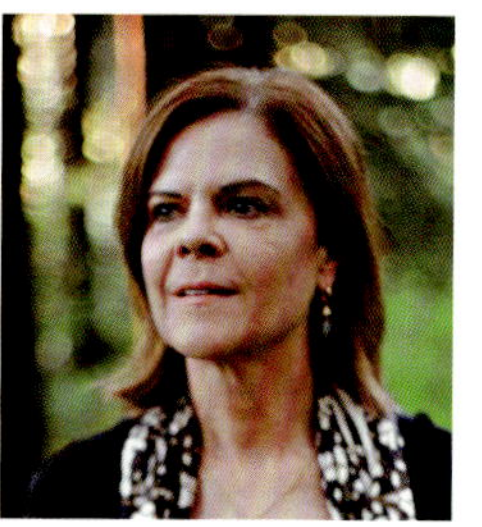

Maude Schuyler Clay was born in Greenwood, Mississippi, where her family had lived for five generations. After attending the University of Mississippi and the Memphis Academy of Arts, she was an intern for her cousin, photographer William Eggleston. She then moved to New York City, where she worked at Light Gallery and as a photography editor and photographer for *Esquire*, *Fortune*, *Vanity Fair*, and other publications. After returning to the Mississippi Delta in the late 1980s, she continued her color portrait work and began a series of black-and-white photographs. The University Press of Mississippi published her monographs *Delta Land* in 1999 and *Delta Dogs* in 2014. Steidl published her book of color portraits, *Mississippi History*, in 2015, with a foreword by Richard Ford. She has received five awards for her photography from the Mississippi Institute of Arts and Letters and the 2015 Governor's Award for Excellence in Visual Art. Her work is in the collections of the Museum of Modern Art, the Museum of Fine Arts, Houston, and the National Museum for Women in the Arts, among others. She lives in Sumner, Mississippi, with her husband, the photographer Langdon Clay.
PHOTO BY TERRI LOEWENTHAL

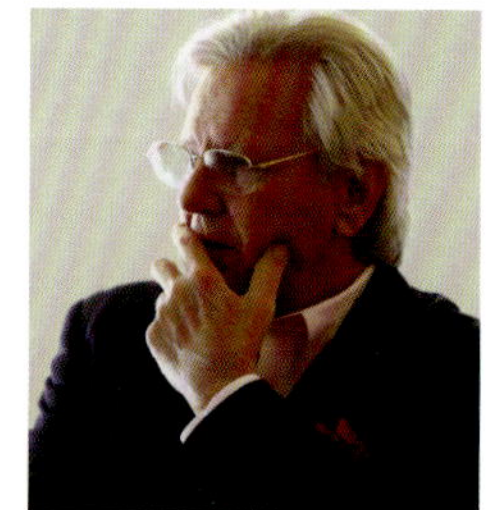

William Dunlap is an artist, writer, arts advocate, and commentator. In a career spanning more than four decades as a painter, printmaker, sculptor, and photographer, Dunlap has exhibited internationally and is included in numerous public and private collections, including the Metropolitan Museum of Art and the National Gallery of Art. He has received awards and honors from the Danforth, Rockefeller, Lila Wallace, and Warhol Foundations, as well as from the Mississippi Institute of Arts and Letters, and the Mississippi Governor's Award for Excellence in the Arts. *Dunlap* (University Press of Mississippi, 2006) is a comprehensive survey of the artist's work. *Short Mean Fiction: Words and Pictures* (Nautilus Press, 2016) is his initial foray into literary fiction, with stories drawn from decades of sketchbooks accompanied by reproductions of original drawings. Dunlap maintains studios in Coral Gables, Florida; McLean, Virginia; and Mathiston, Mississippi. PHOTO BY ELMO THAMM

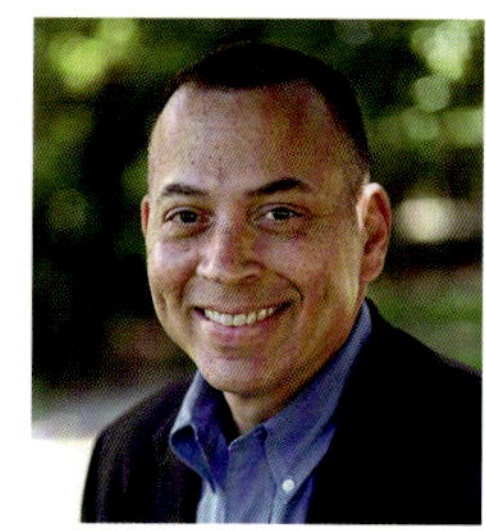

W. Ralph Eubanks is the author of *The House at the End of the Road: The Story of Three Generations of an Interracial Family in the American South* (2009) and *Ever Is a Long Time: A Journey into Mississippi's Dark Past* (2003), which *Washington Post* book critic Jonathan Yardley named as one of the best nonfiction books of the year. He has contributed articles to the *Washington Post* Outlook and Style sections, the *Wall Street Journal*, *Wired*, the *New Yorker*, and National Public Radio. After receiving a BA from the University of Mississippi and an MA at the University of Michigan, he worked in book publishing at Tucker and Francis USA and for the American Psychological Association and served as director of publishing at the Library of Congress from 1995 to 2013. He edited the *Virginia Quarterly Review* at the University of Virginia and has been an advisor and adjunct professor at the University of Virginia and George Mason University. In 2016 he was the Eudora Welty Visiting Professor in Southern Studies at Millsaps College and is currently visiting professor of Southern Studies and English at the University of Mississippi. PHOTO BY STACEY VAETH

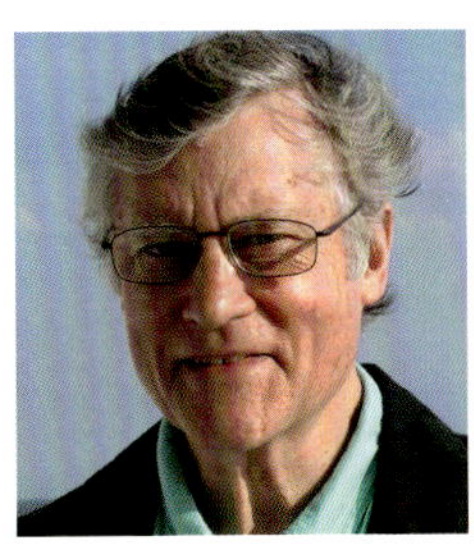

William Ferris is Joel R. Williamson Eminent Professor of History at UNC–Chapel Hill and an adjunct professor in the Curriculum in Folklore. He is senior associate director of the Center for the Study of the American South and the former chairman of the National Endowment for the Humanities. Prior to his role at NEH, Ferris served as director of the Center for the Study of Southern Culture at the University of Mississippi, where he was a faculty member from 1979 to 1997. Ferris has written and edited ten books and created fifteen documentary films. He coedited the award-winning *Encyclopedia of Southern Culture*, which contains entries on every aspect of Southern culture and is widely recognized as a major reference work linking popular, folk, and academic cultures. His last three books—*Give My Poor Heart Ease: Voices of the Mississippi Blues*, *The Storied South: Voices of Writers and Artists*, and *The South in Color: A Visual Journey*—provide an extraordinary trilogy of his documentation of life in the South through nearly six decades of photographs and interviews. He received the Mississippi Governor's Award for Lifetime Achievement in the Arts in 2017. PHOTO BY MARCIE COHEN FERRIS

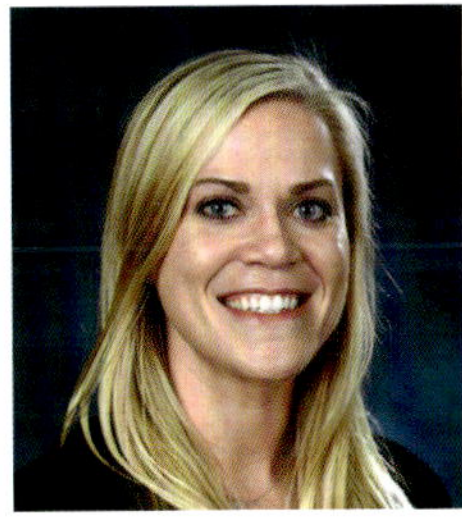

Marti A. Funke is a researcher for University Development. She was collections manager and exhibitions coordinator for the University of Mississippi Museum from September 2011 to June 2018 and received the 2016 Southeastern Museums Conference's Emerging Museum Professionals Award. She had administrative responsibility for the University Museum's artworks and artifacts, a collection of more than 20,000 objects, and coordinated all its exhibitions. Funke earned a bachelor's degree in history with a minor in art history and a master's degree in museum studies, both from the University of Kansas, and has participated in George Washington University's Museum Leadership Seminar. She was assistant curator at the Ulrich Museum of Contemporary Art at Wichita State University and assistant registrar at the Wichita Art Museum before moving to Oxford. PHOTO BY UM COMMUNICATIONS

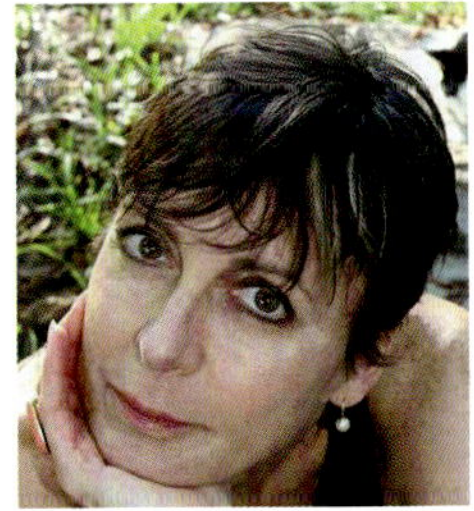

Lisa Howorth, born in Washington, DC, has lived in Oxford, Mississippi, since 1972. She and her husband, Richard Howorth, founded Square Books in 1979, opened an annex store, Off Square Books, in late 1993, and Square Books Jr., a children's store, in 2003. *Publishers Weekly* named the enterprise Bookstore of the Year in 2013. After earning an MS in library science and an MA in art history, she was a reference librarian and an associate professor of art and Southern Studies at the University of Mississippi. Howorth is coeditor of *The Blues: A Bibliographic Guide* and editor of *The South: A Treasury of Art and Literature*; *Yellow Dogs, Hushpuppies, and Bluetick Hounds*; *and The Southern I.Q. Quiz Book*. She has written for *Garden and Gun* magazine and the *Oxford American*, among others, and is a contributor to the *Encyclopedia of Southern Culture*. She is the author of *Flying Shoes* (2014) and a second novel, *Summerlings*, set in DC in 1959, forthcoming summer 2019 from Doubleday. She was awarded the Governor's Award for Excellence in the Arts in 1996 and a MacDowell Colony Fellowship in 2007. PHOTO BY MAUDE SCHUYLER CLAY

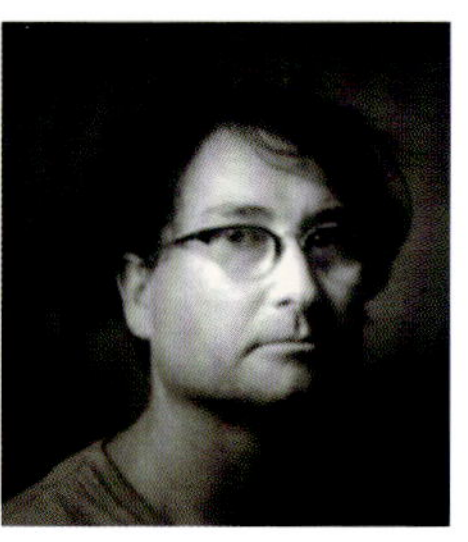

Richard McCabe has worked within the curatorial department of the Ogden Museum of Southern Art since 2005 and was named its curator of photography in 2010. He has curated over twenty-five exhibitions, including *Seeing beyond the Ordinary*, *The Mythology of Florida*, *Contemporary Alabama Photography*, *The Colourful South*, *Eudora Welty: Photographs from the 1930s and 40s*, and *A Place and Time Part 1: Photographs from the Collection 1864–1945*. He is also curator of *New Southern Photography*, a large-scale exhibition featuring the work of twenty-five photographers that debuted at the Ogden in the fall of 2018 and is available for travel to other institutions through 2021. McCabe received an MFA in studio art from Florida State University in 1998. That year he also received a fellowship to the American Photography Institute's National Graduate Seminar at New York University. From 1998 to 2005 he lived in New York City, where he worked for numerous art galleries and museums, including the International Center for Photography. He has also taught photography at Pratt Institute in New York City, Fairfield University in Connecticut, Montclair State University in New Jersey, and Xavier in New Orleans. His photographs, paintings, drawings, and installation art have been exhibited in numerous galleries and museums throughout the United States. In 2017, AINT–BAD press published *LAND STAR*, a monograph of McCabe's photography. PHOTO BY DAVID HALLIDAY

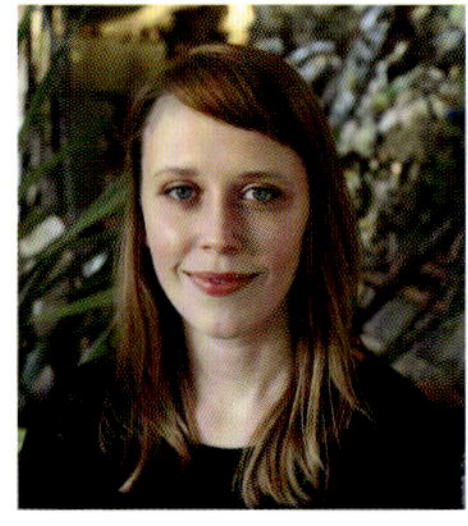

Amanda Malloy received two degrees from the University of Mississippi, a BA in liberal studies, focusing on art history and classics, and an MA in Southern Studies, concentrating on visual arts of the South and documentary filmmaking. The title of her master's thesis is "*William Eggleston's Guide* to the Suburban South." While pursuing her education, she worked at Square Books and for the University Museum as an assistant to the curator of Rowan Oak, William Faulkner's Oxford home. She also worked as a graduate intern for the Mississippi Arts Commission's Folk and Traditional Arts program, where she documented visual artists on the Mississippi Gulf Coast and in the Piney Woods region. She is the visual arts editor of the digital journal *Mississippi Folklife* and has written for several publications. She currently lives in Santa Fe, New Mexico, and works at Gerald Peters Gallery and Peters Projects. PHOTO BY AMANDA MALLOY

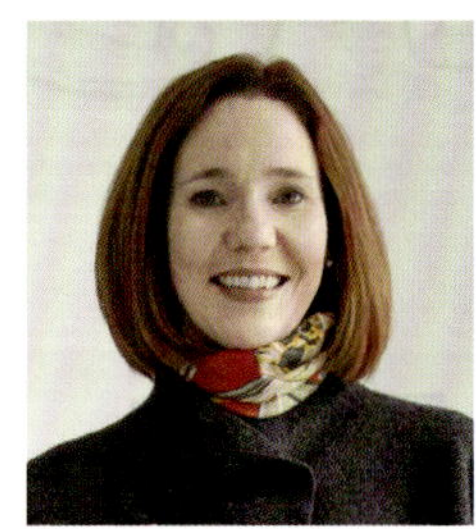

Emily Ballew Neff was named the fifteenth executive director of the Memphis Brooks Museum of Art in April 2015 after spending twenty years at the Museum of Fine Arts in Houston as its first curator of American painting and sculpture, organizer of more than twenty exhibitions, and coordinator of fourteen traveling exhibitions from other institutions. She holds a BA from Yale University, an MA from Rice University, and a PhD from the University of Texas at Austin. Neff is a recent Fellow of the Center for Curatorial Leadership in New York City and was president of the Association of Art Curators in 2013–2015. In May 2016, she launched a yearlong celebration of the Brooks Museum's hundredth anniversary and also initiated the institution's next phase, to be not just "a repository and conservator of precious objects," but "to expand that role into more educational and community-enhancing areas," to "be everybody's museum" and "respond to the city's vitality and diversity." In November 2017, Neff announced plans for moving the Brooks from Overton Park to the Mississippi Riverfront in downtown Memphis. "We are excited about what the future holds," she said, "even as our century-old mission remains consistent: to serve the greater Memphis region as a truly world-class art museum." In January 2018, the *Commercial Appeal* named Neff as the first of the top eighteen leaders in Memphis during the previous year. PHOTO BY BRANDON DILL

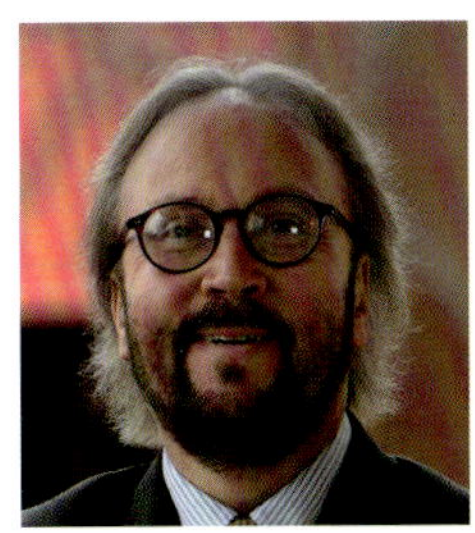

Robert Saarnio has been director of the University of Mississippi Museum and Historic Houses since 2012. In addition to holding the largest and finest collection of Greek and Roman antiquities in the South, an outstanding collection of nineteenth-century scientific instruments, and major holdings of Southern Folk Art and American Fine Art, the Museum owns and operates historic house museums of Mississippi authors William Faulkner and Stark Young. The Museum was named No. 12 of the 35 Best College Art Museums in the United States and No. 17 of the Top 20 list of college museums in the country, including Harvard, Princeton, and Yale. Saarnio received a BA degree in fine arts and architectural history from Harvard University in 1992 and an MS in historic preservation from the University of Pennsylvania in 1995, attended the Getty's Museum Leadership Institute in 2004, and was a National Endowment for the Arts Rome Prize Fellow in Historic Preservation at the American Academy in Rome from September 2005 to September 2006. He began his career at the Peabody Essex Museum in Salem, Massachusetts, and has since held a number of museum positions, including director of museums at Johns Hopkins University and deputy director of the Honolulu Academy of Arts. PHOTO BY UM COMMUNICATIONS

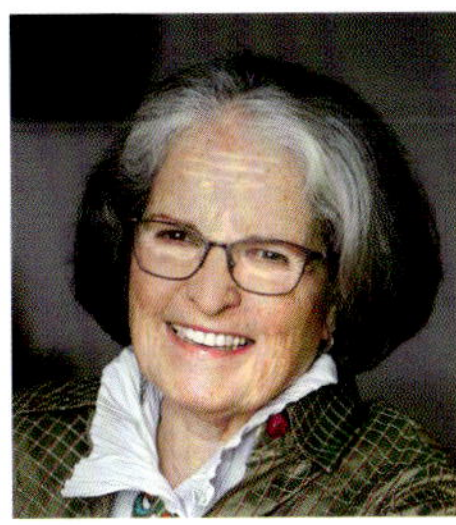

Anne Wilkes Tucker, a native of Baton Rouge, Louisiana, received a BA in art history from Randolph-Macon Woman's College, an AAS from Rochester Institute of Technology, and an MFA from the Visual Studies Workshop in Rochester, New York. While at VSW, she worked part time at the Eastman House and studied under Beaumont Newhall, who wrote *The History of Photography*, and photographer/curator Nathan Lyons. After interning with John Szarkowski, the director of photography at the Museum of Modern Art, she was the founding curator of the photography collection at the Museum of Fine Arts, Houston. In 2001, *Time* magazine named her America's Best Curator, one of her many accolades. While expanding the Museum's collection from 141 works in 1976 to more than 30,000 works by 4,000 artists by the time of her retirement in June of 2015, Tucker raised funds for acquisitions, staged more than forty exhibitions, and contributed to more than 130 books and catalogs. Recently she curated an exhibition from the Library of Congress photography collection for the Annenberg Foundation in Los Angeles. *Not an Ostrich: And Other Images from America's Library* was exhibited April 21 to September 9, 2018. Tucker viewed almost a million images to select almost 500 images for the show. PHOTO BY TODD FRANCE

Works in the Exhibition

All works are by William Eggleston (b. 1939) and are listed chronologically. Dimensions are in inches; height precedes width. © Eggleston Artistic Trust; courtesy Eggleston Artistic Trust and David Zwirner.

The works on this checklist are those that were shown at the University of Mississippi Museum in Oxford, September 13, 2016–February 18, 2017. William Ferris donated the collection to the University Museum.

Page 15
Untitled (Memphis, Tennessee), 1961. Gelatin silver print on fiber-based paper mounted on board, 15⅛ × 12⅜. 1988.5.56.

Page 16
Untitled, 1962 (Memphis, Tennessee), 1962. Gelatin silver print on fiber-based paper, 15⅛ × 12⅜. 1988.5.54.

Page 17
Untitled (diner, Memphis, Tennessee), 1963. Gelatin silver print on fiber-based paper mounted on board, 15⅛ × 12⅛. 1988.5.13.
Lower edge reads, "To Bill Ferris 1963."

Page 18
Untitled, 1964. Gelatin silver print on fiber-based paper mounted on board, 15⅛ × 12⅛. 1988.5.57.

Page 19
Untitled (Memphis, Tennessee), 1964–1965. Gelatin silver print on fiber-based paper, 12⅜ × 15⅛. 1988.5.58.

Page 20
Untitled (Wrightsville Beach, North Carolina), 1968. Gelatin silver print on fiber-based paper, 15⅛ × 12⅛. 1988.5.55.
"Bill Eggleston drove his mother to the beach to visit a friend and 'took a bunch of pictures' while there." —Maude Schuyler Clay

Page 21
Untitled (Union Avenue, Memphis, Tennessee), 1969. Gelatin silver print on fiber-based paper, 12⅜ × 15⅛. 1982.5.12.

Page 22
Untitled (Sid Selvidge's grandmother's home near Greenville, Mississippi), n.d. Resin-coated photograph, 18⅛ × 15⅛. 1988.5.50.

"Sid Selvidge, musician and lead singer of the famed Memphis band Mudboy and the Neutrons, and Bill Eggleston were good friends. Bill made the photos used on several of Sid's album covers, and Sid used many of Bill's photos for covers of other albums he produced." —Maude Schuyler Clay

Page 23

Untitled (Huntsville, Alabama), c. 1970. Dye transfer, 21⅛ × 17⅛. 1988.5.53.

Page 24

Untitled (near Marks, Mississippi), c. 1971. Dye transfer, 17¹⁄₁₆ × 21¼. 1988.5.51.

Page 25

Untitled (Nashville, Tennessee), mid-summer 1971. Dye transfer, 17¹⁄₁₆ × 21. 1982.1.1.

Page 26

H. C. Varner Grocery, 1971. Dye transfer, 17⅛ × 21⅜. 1982.1.4.

"Photograph made near Oxford, Mississippi, off Hwy 7 towards Holly Springs, Mississippi." —Maude Schuyler Clay

Page 27

Untitled (rural Mississippi), 1972. Dye transfer, 21¹⁄₁₆ × 17¹⁄₁₆. 1982.1.2.

Page 28

Moose Lodge (Greenwood, Mississippi), 1972. Dye transfer, 17¹⁄₁₆ × 21⁵⁄₁₆. 1982.1.3.

"Photograph was made on Highway 82 outside Greenwood, Mississippi, going towards Winona, Mississippi. It reflects the very last rays of late, late afternoon light, just minutes before the sun went down. Likely, this image was the first dye transfer Bill Eggleston had made in Chicago. I was there when he took this photograph." —Maude Schuyler Clay

Page 29

Maid's White Uniform with Bees (Memphis, Tennessee), 1972. Dye transfer, 21⅜ × 17⅛. 1988.5.82.

Page 30

Untitled (Blue Parking Lot), 1973. Dye transfer, 17⅛ × 21⅜. 1988.5.60.

Page 31

Untitled (near Plains, Georgia), 1976, from the series *Election Eve*. Resin-coated photograph, 9⅛ × 11⅜. 1988.5.10.

"Eggleston was commissioned by *Rolling Stone* to photograph Plains, Georgia, before the 1976 election of President Jimmy Carter. This photograph is one of one hundred in *Election Eve* (1977), the first of the artist's books of original photographs published by Caldecot Chubb." —Maude Schuyler Clay

Page 32

Untitled (near Plains, Georgia), 1976, from the series *Election Eve*. Resin-coated photograph, 9⅛ × 11⅜. 1988.5.46.

Page 33

Untitled (near Plains, Georgia), 1976, from the series *Election Eve*. Resin-coated photograph, 15⅛ × 18⅛. 1988.5.47.

Page 34

Untitled (near Plains, Georgia), 1976, from the series *Election Eve*. Resin-coated photograph, 15⅛ × 18⅛. 1988.5.48.

Page 35

Untitled (near Plains, Georgia), 1976, from the series *Election Eve*. Resin-coated photograph, 15⅛ × 18⅛. 1988.5.49.

Page 36

Untitled (near Plains, Georgia), 1976, from the series *Election Eve*. Resin-coated photograph, 9⅛ × 11 ⅜. 1988.5.41.

Page 37

Untitled (near Plains, Georgia), 1976, from the series *Election Eve*. Resin-coated photograph, 11⅜ × 9⅛. 1988.5.42.

Page 38

Untitled (near Plains, Georgia), 1976, from the series *Election Eve*. Resin-coated photograph, 9⅛ × 11 ⅜. 1988.5.45.

Page 39

Untitled, 1981. Resin-coated photograph, 15⅛ × 18⅛. 1988.5.7.

Written by William Eggleston along the lower edge, "1st Image Louisiana Pro."

"Photograph taken as part of *The Louisiana Project* on New Orleans fairgrounds, which later hosted the 1984 World's Fair." —Maude Schuyler Clay

Page 40

A Good View, 1981. Resin-coated photograph, 15⅛ × 18 ⅛. 1988.5.2.

Along lower edge reads, "For Bill Ferris Oxford 6/82."

"Photograph of the construction of the Superdome in New Orleans, Louisiana. This photograph is included in Eggleston's *Louisiana Project*." —Maude Schuyler Clay

Page 41

Oh, No! (Oxford, Mississippi), 1981. Resin-coated photograph, 15⅛ × 18⅛. 1988.5.3.

Photograph along lower edge reads, "For Bill Ferris—Oxford 6/82."

Page 42

Untitled, 1981. Resin-coated photograph, 21 × 17⅛. 1988.5.1.

"Photograph made at Monmouth College, West Long Branch, New Jersey. Shot with 6x9 cm Mamiya Universal Camera, hand held or with a tripod, using Ektachrome 74 film and existing light. Photograph commissioned by Ray Stark, producer of *Annie*, as part of project in which nine photographers were invited to photograph whatever they liked at the making of the movie *Annie* by Raystar Productions. Photographs taken as if through the eyes of a child, Annie, who sees the mansion of her benefactor for the first time. Photographed after movie crew had left.

While on the set of *Annie*, Bill Eggleston said he hated this assignment and "did not enjoy one minute of the filming and wanted to come home." The story reminds me of Faulkner in Hollywood, when he asked the studio execs if he could work at home, and they said yes. Faulkner left and went back to Oxford." —Maude Schuyler Clay

Page 43

Untitled (Monmouth College, West Long Branch, New Jersey, on the set of *Annie*), 1982. Resin-coated photograph, 9⅛ × 11⅛. 1988.5.30.

Page 44

Untitled (Monmouth College, West Long Branch, New Jersey, on the set of *Annie*), 1982. Resin-coated photograph, 9⅛ × 11⅛. 1988.5.39.

Page 45

Holly Springs Road at Waterford, Mississippi, 1982. Resin-coated photograph, 15⅛ × 18⅛. 1988.5.6.

Written by William Eggleston along the lower edge, "For Bill Ferris, present when taken on Holly Springs Road—at Waterford, Miss."

"These photographs were made in 1982 in Waterford, Mississippi, on the same day that I interviewed and filmed both Bill Eggleston and Bill Christenberry for my film *Painting in the South*. I did interviews with both Bills on camera and also filmed them as they took photographs in Waterford. *Painting in the South* was funded by Philip Morris as part of an exhibition of Southern painting they sponsored at the Virginia Museum of Fine Arts. Philip Morris did not allow me to include Bill Eggleston in the film, because they said he was not a painter. They did allow me to include Bill Christenberry, because he taught painting at the Corcoran." —William Ferris

Page 46

Untitled (Waterford, Mississippi), 1983. Resin-coated photograph, 9 ⅝ × 12 ⅛ . 1983.24.1.

Page 47

Untitled (Palmer's Grocery, Waterford, Mississippi), 1983. Resin-coated photograph, 9 ⅝ × 12 ⅛ . 1983.24.2.

Page 48

Untitled (Waterford, Mississippi), 1983. Resin-coated photograph, 9 ⅝ × 12 ⅛. 1983.24.3.

Page 49

Untitled (Waterford, Mississippi, 1983. Resin-coated photograph, 12 ⅛ × 9 ⅝. 1983.24.4.

Page 50

Untitled (Waterford, Mississippi), 1983. Resin-coated photograph, 12 ⅛ × 9 ⅝. 1983.24.5.

"The man leaning against the tree is noted photographer and friend of William Eggleston, William Christenberry." —Maude Schuyler Clay

Index

Page numbers in **boldface** refer to illustrations. All works are by William Eggleston unless otherwise indicated.